I0126214

Policing's Problems in the Twenty-First Century

Policing's Problems in the Twenty-First Century

Misconduct, Malfeasance, and Murder

Tom Barker

ROWMAN & LITTLEFIELD
Lanham • Boulder • New York • London

Published by Rowman & Littlefield
An imprint of The Rowman & Littlefield Publishing Group, Inc.
4501 Forbes Boulevard, Suite 200, Lanham, Maryland 20706
www.rowman.com

86-90 Paul Street, London EC2A 4NE

Copyright © 2025 by The Rowman & Littlefield Publishing Group, Inc.

All rights reserved. No part of this book may be reproduced in any form or by any electronic
or mechanical means, including information storage and retrieval systems, without written
permission from the publisher, except by a reviewer who may quote passages in a review.

British Library Cataloguing in Publication Information available

Library of Congress Cataloging-in-Publication Data on File

ISBN 978-1-5381-8819-4 (cloth)
ISBN 978-1-5381-8820-0 (pbk.)
ISBN 978-1-5381-8821-7 (electronic)

Contents

Preface: Looking in the Rearview Mirror

In the 1960s, America went through a national police crisis, not unlike the current national police crisis. Police misconduct, malfeasance, and questionable homicides were rampant in American police agencies, but I didn't know much about it. I was oblivious to the harmful effects of segregation and the hidden brutality of the police. "That's the way it is and always has been," I was always told. I never saw police brutality happen, although I was aware of the numerous fatal shootings of "n—" by cops, Ku Klux Klan members, and offended white persons. "That's the way it is and that's the way it will always be," the politicians would say. I had no reason to doubt them. That changed when I enlisted in the US Navy out of high school to avoid the draft.

College was not an option for people like me, my father said. Poor white people like me lived in segregated neighborhoods with whites in the front facing the streets and blacks, also known as "n—," in the alleys, living in dilapidated shotgun houses. We didn't socialize with one another, although I did receive several whippings for shooting marbles with black friends and twice for saying, "Yes, ma'am" to black women. I remember one of the black women crying when I got whipped, not by my father but by a neighbor who was a known Klan member. My father, who was a maintenance man at a local bank and part Chickasaw Indian and whose father was born in Indian country, would never have done such a thing. I have a vague memory of being slapped by a white woman for getting up and trying to give my seat on a bus to a black woman. *That's just the way it was and always will be.* I frequently tell others that I knew George Wallace when he was a racist. I remember when being a "law and order" man meant using the law to enforce your brand of order.

In the Navy, I had my first contacts with persons of color and learned that discrimination was not just a problem in the South, where I was raised. Blacks and other persons of color or minority status were subjected to discrimination and prejudice in the North, in the South, and from coast to coast. And I was expected to be a racist because I had a southern accent and was from Alabama. My peers labelled me and assumed I was a racist. Most were surprised to learn that my mother, my brother (who also became a police officer), and my maternal relatives were born in New York City. We moved to Alabama when I was a child. I still have fun when people ask me where I'm from and I tell them, Brooklyn, New York. I know I shouldn't do it. I just can't help myself. Quick judgments are often wrong. For example, my career of researching and writing about bad cops leads many to believe that I am a cop hater. Nothing could be further from the truth. I am proud of being a former cop and police trainer; however, I, like most good cops, hate bad cops and think something should be done about them. Nevertheless, in the South, where I was raised, segregation and discrimination were both social and legal forms of injustice. The police were the instruments to enforce legal injustice. According to some today in the United States and the United Kingdom, they still are.

My first experience with police injustice came as a member of the Navy Shore Patrol at the Naval Air Station at Meridian, Mississippi. Even though I personally knew Klan members and rabid "n—" haters while growing up, I was shocked by the treatment of the black sailors and marines by the local police. We had to get the servicemen out of the jails and back to the base, often to the hospital, as quickly as we could. Horrible beatings accompanied every arrest.

Then the unimaginable happened. I was part of the search party looking for the slain civil-rights workers—two white and one black—in Neshoba County, Mississippi, in 1964. As it turned out, from my Navy Shore Patrol duties, I knew several of the police officers and Klan members who were later convicted of murdering the innocent civil-rights activists. I knew one brutal Klan member personally. He assaulted me before the activist murders in an unrelated incident. We both sustained serious injuries. When my enlistment was up, I left Mississippi with a new understanding of racial injustice and police brutality. However, I went from the frying pan into the fire.

I became a police officer for very practical reasons, as did most police recruits in the 1960s. Police work was a well-paying, civil-service, secure job for a veteran with no special skills and only a high-school diploma. Besides, veterans received civil-service points on the qualifying exams. The police department I joined was in transition from being a legal and enforced system of segregation, enforcing Jim Crow laws, to a system in which all citizens supposedly enjoyed the civil rights guaranteed in the US Constitution. That was what I was told.

The reality of the police-work setting was quite different from that described in popular political rhetoric. Some of the officers I worked with were known

Klan members and proud of it. One even asked me to become a white-sheet brother and then withdrew the offer when he found out I was Catholic. He was also appalled when I told him that I had "kicked the shit" out of a Mississippi Klansman when I was on Navy Shore Patrol. He never spoke to me again.

Brutality, up to and including murder, based on race was routine in my department. However, a real shock came when I learned of the systematic police corruption. I expected some cops to take bribes. Every cop I worked with said he took a little money now and then and asked if I had. I learned that a network of corruption from top to bottom existed in my department and others in the surrounding cities and states. It was common and accepted, provided that the "taker" didn't get greedy. *That's just the way it is and always had been.* Later, my academic research and a plethora of nonfiction "crooks" books I read revealed that, in the 1960s, systematic police corruption, violence, and criminal behavior existed in numerous American cities—cities of all sizes—particularly New York City, Chicago, Philadelphia, Los Angeles, Detroit, Miami, New Orleans, and Portland, Oregon. Other American police agencies, located from coast to coast and too numerous to list, also shared these features (Graham and Gurr, 1969; Ahern, 1972; Cray, 1972; Barker and Roebuck, 1973; Shecter and Phillips, 1973; Goldstein, 1975; Fogelson, 1977; and an endless number of others). These researchers documented that brutal, corrupt, and criminal behaviors among American police officers was *just the way it was and had always been.* It soon became clear that police misconduct, malfeasance, and homicide also occurred in other countries, particularly those that had adopted the paid-public police model adopted in England in 1829 (Emsley, 1991; Morton, 1993; Chan, 1997; and others). Police misconduct was an occupational thing, not a people thing.

My studies and research revealed that every occupation, no matter how menial or lofty, has its distinct patterns of corruption and misconduct. It showed that police work was a morally dangerous occupation, one that could have devastating effects on its practitioners, a fact that its practitioners knew and always had known. The current emphasis on officer wellness stresses that more officers lose their souls and moral compass than lose their lives. Anyone who has carried a badge for any length of time knows that (see Barker, 2006). After five years "on the job," a cop will never be who he or she was. I had been forewarned when I took my oath that police work was a morally dangerous occupation, but I didn't fully realize it at the time. When a grizzled veteran police captain, whose breath reeked of cigars and whiskey, swore me in, he leaned forward and, in almost a whisper, as if he was telling me something he wasn't allowed to tell me, he said, "There are three things that ruin most police officers—money, women, and liquor. If you avoid them, you will make a good cop." He dismissed me with a wave of his hand. He, like most cops I have known, don't have a lot of empirical data to document that police work is a morally dangerous occupation. All he knew and all I know came from lived experiences of being "on the job."

The full impact for me would come after seeing its effect on my peers and after doing fifty years of research on cops and their world. It came from talking to more than one devout Christian who quit going to church when he was told absolution required him to turn himself in. It came from knowing cops who "ate their" guns because they could not live with what they'd done and cops who were told "massaging the evidence" wasn't really perjury. Where did they learn these "rules"? They are not written down and handed out with the badge.

The sisters had always told me that, in order not to sin, "you must avoid the near occasion of sin." How do you do that when you work in the "world of the sinners"? There were other secrets to be told. The captain knew them but he didn't tell me. My peer group of fellow cops picked up where the captain left off. During my first years "on the job," the good cops and the bad cops taught me the "rules"— the written rules and the ones they lived by on a day-to-day basis. I learned what a police officer in my department could do or not do. The cops of today who claim that was then and not now are just like the captain. They know that the sins of yesterday come back today and tomorrow. The cops in the twenty-first century know that, but they lie, deny, or won't tell. Anyway, I lived by their rules until a life-changing event occurred and turned my blissfully ignorant life upside down.

I, like hundreds—maybe thousands—of American police officers, took advantage of federal funds made available through efforts to "professionalize" the American police after the national police crisis of the 1960s. The money I received from federal grants and the GI bill allowed me to quit my extra jobs and attend college. I got a bachelor's degree, then a master's degree, and I finished off with a PhD. I took classes in sociology and the other behavioral sciences. My view of what I'd seen and done during my "on the job" experiences changed with my classes. Some of my on the job experiences could be classified into categories of police behavior that the sociology and psychology instructors called deviant or norm-violating behaviors.

First Attempt at Police Deviance Classification

My first attempts to identify the types of and patterns in police occupational deviance and control of police deviance began in graduate school. My first published work was based on my master's thesis, in which my mentor, Dr. Julian Roebuck, and I outlined the first scholarly typology of police corruption. The typology, titled *Typology of Police Corruption*, was a retrospective reexamination of my police-work experiences and my research of the limited number of scholarly works on police corruption (Barker and Roebuck, 1973).

My PhD dissertation, "Peer Group Support for Police Occupational Deviance," sought to explain police occupational deviance and classify it into categories, such as police corruption with a material reward; and police deviance, other than corruption, such as misconduct, crimes, and intentional homicides. It was obvious to me from my past experiences that the various types of police deviance could not be explained by the moral failure of individual officers—"rotten apples." There were occupational and organizational factors that influenced police deviance. However, it was evident that the particular workplace setting and its opportunities, buttressed by the cultural support, were factors to be considered.

Intersection of Occupational and Organizational Factors: Workplace Setting

I was lecturing a group of local police officers from all over one state on police integrity and the types of police corruption when one of them said, "I wish we had all that shit in my city." The light bulb went on. He was correct; some cops "want to be crooks" but just don't have the opportunity in their particular workplace. Police misconduct, malfeasance, and crime result from the intersection of the law-enforcement occupation's opportunities *with* the social setting or workplace culture. A truism recognized by many cops is that the latent inclination to break the rules and the law is present, but they lack the opportunity. It was obvious from my research and experiences that the nature of the occupation provides the opportunities, but the workplace presents the available temptations and support. There was once a distinction between "clean" and "dirty" graft, a distinction that is absent today.

As one leading expert on police misconduct, Professor of Law Joanna Schwartz at the University of California, said in her recent groundbreaking book, *Shielded: How the Police Became Untouchable,*

> It is common wisdom that individual acts of police misconduct can't be wholly separated from the culture of a department or from leaders who encourage that misconduct or look the other way when it occurs. ***There may be bad apples, but they often come from rotten trees.*** (Schwartz, 2023, p. 93; italics added)

Policing's Dark Side

Every occupation or distinct work activity has a dark side where deviant behavior occurs. Often this deviance is supported or encouraged by the work group. Certain occupations, such as the religious occupations, political occupations, and criminal-justice occupations, have more opportunities for deviant behavior. For example, worldwide, there is a similar occupational culture common to police agencies in diverse work settings and different political settings. This criminal-justice phenomenon appears to be pronounced in democratic societies. Therefore, the nature and extent of different categories of police deviance in any particular American police agency vary according to the opportunity, social setting, and demographics specific to that agency—ergo, the term "workplace deviance." An issue to be reckoned with in American police workplace culture is that the typical American police senior officers and supervisors have experienced the same on the job socialization culture. Consequently, a quick solution to pervasive police problems may be to fire everyone and start all over. Unfortunately, that is a necessary and plausible action in some circumstances. This solution has been proposed and taken on occasion, in dire situations. Obviously, this is not possible in all cases because of civil-service regulations, due process, and police unions. Nonetheless, some cities with police agencies resembling criminal enterprises have disbanded or have had their police agencies disbanded and have contracted with other agencies for police services and protection.

American police reform is a historical and contemporary issue (Barker, Burton, and Woods, 2024). We, as a society, continue to keep police deviance on the "dark side," denying its existence and hoping it will go away. But it exists and will not go away, at least not entirely, because police misconduct, malfeasance, and unjustified homicides are a part of the occupation's nature and the police-work setting. Nevertheless, we can, and must, expose the dark side and take action against it. That action involves a three-step process: 1) assessing the problems; 2) proactively planning to deal with the problems; and 3) suggesting ways to monitor the progress. That is the purpose of this book.

PART I

THE GENESIS

The genesis for this book or my interest in policing's dark side did not spring forward as a well-defined pursuit; like most human endeavors, it incrementally developed from a simple question that I asked and the answer I was given. "Why are we doing this?" I asked one day while we were pushing back civil-rights demonstrators. "It's our job and that's the way things are and always have been." The answer was similar to those I had received every time I had asked this question when I saw someone being mistreated or abused by my fellow police officers. Then I continued to ask why and discovered that the three-letter word was the key to social change. It was revealed to me that American police work has a sinister dark side of misconduct, malfeasance, and homicide that needs to be exposed. That's what this book does. The book is divided into three parts. The first part—the preface, Chapter 1, and Chapter 2—is the bedrock for the book and the foundation for the dark-side argument. The second part—chapters 3 to 6—outlines and discusses the patterns of occupational/workplace deviance that comprise American policing's dark side and provides theoretical explanation of the behavior. The third part, beginning with Chapter 7, rounds out the discussion with examination of the serious criminal nature of American policing's dark side. The book does not provide a silver-bullet solution for American policing's misconduct, malfeasance, and homicides because there are no silver bullets.

CHAPTER 1

Overview of Police Deviance

Key Terms:
Police deviance
Police misconduct, malfeasance, and homicide
Police profession versus police occupation

Chapter Objectives:
After reading this chapter, the reader should be able to analyze and discuss the following:

- The definition of deviant behavior and occupational deviance
- The American police-work crisis
- The issues that complicate the study of the American police-work occupation
- The three categories of police deviance

If deviance is considered to be "*any behavior or attribute for which an individual is regraded as objectionable in a particular social system*" (Glaser, 1971, p. 11; italics supplied by Heeren and Shichor, 1993), then every organization and every occupation context provide opportunities for illegal and/or ethical deviance.

If one accepts Glaser's hypothesis as true, the American law-enforcement occupation provides myriad opportunities for deviant behavior (i.e., norm-violating behavior), particularly misconduct, malfeasance, and homicide. The American law-enforcement occupation sometimes is referred to as a profession that performs "policing" for identified state-designated agencies. Broadly speaking, "policing" is the exercise of state power (Waddington, 1999). The nature of what police workers do is tainted and morally dangerous because of policing's structure and setting, in which opportunities for deviance are inherent; this is commonly referred to as the "dark side" of policing. Complicating the dark side of American policing are three issues. First, American law-enforcement practitioners and professional organization officers at all levels of government refer to the occupation as a profession. This leads to a lively discussion that will be explored later in more detail. Nevertheless, when discussing the police profession or occupation, we are using different terms to describe the same work duties.

The second issue is more complicated: the federal government and most states define detention or corrections officers as peace officers and law-enforcement officers (Barker, Hunter, and Rush, 1994). Although this book briefly examines law-enforcement officers at the federal level and detention and corrections officers with limited duties and arrest powers, its main focus is on local law-enforcement officers with the duties of patrol, traffic, and investigation—in other words, the law-enforcement officers most likely to be in uniform and easily identified as police officers. Finally, the American fragmented policing system of law enforcement leads to a motley alphabet soup of law-enforcement agencies at all levels of government with overlapping jurisdictions. One federal agency, the Transportation Security Administration, performs what are considered policing duties but is not a defined law-enforcement agency. At the local level, there are eighteen thousand defined law-enforcement agencies. These local agencies are independent of each other, with no standard qualifications or control. However, despite their differences, American law-enforcement entities face similar categories of deviance—misconduct, malfeasance, and homicide.

Local American Police-Work Misconduct, Malfeasance, and Homicide

American police work, or policing, at the local level, occurs in most cases in low-visibility settings of high-discretion decision-making. That work setting is full of drug dealers, vice operators, marginalized persons, and criminals. This dark side of the police occupation makes it a morally dangerous occupation with myriad opportunities for those in it to engage in deviant behavior (Stamper, 2005; Caless, 2008; Barker, 2011). Police work has always been a deviance-prone occupation and will always remain so. Nevertheless, those who practice police work view it in a variety of ways. Some see the occupation as just a job and others view police work as a profession akin to law, medicine, and education. Others view police work as almost a "calling" to do good work for others. These views have supporters and critics. Whichever view is subscribed to, police workers perform society's dirty work and do what must be done to provide safety and security, however defined. As Bittner said, the police are the fire that is used to fight fire (Bittner, 1970).

Police deviance includes the murders of George Floyd and Walter Scott, the excessive force used against Rodney King, sexual assaults and rapes of runaway girls and sex workers, thefts from crime scenes or victims, and claims for overtime pay for work not done.

CATEGORIES OF POLICE DEVIANCE

This book addresses the dark side of American policing and, by necessity, deals with egregious police practices. The deviance in American policing is divided into three categories—misconduct, malfeasance and police-caused homicide. The categories are contemporary problems with historical roots. The three categories were always present in police work, but secrecy kept them in the shadows. Secrecy in policing is anathema to democratic policing in which police actions are always subject to civilian or citizen oversight. A lack of transparency is disturbing, because law enforcement is the only social-control institution in the United States that is legally justified in using coercive force against citizens. This violent street justice, perpetrated by police officers, has become visible to some extent (see the seminal work of Johnson, 2003). The use of coercive force by police officers occurred outside the view of neutral parties until cell-phone videos appeared on social media platforms like Facebook, Instagram, and Twitter.

The recent civil protests and official and open-source examinations of questionable homicides committed by publicly paid law-enforcement agents shined a faint light on policing's dark side but did not provide total illumination. Police misconduct, malfeasance, and police-caused homicide still occurred behind a dark cloak, primarily because there was no official record of it happening and the police could arrest and charge anyone complaining about such police behavior without fear that fellow officers would contradict what they said. They were not held accountable. To some extent, this lack of accountability has changed with body-worn cameras and cell phones in the hands of "citizen journalists"; however, the dark side has not disappeared. There are still vague shadows and locked closets known only to the police, their victims, or their ghosts. This is particularly true of police-caused homicides. Police homicides are often not officially reported as such. For example, in some areas, such as in some small towns or rural areas, those filling out official death certificates may be physicians with no forensic training, sheriffs, or morticians. They may classify the death as a homicide and not mention police violence as a cause in error or may have implicit biases based on race or social status (Anon, October 21, 2021). There is considerable evidence to support this statement (Barker, 2020).

Police Misconduct Is a Social-Justice Issue

Not all American police officers indulge in misconduct, malfeasance, and homicide. To say that all do flies in the face of reality. Most American police officers are not corrupt or brutal. They perform their almost impossible tasks courageously and exemplarily. Their stories of police deviant behavior that no longer occurs are taken to the grave with them. These officers receive little publicity. I have attended and spoken at many of their funerals. I am extremely proud to have served with them. However, American police as deviant actors receive 24/7 publicity, creating the impression that *all* police officers commit misconduct, malfeasance, and homicide. On the other hand, the vociferous denials from police apologists and deniers, who claim that police misconduct, malfeasance, and homicide are rare events, confined to a small group of rogue and rotten apples, are also wrong. Police deviance, including serious criminal behavior by individuals, groups, and entire law-enforcement agencies, is and always has been an American social-justice problem that needs to be addressed. Good American cops abhor bad American cops. Unfortunately, good cops and others know there is an unknown and surprising number of bad American cops.

POLICE CRIMINAL BEHAVIOR

The Henry A. Wallace Police Crime Database, which is directed by a former police officer with a JD and a PhD at Bowling Green State University, is the only national database of *nonfederal* American law-enforcement officers who have been arrested for assault offenses, driving offenses, drug offenses, fraud offenses, gambling offenses, homicide offenses, larceny/theft offenses, offenses against the organization, sex crimes, and the catchall category of other offenses (http:/policecrime.bgsu.edu). The database reports that, from 2005 to 2019, at least 13,600 nonfederal American officers were arrested for those listed offenses. During that same period, 104 nonfederal law-enforcement workers with the general powers of arrest (police officers, deputy sheriffs, state troopers) were arrested for murder and manslaughter. The data for this text include arrests of federal and nonfederal officers and examples from other official and open-source information. The nature and extent of arrests for police crimes in 2023 in my files of Google and Yahoo alerts and official press releases are mind-boggling (see Textbox 1.1).

Textbox 1.1. Arrests for Selected Police Crimes (October to December 15, 2023)

THE "SLEAZY" BLUE LINE: POLICE SEXUAL MISCONDUCT

* A New York Police Department (NYPD) officer was indicted on child sex offenses (Office of Public Affairs, Department of Justice, December 14, 2023). According to the indictment, the officer, Terranova, used social media to engage in sexually explicit conversations with underage boys and attempted to entice the victims into taking sexually explicit photographs of themselves and sharing them with him. It is alleged that he used popular social media applications, such as Snapchat, to message with underage boys whom he encountered socially or through his job as a police officer. After establishing a relationship with the boys, he solicited nude photographs from them. It is alleged that on one occasion he drove a boy to a secluded location where he directed the victim to engage in sex acts with him.

*A Rock Hill, South Carolina, police department detective, who served as a school resource officer, was indicted on twelve counts of distributing child pornography and six counts of child sexual abuse materials (US Attorney's Office, District of South Carolina, Department of Justice, December 13, 2023).

*A former Allentown, Pennsylvania, police officer was sentenced to five years in prison after pleading guilty to distributing child sex abuse materials (US Attorney's Office, DOJ, December 12, 2023).

*A lieutenant with the Clarkesville, Iowa, police department met a minor girl while he was investigating a sex offender who had offered cigarettes and alcohol to minors in exchange for nude photos of them. The girl later joined the police department's ride-along program. The police lieutenant had sex with the girl and solicited nude photos of her and her friends. He was arrested, found guilty of eleven felony and misdemeanor counts of child sexual exploitation, and sentenced to fifteen years in prison (Anon, December 12, 2023).

*In November 2023, a Knoxville, Tennessee, officer was arrested for the production of child pornography (US Attorney's Office, Eastern District of Tennessee, Department of Justice, November 6, 2023).

*A campus law-enforcement officer for the Moss Point, Mississippi, school district who had previously run for mayor was arrested and charged with three counts of sexual battery and enticing a child for sexual purposes (Buchman, November 13, 2023).

*A Philadelphia police officer, who was a serial rapist in uniform from 2005 to 2017 and whose crimes involved at least two hundred women and minor girls, pleaded guilty to two offenses and was sentenced to seven years in prison (Mitman, October 23, 2023).

LAW-ENFORCEMENT CRIMES THAT ARE NOT SEXUALLY RELATED

*Three former San Antono, Texas, officers were indicted for the fatal shooting of a woman having a mental crisis. Two were indicted for murder, and the third was indicted for aggravated assault with a deadly weapon by a public servant (Nowlin, December 15, 2023).

*A former Federal Bureau of Investigation (FBI) "special agent in charge" pleaded guilty to betraying the United States of America by entering into a conspiracy to avoid sanctions and launder money with a Russian oligarch who acted as an agent for Putin (Office of Public Affairs, Department of Justice, December 14, 2023). As we shall see, at least two FBI special agents have been convicted of treason. No American law-enforcement officer is immune from deviant behavior related to his or her occupational duties. This particular agent was sentenced to fifty years in federal prison.

*A Gastonia, North Carolina, police officer, Xana Dove, was arrested and charged for using her access to official computer databases to send information to suspects (Fohner and Collins, December 14, 2023). The black female officer was also charged with drug trafficking.

*Police deviance became a family matter when the father of a Texas state trooper became the leader of a drug trafficking organization transporting methamphetamine, heroin, and cocaine from the Rio Grande Valley to Tennessee (US Attorney's Office, Southern District of Texas, Department of Justice, December 14, 2023). The trooper began running license plates on suspected law-enforcement officers to identify possible undercover officers. The former trooper was convicted and sentenced to eighteen months in prison.

*Two Massachusetts state police troopers, a lieutenant and a sergeant, were convicted of overtime theft (US Attorney's Office, District of Massachusetts, Department of Justice, December 13, 2023). The two troopers and other troopers from the headquarters traffic program section stole thousands of dollars from federally funded overtime programs by claiming pay for hours they did not work.

*A four-year veteran of the Glastonbury, Massachusetts, police department, with only one minor complaint against him, was accused of committing more than forty burglaries in Massachusetts, Connecticut, and Rhode Island (Dehnel, December 11, 2023).

*A Los Angeles County Sheriff's Department deputy was sentenced to twenty-four months in jail for making a false arrest and lying to cover it up (US Attorney's Office, December 11, 2023).

*A Miami police officer was arrested by the FBI for stealing cash and drugs during traffic stops (Hamacher, November 17, 2023).

*Two Drug Enforcement Administration (DEA) special agents were convicted of bribery for "selling" confidential information to drug traffickers (US Attorney's Office, Southern District of New York, Department of Justice, November 9, 2023).

The Monetary Cost of Bad Cops Is Staggering

Deviant cops and their abuse of authority are not rare in American police agencies that have a long history of police misconduct, such as New York City, Los Angeles, and Chicago. In such police agencies, they are a real burden on taxpayers. According to High Rise Financial, a presettlement company, the states in which these three cities are located had the highest settlement totals in police-misconduct litigation from October 2009 to July 2023—New York, $1 billion and 94 million; California, $332 million; and Illinois, $320 million (Cheek, December 9, 2023). The top ten states, in order, are New York; California; Illinois; Maryland, $81 million; Pennsylvania, $59 million; Colorado, $51 million; Massachusetts, $39 million; Minnesota, $37 million; Ohio, $33 million; and the District of Columbia, $32 million. The database listed 217 publicly reported settlements for the years 2020, 2021, and 2022. The same report revealed that Virginia averaged $237,000 a year in police-misconduct settlements, for a total of $3 billion since 2009. Table 1.1 lists selected settlements reached in 2022.

REPEAT OFFENDERS

As disturbing as the foregoing cases are, equally disturbing is the prevalence of repeat offenders; some police officers appear repeatedly as defendants in civil suits. Many American police agencies ignore or fail to identify problematic officers. For example, Derek Chauvin, the officer who was convicted of murdering George Floyd, had eighteen civilian complaints and two civil suits brought against him, resulting in the expenditure of almost $9 million, before the killing of Floyd (Hohnstadt, May 29, 2020; Anon, April 13, 2023). A Chicago police officer who had cost the city $200,000 in resolving civil suits and had thirty-one citizen complaints brought against him was on the district attorney's "do not

Table 1.1.   Selected 2022 Police-Misconduct Settlements

Location	Compensation	Description
Chicago, Illinois	$200,000.00	A man alleged that he was framed by an off-duty Chicago police officer.
Chicago, Illinois	$400,000.00	A man alleged that he was run over and injured by the negligent operation of an unmarked police vehicle.
Los Angeles, California	$300,000.00	A man was shot and injured by a police projectile during a George Floyd-related demonstration.
Palo Alto, California	$136,000.00	A man alleged that a K-9 officer allowed his dog to attack him during a search.
Antioch, California	$180,000.00	Man was punched and arrested for suspicion of resisting arrest. The prosecutor refused to file charges.
Baltimore, Maryland	$8,000,000.00	A man spent seventeen years in prison for a crime he did not commit. His wrongful conviction was the result of police misconduct.
Baltimore, Maryland	$195,000.00	Baltimore City approved the settlement for two victims who spent two years in prison after members of the Police Gun Trace Task Force planted drugs on them. Thus far, Baltimore has paid over $13 million in settlements for the illegal activities of this task force.
Minneapolis, Minnesota	$500,000.00	A photographer alleged that a Minneapolis Police Department officer fired a rubber bullet that left her with permanent and temporary injuries.
Minneapolis, Minnesota	$645,000.00	A man alleged that he was beaten and tased while trying to surrender to the police.
Minneapolis, Minnesota	$600,000.00	A photojournalist alleged that she was left blind in one eye after a Minneapolis Police Department officer fired a foam bullet at her during a George Floyd-related demonstration.
Minneapolis, Minnesota	$50,000.00	A seventeen-year-old boy alleged that a Minneapolis Police Department officer used excessive force on him and violated his civil rights. The teenager was never charged with any offense.

Location	Amount	Description
Brooklyn Center, Minnesota	$3,250,000.00	A Brooklyn Center Police Department twenty-six-year veteran officer shot and killed a misdemeanor offender after mistaking her gun for a taser. The officer was later sentenced to two years in prison for manslaughter.
Springfield, Massachusetts	$249,997.00	A police officer pepper sprayed and beat (with a baton) a man during a domestic violence incident. The civil jury found that the responding officers engaged in the use of excessive force and that the city had a custom of failing to discipline officers.
Austin, Texas	$850,000.00	A volunteer medic was injured by a police bean bag gun while giving aid to a police victim during a racial-justice demonstration.
San Antonio, Texas	$466,300.00	The jury found three San Antonio Police Department officers liable for an in-custody death. According to testimony, the officers put their weight on the man for five-and-a-half minutes and waited an additional three minutes before giving medical aid. The medical examiner ruled the death a homicide.
San Antonio, Texas	$449,000.00	A black man was shot and killed by a white officer. The officer claimed that he believed the cell phone the man had in his hand was a gun. The officer was never charged.
El Paso, Texas	$1,200,000.00	A man was shot and killed by an El Paso officer after allegedly attacking the officer with a box cutter. The box cutter was revealed to be a brake pad, and the medical examiner found that the alleged assailant had been shot three times in the back of the head. This indicated that the man, when he was shot, was running away from the officer.
Graham, North Carolina	$336,900.00	A group of complainants alleged the excessive use of force during a voting-rights-related march.
Raliegh, North Carolina	$37,000.00	The victim alleged that she was subjected to excessive use of force during a Black Lives Matter demonstration.

(Continued)

Table 1.1. Selected 2022 Police-Misconduct Settlements (Continued)

Location	Compensation	Description
Greensboro, North Carolina	$2,570,000.00	It was alleged that a homeless man asked the police to take him to the hospital and that, while waiting for emergency medical technicians to arrive, eight officers threw the man to the ground and "hogtied" him. The man complained that he could not breathe and asked for help. He died, and the family filed suit.
Fairfax, Virginia	Amount undisclosed	A black man alleged that a white officer tasered him and struck him without provocation. The city settled the case, and a grand jury declined to indict the officer.
Westover, West Virginia	$750,000.00	A man claimed he was kicked, punched, pepper sprayed, and falsely arrested by Westover officers after he attempted to record them during an arrest. The entire incident was recorded on a nearby security camera.
Westover, West Virginia	$350,000.00	The complainant alleged that the police chief and two officers took him from his house and beat him.
Nome, Alaska	$750,000.00	A sexual assault victim sued the police department for mishandling her assault. In addition to the monetary settlement, she received an apology from the city.
Atlanta, Georgia	$1,500,000.00	A federal jury awarded a black transgender woman this amount for her unlawful arrest and the six months that she spent in jail on false drug charges.
Gwinnett County, Georgia	$400,000.00	A black man was assaulted by two white officers following a traffic stop. Both officers were fired and charged with assault. One officer plead no contest, and the other was convicted at trial.
Camden County, New Jersey	$10,000,000.00	A man alleged that he was left paralyzed by his encounter with three Camden County officers.
Elkhart, Indiana	$7,000,000.00	A man alleged that he was framed for an armed robbery by a police detective who used false testimony. The settlement was the largest ever paid in Indiana history for a wrongful conviction.

Tacoma, Washington	$4,000,000.00	It was alleged that white Tacoma police officers shot and killed an unarmed black man without provocation.
Redmond, Washington	$7,500,000.00	The city settled with family members before they filed suit. A police officer shot and killed an unarmed woman with mental issues as she lay on the ground. The medical examiner found six rifle bullets in the woman and ruled that her death was homicide.
Denver, Colorado	$14,000,000.00	A federal jury awarded this amount to twelve activists who claimed that Denver police officers used excessive force and unnecessary violence against them during George Floyd–related demonstrations.
Colorado Springs, Colorado	$2,970,000.00	The allegations were that police officers tried to question a nineteen-year-old teenager and that he ran away. He was shot in the back.

Source: National Police Funding Database (July 17, 2023).

call as a witness" list because he was untrustworthy (Blaidsdell, May 24, 2023). Chicago taxpayers paid $91 million to resolve multiple civil suits in which plaintiffs alleged misconduct by Chicago Police Department officers from 2019 to 2021 (Cherone and Rutecki, August 22, 2023). Two officers were defendants in ten different suits, and two officers were defendants in twelve suits. The two officers who were defendants in twelve suits were tactical officers who created search warrants to raid houses and steal cash and drugs. These officers were convicted of felonies and received prison sentences. Twenty-six officers were named in three suits; one of them, a detective, was accused of framing more than fifty victims. One of the corrupt detective's victims was sentenced to death based on fabricated evidence. She was exonerated after serving a decade in prison. The settlement paid due to this corrupt detective's activities totaled $33.3 million in 2019, 2020, and 2021. Thirty of his wrongfully convicted victims were eventually exonerated. An ongoing investigation into the activities of a corrupt Chicago sergeant who was in charge of a drug task force has resulted in 230 conviction revocations and payment of $80 million in settlements (Mitchell, December 7, 2023).

New York City also has problems with repeat offenders being named as defendants in civil suits. Ten NYPD officers are responsible for payment of $68 million in police-misconduct settlements from 2013 to 2023, according to a report by the Legal Aid Society (Khalfeh, September 25, 2023). One NYPD sergeant has had forty-eight cases against him settled for $1.1 million since 2013. Another officer has had three cases against him settled for $12.1 million in the past decade.

Recommended Action Based on Liability Settlements

It is too early to grasp the link between civil suits and police misconduct (Barker, Burton, and Woods, 2024). However, the available evidence is disturbing. At a minimum, more research on this issue, especially on officers who are repeat offenders and on the nature and patterns of the alleged police misconduct, is needed. The preliminary data strongly suggest that civil suits—the number, the allegations made, and the settlement amounts—need to be a factor incorporated in early warning systems and early intervention systems. I have known police officers who could start a riot in a church. Is that what we have here? Maybe, but what we also have is a need for American police reform.

American Police Reform

The enlightened public, sometimes via social media, has called for American police reform. To do that, we must explain what needs to be reformed, how we arrived at this need for reform, and what reform would look like. We must ask, "What is wrong with American policing?" The short answer is that *some* American police officers' conduct is not fair, "professional," or legal in their interactions with the public or each other. The American police occupation must rid itself of deviant (criminal and noncriminal) members and ensure the fair, equal, and transparent treatment of the public and each other; internal and external procedural justice are necessary. Do we need to engage in this exercise to identity what is wrong with American policing and what needs to be done? Consider the following.

A two-year investigation of the Antioch and Pittsburg, California, police departments has led to allegations that ten members of those two police departments engaged in falsifying official records to receive promotions and raises, participated in drug distribution, and deployed K-9 dogs on citizens. They violated department regulations by not wearing body cameras. It is alleged that at least forty-five members of these departments sent racist, homophobic, and sexist texts to one another. Five of the officers are charged with fixing traffic tickets, and another is under suspicion of interfering in a murder investigation (Medina, August 17, 2023; Byik, August 18, 2023).

TRANSPARENCY AND ACCOUNTABILITY

The first step toward American police reform requires a commitment to transparency and accountability—lifting the veil of secrecy surrounding what the police do and how they do it. We may not like what we find, but viewing it is necessary. For example, a proposed Delaware house bill requires that a public report be made of any incident, "involving an officer's discharge of a firearm, an officer's use of force that results in serious physical injury, a sustained finding of sexual assault, a sustained finding of dishonesty related to the reporting, investigation or prosecution of a crime, or to the reporting, or investigation of misconduct by another law enforcement officer, a sustained finding of domestic violence" (Steele, June 9, 2023). Delaware is one among many states attempting to light up the dark side of American policing. In other words, what Delaware lawmakers are signaling here is that there is a problem, and they are suggesting some ways to address it.

The guiding definitions for this book are presented below, with the caveat that definitions of who is and who is not an American law-enforcement officer in our fragmented system vary as do the definitions of what are proscribed behaviors. Our fragmented system, which prioritizes local control, makes generalizing difficult. Furthermore, in addition to there not being common definitions, there are no national databases on American police agencies and their operation. What we know or what we find may lead to more questions. For example, the only two studies that provide data on police terminations for misconduct—one concerning the NYPD from 1975 to 1996 and the second concerning Florida police departments from 1988 to 2016—found that black officers (their term) were more likely to be terminated for misconduct than were white officers. However, both studies concluded that this may not be the operation of racial discrimination. It could be due to the assignment of black officers to socially disorganized areas with more opportunities for misconduct. We need more research on this issue to come to definitive conclusions. We will see other areas where more research is needed. This book presents the best evidence available at this time. It follows the guiding principle on police reform, as expressed by the eminent police scholar Egon Bittner in 1970: "Clearly it is *necessary* that it be known that *what* needs to be done before anyone can venture to say *how* it is to be done well" (Bittner, 1970, p. 2).

Textbox 1.2. Guiding Definitions

Law enforcement Officers (LEOs) in the American federalist system are publicly paid federal, state, local, and special district officials of social control. They have general powersof arrest and perform one or more of the direct police services of traffic, patrol, crime investigation, or detention in their defined jurisdiction. Law enforcement officer (LEO) and police officer (PO) are used interchangeably.

POLICE OCCUPATIONAL/WORKPLACE DEVIANT BEHAVIORS:

Misconduct—behavior that is rule violating and unethical. The police department's definition always includes criminal behavior but is heavily weighted to violations of policies, rules and procedures and conduct that brings discredit to employee or department. This behavior undermines the legitimacy of the police agency. Typical reaction is internal through an Internal Affairs or professional standards division—internal accountability. Widespread violations range from moral character violations (sexual misconduct) to rules and regulations misconduct (sleeping or drinking on duty).

Malfeasance—illegal actions by a public official for personal gain. External civil and criminal reaction. Individual, group, and systematic behavior ranging from profit-motivated crimes to payoffs and shakedowns.

Police-Caused Homicides—murder and manslaughter (voluntary and involuntary). External reaction. A persistent occupation/workplace police problem, ranging from the motives of robbery, jealousy, vengeance and reckless disregard for human life to serial killers and contract hitmen. Some of these intentional homicides remain unrecorded in the dark side because the officers were charged and convicted of civil rights violations and excessive use of force. Gross misconduct charges include egregious abuse of power that shows a disregard of the sanctity of life.

IS AMERICAN POLICE WORK A PROFESSION OR AN OCCUPATION?

The above question is more than an academic debate; one's position on the answer has consequences. During the early twentieth century, police reformers were divided into two camps on this issue (Reppetto, 1978). The first camp of police reformers, like Raymond Fosdick, Bruce Smith, and other "progressives," were upper-middle-class, Ivy-League–educated public-administration–minded men who thought that the police chief executive officer must be college educated in the latest management techniques (Reppetto, 1978, p. 244). They believed that the unskilled but tightly supervised workers were different. College education for the menial police workers was not necessary and was a waste of time. On the other hand, August Vollmer and the police reformers who followed his philosophy came from the ranks of police workers. They thought police workers should be highly educated and well-trained decision-making professionals dealing with social issues. Vollmer's ideal, a profession of police workers akin to social workers, required that all police workers have a college education. This idea was ironic for a man who had only a grade-school education. He went on to become a college professor and to establish or help to establish three law-enforcement college programs from 1905 to 1932. He became known as "the father of modern policing" (Reppetto, 1978; Gardiner, September 2017).

Is a College Degree Necessary for All Police Workers?

I have been reluctant to join in that debate; however, college education for all social-issue decision-makers in today's complex society appears to be a necessity. My primary interest was always in police behavior, not in police work as a profession. Some years ago at a professional meeting, I was heckled by a police chief who kept yelling, "The only reason why you support a college degree for cops is because you are a dean of a college of law enforcement!" (The name was later changed to a college of "criminal justice," at my insistence.) Finally, I got the chance to reply, "That is not true.

I am a dean of a college of law enforcement, because I believe that all cops should be college educated with at least an associate's degree." Furthermore, I knew at the time that no American occupation not requiring a college degree has ever been recognized as a profession (Barker, 2011). I am not aware that that has changed. I was, and still am, more interested in police behavior than professional status. That is why this book focuses on police deviance.

Professional Behavior

Police practitioners and other police experts routinely describe police work as a *profession* whereby the law is the basis of all *police workers'* official acts. That is, police workers are *professional* in their behavior. That is not true today and probably will never be true in the American police-work occupation, as long as there are eighteen thousand independent local police agencies. As I see it, in the first case, "profession" is a noun describing a person, place, or thing. However, the use of *professional* to describe the police worker's behavior simply describes how the police worker performs the occupational duties of police work or law enforcement. The temptations, or opportunities if you will, to break the law or go outside the law in their official actions are always present in police work. This distinction leads to two different discussions concerning the education required for an occupation to be a profession.

In 1905, August Vollmer said that all American police officers should have a college degree, and he outlined a course curriculum for this degree (Stamper, 2005). Has American policing made any progress on this requirement? The most recent report from the Center for Public Policy at California State University, Fullerton, reveals that, 118 years later, only two local American police departments—in Arlington, Texas, and in Tulsa, Oklahoma—require all police officers to have a four-year college degree (Gardiner, September 2017). The overwhelming majority of local American police agencies require entry-level applicants to have a high-school diploma or a high-school equivalency diploma (i.e., a GED). At the national level, various commissions have recommended a confusing array of educational requirements.

The 1967 President's Commission on Law Enforcement and Administration of Justice reported that only 70 percent of the nation's police departments required officers to have a high-school diploma. The commission went on to divide police officers, relabeled as community service officers, into categories: police officer and police agent (President's Commission on Law Enforcement and Administration of Justice, 1967, p. 106). Becoming a police officer would require at least two years of college and, preferably, a baccalaureate degree in the liberal arts or social sciences. He would perform all police duties. The police agent would be an apprentice police officer under close supervision until he gained experience and got his two years of college. The 1973 National Advisory on Criminal Justice Standards and Goals made a series of recommendations: 1) every police organization should require at least one year of college of any applicant; 2) by 1975, the applicant must have completed three years of education at an accredited college or university; and 3) by 1982, every applicant must have four years of education (1973 NACJSA). Obviously, none of these recommendations were adopted.

Nevertheless, the number of college-educated police officers is increasing. Many local police agencies state that applicants with college degrees are preferred, and 6.6 percent of American local or municipal police agencies require some college credit or a two-year degree. Many American police agencies require college degrees for promotion to senior positions. Other local police agencies (for example, California and Massachusetts) require master's degrees for chief executive officer positions (Gardiner, September 2017).

The latest statistics on educated police officers are encouraging. When I joined the Birmingham, Alabama, police department in the 1960s, only one officer had a college degree. Furthermore, there were no black or women officers. That has changed dramatically in Birmingham and throughout the country. Today, according to the 2017 Fullerton report, almost 52 percent of sworn municipal American police officers have at least a two-year degree. Thirty percent have a four-year degree, and over 5 percent have a graduate degree (Gardiner, September 2017). The states with the highest percent of officers with at least a four-year degree are Massachusetts (49 percent), New Jersey (46.1 percent), Minnesota (42 percent), and California (39.5 percent). Massachusetts and New Jersey have the highest percentage of officers with a master's degree or a higher degree (14.6 percent and 13.6 percent, respectfully). Almost 29 percent of the chiefs and sheriffs have a four-year degree, and 32.1 percent have master's degrees.

Conclusion

American police misconduct is a major social issue that exists in the dark side of the police-work occupation, also known as the police profession. This deviant behavior has three categories: misconduct, malfeasance, and police-caused homicide. This book addresses each category and provides timely examples of each. Reform strategies are presented within the discussions whenever possible.

The profession/occupation debate will continue along with the value of police education as an overall reform strategy; however, we should not divert attention away from an examination of police deviant behavior. Police officers having varying degrees of education does not affect police deviant behavior. American law-enforcement officers with college degrees commit misconduct, malfeasance, and police-caused homicide. Police deviance has its roots in the police occupational structure and its culture.

Discussion Questions

1. Is American policing a profession or an occupation? Does it make a difference? Or is the debate much ado about nothing? Once you form your opinion, ask the question of a working police officer and share his or her answer along with supporting statements with the class.

2. The author believes that all occupations have a dark side and that police work has a LARGE ONE. Do you agree or disagree? Share your answer with your classmates. I suggest that you think of previous occupations you may have had and identify their dark sides. No confessions, please. If you have never worked before, consider being a student as an occupation and identify its dark side, where deviance appears.

3. If, as some argue, police deviance (criminal and noncriminal) is the result of a *few* rotten apples, then police misconduct, malfeasance, and homicide are not real police occupational or organizational problems. If that statement is true, what is the number of misconduct, malfeasance, and homicide incidents (or the percentage of such incidents in relation to all police actions) in a police organization that makes their occurrence a problem? What is the number of police deviance incidents that make their occurrence a national police crisis? Ask your local police chief. See if he or she will come to class to discuss the issue.

CHAPTER 2

Policing's Paradox

Key Terms:
> Sir Robert Peel
> Peel's nine principles of policing
> Code of ethics
> International Association of Chiefs of Police (IACP)
> United Kingdom College of Policing
> Constitutional policing
> Master status
> National police crisis
> Rogue police officers

Chapter Objectives:
> After reading this chapter, the reader should be able to analyze and discuss the following:

- The history and development of the police-work occupation
- The code of conduct for police agencies in the United Kingdom and the United States
- Rogue police officers and the dark side of policing
- The national police crises of the United Kingdom and the United States
- The American policing paradox

Textbox 2.1. The Beginning: The Blue Parade

On Saturday, September 26, 1829, approximately one thousand men divided themselves into six divisions and, at two-hour intervals, were read the conditions of work for London Metropolitan Police Service officers. They were then sworn in by the newly appointed police commissioners. They were given uniforms. On Monday morning, the officers were told where to report for food and lodging. On Tuesday evening (at 6 p.m. on September 29, 1829), the six companies of the Metropolitan Police Service, the first publicly paid police agency in world history, paraded in Old Palace Yard, Westminster, and marched, single file, on the outer edge of the pavement from their barracks to their new station houses.

Sources: Colquhoun (1806 and 1969), Browne (1956), and Mason (2004).

The American police occupation/profession has its foundation in England, where policing, or the exercise of the state's power and authority over its citizens, evolved. American police misconduct and crime have their roots in England despite the creation there of a culture of integrity for the occupation/profession in the form of codes of conduct. Deviant police behavior represents policing's dark side and presents a contradiction between what the police do and what the occupation's spokespersons say they should do. This is a real paradox, as we shall explain. First, we address the development of the law-enforcement occupation/profession.

Evolution of Policing

Policing as a publicly paid occupation became a reality, a defined jurisdiction with accepted workplace standards and expectations of workers' behavior, in London in 1829. For the first time in history, there were full-time salaried police employees who were accountable to a central government. The idea behind the creation of this new occupation was prevention of crime and disorder—deterrence. Deterrence was narrowly defined as preventing the illegal street-level incidents committed by members of the lower classes and minority and marginalized members of the London community. The American police occupation/profession has its foundation in England where policing, or the exercise of the state's power and authority over its citizens, evolved (Waddington, 1999).

The roots of American police misconduct and crime have their roots in England despite the creation there of a culture of integrity for the occupation/profession. Policing's dark side in both countries presents a contradiction between what the police do and what the occupation's spokespersons say they should do. This is a real paradox.

THE CONTROVERSIAL BEGINNING

The movement to create this new public-service occupation was not without controversy. Members of the English public feared the loss of their autonomy and subjugation by the monarchy with a new police system. In the nineteenth century, the only European organized police agencies that could serve as models were armed and often used by autocratic leaders to target their opponents and suppress opposition. The English public feared that enabling oppressive police actions to enhance political control was the reason for creation of a centralized police organization. This new police occupation challenged England's history of community policing, that is, policing by the people and the people being responsible for social order and apprehending criminals. However, that system had broken down with the industrial revolution and the growth of the cities (Browne, 1956; Mason, 2004).

London was chaotic with crime and homeless and landless former serfs. England, particularly London, called for a new system of policing. Sir Robert Peel, the founder of the first publicly paid police agency, introduced a London Metropolitan Police bill to the House of Commons on April 15, 1829, and said, "It is no longer possible to leave all the responsibility in connection with the detection of offenders, or the prevention of crimes, in the hands of the parochial authorities" (Ascoli, 1979, p. 1). To overcome opposition, Sir Robert Peel stressed that the new police would serve the public, not the government, as was common in the European police forces. The new police would be citizens in uniform and would police by consent, not by force or repression. These ideas were incorporated in the principles of behavior for the new police officers and their organizational structure.

To ensure their deterrence value, the new police officers were highly visible, wearing bright uniforms during the day and night. The uniforms were designed to let potential criminals and disorderly members of the public know of their presence. The visible Met officers walked a small, regular route at a pace of 2.5 miles per hour (Bindler and Hjalmarsson, 2021). Nonetheless, despite their visible appearance, their interactions with the public were largely invisible and not subject to review. The inherent dark side lacked transparency and accountability. Furthermore, it was an unfortunate reality that police patrols were most frequent and invisible among the groups considered to be the "dangerous classes." According to the English elites, "this lower Rank of people" exhibited a "lower-class culture" where crime and disorder occurred (Colquhoun, 1806, republished in 1969). This same thinking became a part of the reasoning in American policing when the London Met model was adopted in America (Potter, no date; Williams, 2002). Whether or not one was young, poor, transient, an immigrant, or a person of color was not supposed to influence police power in England and America; however, as a practical matter it did—and still does (see Textbox 2.2 and Textbox 2.3).

Textbox 2.2. The 2015 President's Task Force for 21st Century Policing

The 2015 President's Task Force for 21st Century Policing spoke to this issue and its effect on American policing:

[American] Law enforcement culture should embrace a guardian—rather than a warrior—mindset to build trust and legitimacy both within agencies and with the public. Toward this end law enforcement agencies should adopt procedural justice [fair and equal justice for all] as the guiding principle for internal and external policies and practices to guide their transactions with rank-and-file officers and with citizens they serve. Law enforcement agencies should also establish a *culture of transparency and accountability* [italics added] to build trust and legitimacy. (Task Force, 2015, p. 7)

Textbox 2.3. Police Best Practices: Procedural Justice

Procedural justice, the foundation upon which democratic policing is based, is outlined in the Peelian principles. Procedural justice entails the fair, impartial, and transparent treatment of all citizens and each other. The concept can be viewed as an equation (Kunard and Mae, 2015, p. 3):

$$ASSESSMENT = OUTCOME + PROCESS$$

Assessment refers to the citizen's opinion of the fairness of his or her encounter with police. Ultimately, the citizen will be influenced by the *outcome* of the encounter and the *process* to assess the interaction. It makes a difference to citizens as to how the police do what they do as well as what they do. The obvious examples are those officers who talk down to others or use racial and ethnic epithets. Engaging in this behavior affects citizens' willingness to cooperate or trust the police. Every police–citizen contact is an opportunity to build trust and credibility. Whenever possible, police officers must take the time to explain why they stopped the citizen and why they chose the outcome. This can change a constitutional "Terry stop" into a positive outcome. If there is no reasonable suspicion, the officer should not do the stop. Doing justice is not doing injustice.

A second deterrence objective of the new visible state representatives was *incapacitation* (Bindler and Hjalmarsson, 2021). This led to accepted patterns of police misconduct in obtaining false convictions and in providing perjured testimony (Holdaway, 1983; Morton, 1993). If an English police officer caught a criminal in the act, the offender would be sentenced to death, prison, or transportation to Australia. This practice permitted police to remove certain persons, whether caught in the act or not, from London. Suspected criminals who were not caught in the act were "fitted" (framed) with crimes or evidence of crimes. This police strategy would become known in America by the misnomer "noble cause corruption."

A member of the new law-enforcement occupation officer would "fit up" a "known criminal" even if that meant "fudging the evidence" to convict the obviously guilty person. This still occurs in the United Kingdom. A former English police officer and police expert said, British police were always ready to "fit up" a "guilty person" with fabricated evidence or a false confession when necessary (Caless, 2008). "Fitting people up" is identified as a serious police corruption problem in British public surveys. Simon Holdaway, a retired British police officer, a police expert, a scholar, and an author, quotes a British police officer:

> I think it is permissible to thump [beat] a prisoner and get justice. You see we know the officer who brings the person in the station. We know some of the facts and, let's face it we know that most people who are brought to the station are guilty anyway. So what's wrong with giving them a verbal [perjured testimony] or adding some evidence. (Holdaway, 1983, p. 130)

THE NEW POLICING OCCUPATION WAS AN IMPROVEMENT AND A MODEL FOR CHANGE

The new system did prevent some crime and disorder. Bindler and Hjakmarsson (2021) used a highly sophisticated research design, based on statistics from the

London National Archives, a national database located in Richmond, England, and concluded that the London Metropolitan Police system (the Met) prevented crime, especially violent crimes such as robbery. The new occupation and its patrol methods also sought to increase "response time" to crime attempts and completed violations. The new publicly paid police occupation set behavioral standards for the police, which was a vast improvement over the existing police models. There was a change in organizational structure to a more rational bureaucratic model.

Organizational Structure

Prior to the September 1829 Blue Parade, the two commissioners for the Metropolitan Police—Charles Rowan and Richard Mayne—were sworn in in July and tasked with setting up the organization, structure, and rules of conduct for the new police (Ascoli, 1979). Twelve weeks later, they had done the following:

1. Produced an approved establishment for the first six police districts and the supervising headquarters;
2. Devised a pay structure;
3. Devised a detailed divisional organization, broken down into sections, and precise beats;
4. Written a General Instruction Book which remains today a model of its kind[1];
5. Established a central police office at 4 Whitehall Place;
6. Acquired suitable station houses from which each divisional "company" would operate;
7. Recruited upward of one thousand constables and superior grades;
8. Designed, contracted, and arranged the manufacture of uniforms and equipment for the new force; and
9. Provided basic drill and elementary instructions for the force.

The General Instruction Book contains what are known as the "Peelian principles of policing," which are recognized as the standards of ethical police behavior for democratic policing, that is, policing with the consent of the people. Setting the standards for the occupation in effect defines the occupation's deviant behaviors, that is, workers' behavior that is outside the norm. First, the concept of consent in this context refers to "the power of the police coming from the consent of the public, as opposed to the power of the state" (Tudor, 2023, p. 2). That concept explicitly recognizes citizens' oversight of police behavior and

---

1. *General Instruction Book* is one of the main accomplishments of the new policing *Creating a Culture of Integrity* (see McDevitt, Farrell, Wolff, 2008).

that no individual, or the state can withdraw their consent from the police or the law. The publicly paid police model of the United Kingdom and, in turn, of the United States requires public approval and trust. In effect the police are required to apply the law fairly, impartially, and using minimum force.

The nine Peelian principles set the stage for preventive policing and are based on *consent* of the public, *transparency* of power, and *accountability* for police actions. The purpose of the Peelian principles was to ensure that a culture of integrity developed in what was recognized as a morally dangerous occupation fraught with temptations. A culture of integrity would ensure that individual police officers would recognize and resist the temptations inherent in police work.

NINE PEELIAN PRINCIPLES OF POLICING

1. To prevent crime and disorder, as an alternative to their repression by military force and severity of legal punishment. The goal in creating the new police was crime prevention.
2. To recognize always that the power of the police to fulfill their functions and duties is dependent on public approval of their existence, actions and behavior, and their ability to secure and maintain public support. Democracies remain as long as they have the consent of the people.
3. To recognize always that to secure and maintain the respect and approval of the public means also securing of the willing cooperation of the public in the task of securing observance of laws. Having trust in the police to be fair leads to cooperating with the police in the exercise of their duties.
4. To recognize always that the extent to which the cooperation of the public can be secured diminishes proportionally the necessity of the use of physical force and compulsion for achieving police objectives. Having trust in the police's fairness and legitimacy reduces the need for force.
5. To seek and preserve public favor, not by pandering to public opinion, but by constantly demonstrating absolutely impartial service to law, in complete independence of policy, and without regard to the justice or injustice of the substance of individual laws, by ready offering of individual service and friendship to all members of the public without regard to their wealth or social standing by ready exercise of courtesy and friendly good humor, and by ready offering of individual sacrifice in protecting and preserving life. Procedural justice demands transparency and fairness.
6. To use physical force only when the exercise of persuasion, advice and warning is found to be insufficient to obtain public co-operation to an extent necessary to secure observance of law or to restore order, and to use only the minimum degree of physical force which is necessary on any particular occa-

sion for achieving a police objective. Police must respect the sanctity of life and physical integrity.

7. To maintain at all times a relationship with the public that gives reality to the historic tradition that the police are the public and that the public are the police, the police being only members of the public who are paid to give full-time attention to duties which are incumbent on every citizen in the interests of community welfare and existence. Police officers are paid to do what is every person's responsibility.

8. To recognize always the need for strict adherence to police executive functions, and to refrain from even seeming to usurp the powers of the judiciary or of avenging individuals or the State, and of authoritatively judging guilt and punishing the guilty. This principle forbids what would become known as "noble cause corruption" in the United States; however, police officers using unethical or illegal means to accomplish desired goals is as old as the police occupation. The author uses the term "noble cause injustice" to distinguish it from corruption, which is defined to require a personal gain.

9. To recognize always that the test of police efficiency is the absence of crime and disorder, and not visible evidence of police action in dealing with them. This principle endorses preventive policing.

MORALLY DANGEROUS WORKPLACE SETTING

The London Metropolitan Police officer's behavior was prescribed by law, rules and regulations, and ethical standards. The new occupation was morally dangerous and tainted by its connection to evildoers, criminals, perverts, and disorderly persons (Bittner, 1980). As stated, the stigma and moral danger created a dark side to this new occupation, as the officers succumbed to rule breaking and criminal opportunities. The work setting presented the so-inclined or morally weak police worker with the central factor in workplace crime: opportunity. Workplace crime cannot take place without a *motivated offender* and an *opportunity*. The last factor, *a real or perceived low level of risk*, was added as the police culture of a blue brotherhood developed. Police misconduct, corruption, and crime exploded among the ranks of the new occupation.

Workplace Deviance

The opportunity structure for deviance was exacerbated by moral policing among the powerless working classes. Records in the National Archives of the United Kingdom reveal that Met officers were dismissed for drunkenness, neglect, misconduct, and criminal conduct (Bindler and Hjalmarsson, 2021). These acts are referred to as workplace deviance, a term that includes violations of norms, policies, and expected behavior by occupational workers (Martin, Rao, and Soan, 2009). These deviant behaviors expanded as police officers learned how to commit the acts and mask their behavior, in other words, as they created a dark side to policing. Police officers, then and now, learn the techniques and rationalizations for workplace misconduct and crime from their fellow workers. The early evidence of workplace misconduct and crime reveals that almost all police workers in the new occupation engaged in some deviant acts; that a larger number occasionally committed rule violations and thefts; and that a smaller group of London police officers were criminals, taking advantage of any opportunity in the work setting (Browne, 1956).

The members of the new publicly paid police-work occupation, which spread throughout England and Wales and reached the colonies that were to become America, were expected to be of higher moral quality than the average citizen. History would prove this expectation to be wrong. The police's visible presence, although originally intended to prevent crime, instead became a camouflaged cloak of power and respectability in the shadows known only to them, their victims, and history. This was especially true when the new police-work profession was transported to the United States. In the United States, the new police became corrupt and served the interest of the politicians and not the law (Reith, 1952). This behavior contributed to policing's darks side. "The most hideous and perverse police transgressions occur in sheltered backrooms" (Bittner, 1980, p. 99).

The Development of American Policing

The nature of the duties—close contact with the public, control of vice activities, and enormous discretion combined with low-visibility decision-making—overwhelmed the new publicly paid police officers. The extent of this moral failure became most evident in America as the Met model was emulated in New York City (1845), New Orleans and Cincinnati (1852), Chicago and Philadelphia (1855), and Baltimore and Newark (1857) (Uchida, 2015). According to one source, sixty-four American cities formalized a professional police agency from 1840 to 1930: in 1840, eight agencies; in 1850, twenty-six agencies; in 1860, sixteen agencies; in 1870, seven agencies; in 1880, three agencies; and, from 1900 to 1930, four agencies (Salimbene, 2021). The growth from 1840 to 1860—when fifty new American police agencies were created—is explained by the demographic changes in American society at the time. America's population from 1814 to 1860 quadrupled to over 31 million as a result of an influx of immigrants from Ireland and the German states. The foreign-born workers replaced many native-born factory workers, causing competition and turmoil in the expanding urban cities (Jaffee, 2007). This was exacerbated by these groups moving into the working-class sections of cities. Crime, disorder, and riots resulted. The historical events that resulted in policing having a dark side in the United Kingdom and the United States led to efforts to build a culture of integrity, based on the behavioral standards outlined in the Peelian principles.

BUILDING A CULTURE OF INTEGRITY

The nine principles were the first police code of ethics The early founders of the English police envisioned a police occupation that would be similar to practice of medicine, law, and teaching. They envisioned that policing, at some time in the future, would require prolonged training, formal qualifications, and a code of ethics, as had occurred in those other occupations prior to their recognition as professions. The professional behavior of individual officers, groups of officers, and, in turn, all members of the police-work occupation would depend on them subscribing to and following a code of ethical behavior.

Police Code of Ethics

A code of ethical behavior is a code of behavior that is considered correct for a particular group or members of an occupation (Barker, 1996). The code of ethics outlines the culture of integrity. The purpose of a code of ethics is to establish formal guidelines for ethical behavior and eliminate the ambiguity that surrounds individual considerations of what is right or wrong behavior (Department of Justice, 1978, pp. 16–22). Police agencies in the United States and the United Kingdom—England and Wales—have published codes of ethics.

American Police Code of Ethics

The American Law Enforcement Code of Ethics was developed by the International Association of Chiefs of Police in 1987. The Peelian principles are the basis for this code. The International Association of Chiefs of Police (IACP) code of ethics applies to official American publicly paid law-enforcement officers and not to privately employed police. A law-enforcement officer is defined as any public official who has the extraordinary powers of arrest above and beyond those possessed by all citizens in a democracy and who performs at least one of the direct police services of patrol, traffic control, or criminal investigation (Barker, 1996). This definition applies to all public law-enforcement officers at the local, county, state, and federal levels.

Following is the IACP code of ethics, with sections of it interspersed with my analysis (IACP, 1987; all italics are mine):

> AS A LAW ENFORCEMENT OFFICER, *my fundamental duty is to serve the community, to safeguard lives and property, to protect the*

innocent against deception, the weak against oppression, or intimidation, and the peaceful against violence and disorder, and to respect the constitutional rights of all to liberty, equality and justice.

Constitutional Policing. There is no mention of crime, making arrests, writing citations, or investigating crimes in the IACP code of ethics. Why? The American police, operating in a democratic and free society, are considered to have a higher calling. The key words in this statement are "serve," "protect," and "respect." The police in a democracy are—or should be—the most important protectors of individual and group liberties. "If the overall purpose of the police service in America were narrowed to a single objective, that objective would be to preserve the peace in a manner consistent with the freedoms secured by the Constitution" (National Commission on Standards and Goals, 1973, 13). The 2015 President's Task Force on 21st Century Policing echoed the same feeling: "Trust between law enforcement agencies and the people they protect and serve is essential in a democracy. It is the key to the stability of our criminal justice system, and the safe and effective delivery of policing services" (President's Task Force, 2015, p. 1). That means that every citizen should be handled in the same way and fairly to ensure the constitutional rights of all.

> *I **Will** keep my private life unsullied as an example to all and will behave in a manner which does not bring discredit to me or my agency. I **Will** maintain courageous calm in the face of danger, scorn, or ridicule; develop self-restraint; and be constantly mindful of the regulations of welfare of others, Honest in thought and deed in both my personal and official life. I **Will** be exemplary in obeying the law and the regulations of my department. Whatever I see or hear of a confidential nature or that is confided in me in my official capacity will be kept ever secret unless revelation is necessary in the performance of my duty.*

Being a Police Officer Is a Master Status. A status is a social position that we occupy in a group. For example, in a family there can be social positions known as father, mother, daughter, son, and so on. A person can occupy social positions in a variety of groups, including a family group, a work group, a church group, etc. A master status is one that cuts across all the groups a person belongs to and defines his or her expected behavior. Preacher, priest, and teacher are examples of master statuses; each is associated with an expected behavior pattern. Law-enforcement officer is a master status that overshadows all other social statuses; therefore, law-enforcement officers must act accordingly on and off duty. They live in a fishbowl in which what they do is seen, heard, and commented on. A police officer's integrity and credibility must be beyond reproach. Once one has been a cop, one is never not a cop.

> *I **Will** never act officiously or permit personal feelings, prejudices, political beliefs, aspirations or friendships to influence my decisions with*

*no compromise for crime and with relentless prosecution of criminals. **I Will** enforce the law courteously and appropriately without fear or favor, malice or ill will, never accepting gratuities.*

Avenging Angel Syndrome. Police officers are not the law. They are paid to enforce the law. However, their enforcement decisions are mostly discretionary decisions that should never become personal. The "avenging angel" syndrome should be avoided at all costs.

> ***I RECOGNIZE** the badge of my office as a symbol of public faith, and I accept it as a public trust to be held so long as I am true to the ethics of public service. **I WILL NEVER** engage in acts of bribery nor will I condone such acts by other police officers. **I WILL** cooperate with all legally authorized agencies and their representatives in the pursuit of justice. **I KNOW** that I alone am responsible for my own standard or professional performance and will take every opportunity to enhance and improve my level of knowledge and competence. **I Will** constantly strive to achieve these objectives and ideals dedicating myself before GOD to my chosen profession—**LAW ENFORCMENT**.*

Police Code of Ethics in the United Kingdom

In July 2014, the College of Policing in the United Kingdom published a "Code of Ethics: A Code of Practice for the Principles and Standards of Professional Behavior for the Policing Profession of England and Wales" (college.policing .uk). The College of Policing is the official body that sets the standards for all of the police agencies in England and Wales. The chief executive of the College of Policing makes it clear that this code of ethics is based on the Peelian principles. He also recognizes that policing has not adopted all the hallmarks of a profession; however, the adoption of a code of ethics is one step toward obtaining fully professional status for policing, similar to that seen in medicine and law (college .policing.uk). The code contains ten standards of professional behavior.

Standards of Professional Behavior:

1. **Honesty and integrity.** I will be honest and act with integrity at all times and will not compromise my position.
   - Examples of meeting this standard are when you:
   - are sincere and truthful
   - show courage in doing what you believe to be right
   - ensure your decisions are not influenced by improper considerations
   - do not make false, misleading, or inaccurate oral or written statements
   - do not use your position to inappropriately coerce any person or to settle personal grievances

2. **Authority, respect and courtesy.** I will act with self-control and tolerance, treating members of the public and colleagues with respect and courtesy. I will use my powers and authority lawfully and proportionately and will respect the rights of all individuals.
   - Examples of meeting this standard are when you:
   - remain composed and respectful
   - retain proportionate self-restraint
   - recognize the particular needs of victims and witnesses
   - step forward and take control when required
   - keep an open mind and do not prejudge situations
   - use your authority only in ways that are proportionate, lawful, accountable, necessary and ethical

3. **Equality and diversity.** I will act with fairness and impartiality. I will not discriminate unlawfully or unfairly.
   - Examples of meeting this standard are when you:
   - show compassion and empathy to people you come into contact with
   - treat people according to their needs
   - recognize that some individuals who come into contact with the police are vulnerable and may require additional support and assistance
   - take a proactive approach to opposing discrimination so as to adequately support victims
   - consider the needs of the protected groupings
   - promote equality and diversity

4. **Use of force.** I will only use force as part of my role and responsibilities, and only to the extent that it is necessary, proportionate and reasonable in all the circumstances.

5. **Orders and instructions.** I will, as a police officer, give and carry out lawful orders only, and will abide by Police Regulations. I will give reasonable instructions only, and will follow all reasonable instructions.
   - Examples of meeting this standard are when you:
   - give and follow only lawful orders
   - accept restrictions on your private life

6. **Duties and responsibilities.** I will be diligent in the exercise of my duties and responsibilities.
   - Examples of meeting this standard are when you:
   - are aware of unconscious bias
   - consider the changing needs and concerns of different communities

7. **Confidentiality.** I will treat information with respect, and access or disclose it only in the proper course of my duties.

8. **Fitness for work.** I will ensure, when on duty or at work, that I am fit to carry out my responsibilities.

9. **Conduct.** I will behave in a manner, whether on or off duty, which does not bring discredit on the police service or undermine public confidence in policing.
10. **Challenging and reporting improper behavior.** I will report, challenge or take action against the conduct of colleagues which have fallen below the standards of professional behavior.

Code of Ethics Violated from the Beginning

As stated, codes of ethics define what is accepted or not accepted behavior for the police occupation. In effect, they define the occupation's deviant behavior. The "official" codes of conduct for policing in the United Kingdom and in the United States were examined for obvious reasons. The 1829 Peelian principles are the foundation for both codes. Abuse of the police position and its power led to numerous examples of proscribed behavior, including serious criminal behavior in the United Kingdom and in the United States (Browne, 1956). According to the chief counsel of the Knapp Commission, which investigated NYPD misconduct and corruption in the 1970s, police corruption became a problem in 1844, when the New York State legislature created the first American municipal police department in New York City (Armstrong, 2012). The nineteenth-century New York City police department and other agencies that followed the London model copied many of the features of the London-based police. Such agencies were publicly supported, were bureaucratic in organization, and had rules and regulations. However, local American police were not under centralized control. Early American police were corrupt and brutal to a fault. In most nineteenth century cities, the local police were under control of the political parties. The local ward leader appointed the police officers. He was typically a neighborhood tavern owner. The police accepted payoffs to allow illegal drinking, prostitution, and gambling.

Breaking conduct rules, engaging in crime, and having other integrity issues became the dark side of American policing, which continues in the modern era. There were NYC police scandals in 1894, the Lexow committee; 1913, the Curran committee; 1932, the Seabury committee; and 1950, the Harry Gross investigation. In the NYPD, police corruption became "a way of life." In the early 1930s, a New York citizens' committee allegedly said, "[C]orruption is so ingrained [in the NYPD] that the man of ordinary character entering the force and not possessed of extraordinary moral fiber may easily succumb" (Knapp Commission, 1972, p. 62). However, as extensive as corruption was in the early NYPD, there were officers who took no graft.

Even in the most corrupt law-enforcement agencies, there is a continuum of officers, ranging from "white knights," who are considered to be honest to a fault, to criminal cops or rogues; there are even crews or gangs of criminal cops that commit the most serious crime (Barker, 2011). The number of officers in each category varies by opportunity, inclination, and risk. The police occupation supplies the opportunity; the officer brings the inclination to the work setting (his or her actions result from personal and rational choices); and, finally, the police culture defines the risk. Peer group norms and values, such as the "code of silence," influence choice or neutralization techniques. The vaunted and exaggerated code of silence is best looked on as a barometer of how "good" or "bad" the peer group considers the act. It is not immutable. However, the code of silence is an important factor in police occupational deviance, as are opportunity and inclination.

Police work, as discretionary decision-making, in some incidents leads to poor or deviant decisions; however, the peer group defines the acts that police officers in their group, squad, unit, or agency should not engage in. If an individual officer feels that his or her peer group is against a behavior, the malefactor engaging in that behavior is owed no loyalty. There is no absolute code of silence. Although police agencies in the United Kingdom and the United States have struggled with the code of silence since their founding, police officers are often quick to "rat out" a police blue brother under some circumstances. The NYPD officers who testified against the officer who sodomized Abner Louima with a broken broomstick were not ostracized (Benoit and Dubra, 2004). His actions horrified the department's cultural system, which gave implicit support to some acts of misconduct, malfeasance, and murder and not to others. When an officer's outrageous behavior exceeds the bounds of the peer group, the officer is often on his or her own.

The code of silence exists to some extent in all police organizations that follow the paramilitary model, but it varies with police culture, as noted above, and police culture varies by country and police organizations within those countries (Ivkovic, Haberfield, Kang, Peacock, Porter, Prenzler, and Sauerman, 2020). The code is a factor in police occupational deviance, as are opportunity and inclination. It appears from the Ivkovic et al. study that supervisors and the peer group (including the organizational culture and the workplace environment) are important variables that influence the strength or weakness of the code of silence. Respondents were more likely to report deviant behavior when they believed their supervisors or their peers would take action. This has implications for its effect on workplace deviance. In any event, cops do blow the whistle on other cops. One Los Angeles Police Department detective, in her PhD dissertation, says that police whistleblowing exists and is common and provides empirical evidence of such whistleblowing (Gonzales, 2010). Police whistleblowers can report the deviant behavior of fellow workers and be protected from retaliation.

Criminal police officers, with respect to the police code of silence, are just like other criminals, including those in the Mafia, which has a code of omertà; if the penalty is high enough and certain to occur, they rat each other out (Barker, 2011). Police officers will snitch on each other to keep from getting fired, to avoid criminal prosecution, and to avoid civil liability. For example, five corrupt officers identified wrongdoers and gave testimony during the 1970s NYPD Knapp Commission hearing on police corruption (Knapp Commission, 1972). Later, in the Buddy Boys scandal, NYPD officers bumped into each other seeking "get out of jail" cards. Chicago police whistleblowers have sent corrupt cops to prison. A rookie officer, with the Oakland Police Department for fifteen days, turned in officers on a crisis response team drug special unit for murdering a young Hispanic man. There is no honor among thieves. After all, a group of crooked and criminal cops is a group of crooked and criminal cops. Cops don't trust criminals.

POLICE SCANDALS IN THE UNITED KINGDOM

The same periodic pattern of police-corruption scandals that have appeared in the United States have occurred in the United Kingdom. The United Kingdom has one police system, with forty-five local police agencies in England and Wales with separate jurisdictions in Scotland and Northern Ireland. According to Morton (1993), there were police scandals in the United Kingdom in 1855, 1877, 1890, 1911, 1920, 1929, 1955, 1962, 1963, 1964, 1969, and the 1970s. When the new London Metropolitan Police commissioner took office in 1972, he said that the Met was "the most routinely corrupt organization in London (Cox, Shirley, and Short, 1977). From 1969 to 1972, fifty officers were sent to jail and 478 took early retirement. Police misconduct and criminal behavior continue in both countries. The United Kingdom and the United States are currently in the throes of national police crises precipitated by police murders and other questionable police behaviors.

NATIONAL POLICE CRISIS IN THE UNITED STATES

American police violence, including murder of innocents, began with the atrocities of the colonial slave patrols and reached its peak with the Memorial Day massacre, perpetrated by Chicago police officers in 1937 (Barker, 2020). Today, there is a law-enforcement crisis in the United States—a crisis resulting from a lack of ethical behavior, transparency, trust, and accountability. The police crisis is due to American police officers abusing their power and engaging in serious criminal behavior, including murder. The current police crisis in the United States began in 2014 with the August 9th shooting death of an eighteen-year-old black teenager, Michael Brown, in Ferguson, Missouri, and the rise of the Black Lives Matter movement. A little over two months later, a seventeen-year-old black teenager was shot sixteen times on October 20 by a white Chicago police officer who was convicted of murder in this case four years later (Barker, 2020). A third shooting of an unarmed black occurred on November 20, 2014, when a white police officer in Columbus, Ohio, shot and killed a twelve-year-old black child. A spate of police fatal shootings of black males soon followed. A bad policing event anywhere causes a negative reaction everywhere. The American national police crisis picked up steam when a white Oklahoma City police officer was arrested and charged with sexually assaulting fourteen black women in a five-month period from February 2014 to June 2014 (Barker, 2020). Oklahoma also had the highest rates of police violence against non-Hispanic black Americans in 1980 and 2019 (Anon, October 21, 2021). Today, there is a national debate over the alleged murder of Tyre Nichols in Memphis.

Dangerous Classes

It appears that the groups initially identified as members of the dangerous classes in England by the elites in the nineteenth century are once again the targets of police abuse, this time in the United States. Polls indicate that a substantial number of Americans—particularly persons who are part of a minority or marginalized group or who are persons of color—do not support the way the police "do what they do, and how they do it." According to a 2023 report, 89 percent of those responding called for changes in local American policing (21CP Solutions, March 2023). The report goes on to say that a 2022 Gallup survey found that only 45 percent of respondents had a "great deal" or "quite a lot" of confidence in the police—53 percent of white respondents and 34 percent of respondents of other races. This lack of public trust in local police is an American problem. In the words of President Obama, who appointed the Task Force on 21st Century Policing, "When any part of the American family does not feel like they are being treated fairly, that's a problem for all of us." The fair treatment of one citizen matters to all citizens, especially in a nation as diverse as the American republic. The United Kingdom is also in the throes of a national police scandal.

NATIONAL POLICE CRISIS IN THE UNITED KINGDOM

Policing in England and Wales is based on the principle of policing by consent, which relies heavily on a relationship of mutual trust between the police and the public. Trust is essential if the police are to receive information from the public which helps them to detect and

combat crime. It is also essential to enable the public to feel able to
seek the assistance and protection of police officers when necessary.
(IPCC, September 2011)

The quote cited above comes from the United Kingdom's Independent
Police Complaints Commission (the IPCC) in response to a police crisis in the
United Kingdom in 2011. The IPCC became operational in 2004. It investigates
the most serious allegations of police misconduct in England and Wales and re-
views appeals of decisions made by local police agencies. The 2011 IPCC report
was the result of "widespread concern about deaths and serious injuries in police
custody and the policing of black communities" (IPCC, September 2011). The
quote is similar to what President Obama said in 2015 and the reason for the
2015 Task Force Report. The current London Metropolitan Police commissioner, Sir Mark Rowley, indicates that the current Metropolitan Police crisis is
more serious than that of 2011, "We [the Met police] failed as a police service
to show zero tolerance for racism, misogyny, homophobia, and ableism and that
shames us and clearly previous claims of being an organization that shows zero
tolerance have been premature" (quoted in Dodd, October 16, 2022).

Casey Report, 2022

The Casey report, called so because of the commission chairperson, Dame Louise
Casey, was commissioned in 2021 by the UK home secretary after the brutal
kidnapping, rape, and murder of Sarah Everard by a serving UK police officer.
Sarah Everard was a thirty-three-year-old marketing executive who was kidnapped, raped, and murdered by a Metropolitan Police officer, Wayne Couzens,
who was working as a parliamentary and diplomatic protection officer. She was
walking home from a friend's house in south London at about 21:30 BST on
March 3, 2021, when she was abducted. Ms. Everard was a random victim, but
Couzens was a repeat sex offender and had planned the abduction and murder
(Morton, September 30, 2021). He made numerous trips to research the area
and decide the best way to "hunt" for a lone young woman to rape. Several days
before this heinous abduction, he rented a car and bought self-adhesive tape.
When he saw Ms. Everard walking, he showed her his Met police identification
card and arrested her for a bogus coronavirus violation. He handcuffed her and
put her in the rented car. A couple traveling by at the time believed, as Ms. Everard evidently did, that an undercover officer was making a valid arrest. Couzens
then drove the victim and the rented car to where he had parked his own car.
The police officer then drove to a secluded area where he raped and murdered
Ms. Everard. At 02:31, he was spotted at a service station, buying drinks.

The next day he returned to where he had dumped the body and poured gaso-
line on the remains. Then he put the remains in two garbage bags and dumped them

in a pond in a woodland area he owned. Days later, Couzens took his wife and two children on a family trip to the area, where he burned the body. He became a suspect and was briefly interviewed. When the body was found in the pond near the land he owned, he was arrested. He was tried, convicted, and sentenced to life in prison. The Everard murder, done by a serving police officer, created public outrage and called for more action by the police. This led to the Casey review.

The interim Casey review, in October 2022, called the vetting, misconduct, and misogyny in the police service racist and misogynistic. The review found that it took four hundred days to resolve misconduct allegations; that officers with repeated patterns of misconduct were not identified or disciplined; that there was no good definition of what constituted gross misconduct (a firing offense); and that black and Asian officers were over 120 percent more likely to be removed from the police service during the probationary period. The racial and gender bias of the disciplinary system was such that allegations of sexual misconduct and discrimination were less likely to be pursued than were other misconduct allegations (Presse, October 17, 2022). The new Met police commissioner has promised to reform the police service.

The current UK national police crisis and calls for reform have led to calls to disband London's Metropolitan Police Service and break it up into local agencies (Brownsell, March 23, 2023). The social activists who suggest defunding the London Metropolitan Police Service suggest shifting its funding to social services, such as housing, mental-health, and drug-addiction programs. There is also a Back Lives Matter organization in London that claims that the UK police use excessive force against a vulnerable pool of people who are black, Asian, or minority ethnic (BAME). Since 1990, 1,833 people have died in police custody. Persons who are BAME represent 3 percent of the population; however, they represent 16 percent of those who died in police custody or during police contact (Singh, September 27, 2022). The BBC reported that black persons accounted for 8 percent of the deaths. The shooting death of a twenty-four-year-old unarmed black man on September 5, 2022, sparked mass public outrage and demonstrations similar to those in the United States.

The young man was shot in the head through the windshield of his car while his car was blocked by two police vehicles in a narrow residential street (Singh, September 27, 2022). It took two weeks before the officer was suspended and an investigation began. The family was told that it would take six to nine months to complete the investigation. There have been other deaths of black men in recent years, but only one police officer has been convicted of an unlawful on-duty killing since 1986. The 2022 killing, combined with the Casey review, exacerbated the national police crisis in the United Kingdom. London Metropolitan Police commissioner, Sir Mark Rowley, told Parliament's London Assembly Police and Crime Committee that rooting out the hundreds of corrupt officers would take time (Davis, January 25, 2023). He expected two or three officers per week to be charged with dishonesty, sexual offenses, and violence in the coming months. His Majesty's Inspectorate of Constabulary told the BBC that a vetting audit showed that 10 percent of those officers joining the force in 2021 should have never been hired (Boyle, January 26, 2023). They faded into the dark side of British policing.

Conclusion

Police officers have abused their power and have engaged in police occupational deviance that led to misconduct, malfeasance, and murder. When the media and the public focused on police occupational deviance, their attention created police crises and calls for reform; this occurred in the United Kingdom and in the United States. The police reform efforts that resulted from the national police crises in the United Kingdom and the United States are still being determined. The two national crises demonstrate the occupational or workplace nature of police misconduct, corruption, and crime. Police work is a morally dangerous occupation in which officers confront a morally ambiguous work setting. Rule breaking and criminal behavior have always been a part of the dark side of policing. It takes a scandal to reveal the dark side. Every occupation has a dark side where misconduct occurs, but the dark side of policing runs counter to the ethos of democratic policing, which requires transparency and the consent of the public.

In a democracy, the public has a right to know what the police are doing and how they are doing it. The public, or the community, in a democratic and free society should hold powerful law-enforcement institutions, at all levels of government, accountable for their officers' behavior. There should be no dark side.

Discussion Questions

1. What are the similarities and differences between the United Kingdom's College of Police code of ethics and the IACP code of ethics? Are there any common elements? What is missing in each?
2. What are the similarities and differences between the national police crisis in the United Kingdom and that in the United States?
3. The discussions of police deviance in the United States and in the United Kingdom demonstrate that police deviance is more of a law-enforcement occupational hazard than a problem with some individuals being rotten apples. Find in the social media of other countries reports of police deviance similar to what is reported in the American social media. Share your findings with your classmates. To make the discussion even more interesting, look for examples in democratic countries and nondemocratic countries.

PART II

TYPES AND PATTERNS OF POLICE DEVIANCE

POLICE MISCONDUCT

CHAPTER 3

Police Sexual Misconduct and its Types

Key Terms:
> The sleazy blue line
> Sexual-abuse-prone occupations
> Police sexual misconduct (PSM)
> Police sexual misconduct causal equation
> Typology of police sexual misconduct Sex-related police homicides

Chapter Objectives:
> After reading this chapter, the reader should be able to analyze and discuss the following:

- Why police work is a sexual-abuse-prone occupation
- What a typology of police sexual misconduct would show
- What the police sexual misconduct causal equation is
- Why requiring police officers to have a college degree would not be a silver bullet for police reform

History has demonstrated that police work is a morally dangerous occupation with numerous opportunities for police misconduct. Police–citizen encounters often occur in highly discretionary and coercive, private, unsupervised settings (Klockers, Ivkovich, Harver, and Haberfield, 2000). The victims of the resulting misconduct overwhelmingly come from pools of vulnerable persons who lack power or credibility.

Recall that the concept of police misconduct is a heuristic concept for examining the types and patterns of deviant police criminal and noncriminal behavior. That behavior includes but is not limited to violations of agency policies, rules, and regulations.

Police professionals and police organizations have recognized that an agency's culture of integrity begins and ends with reducing the number of opportunities for misconduct and malfeasance through using a viable and *rational* system of administrative rule-making and having zero tolerance for rule violation (see Bureau of Justice Assistance, September 1989). The emphasis is on the *rational* aspect of this rule-making because the tendency of many police agencies is to *irrationally* overemphasize punishment as a tool of reform and become a punishment-oriented bureaucracy in which rules are routinely dismissed and violated.

There are American police agencies with volumes of policies, rules, and regulations that no one follows or even knows exist. I have seen this phenomenon in numerous civil suits I have been a part of as a consultant. In some American police agencies, an officer can be suspended for having unshined shoes but given a pass for having sex in a marked police vehicle or lying on a police report or in court (I personally observed this).

Many police conduct violations with citizen victims are crimes or become crimes if they're allowed to continue. The most frequent patterns of police misconduct of a criminal nature are police sexual misconduct (PSM), police lying, and police involvement in wrongful convictions. These behaviors are breaches of the public trust by *public servants* known and identified as law-enforcement officers. In democratic and free societies, citizens expect and demand that public servants conduct themselves according to personal, occupational, and organizational codes of conduct to insure integrity. In recent years, the concept of police integrity has evolved from a focus on individual integrity in the form of identifying and excluding "rotten apples" to a focus on the occupational and organizational factors that affect and fashion police misconduct (McDevitt, Farell, and Wolff, 2008; Barker, 2011).

Citizens trust that a police officer's individual integrity, defined as a sincere devotion to honesty, justice, and allegiance to an occupational code of conduct, will stop the officer from engaging in police misconduct even when he or she is not observed. Citizens also expect an agency to prevent or take action when transgressions are discovered (Bureau of Justice Assistance, 1989; see Textbox 3.1). Silence protects these behaviors and encourages their occurrence. American police officers *must* understand that "a code of silence is nothing more than a code to protect Corruption [and other patterns of police misconduct]" (Bureau of Justice Assistance, 1989, p. 45). It is easy to understand why police executives and fellow officers would be reluctant to disclose their failure to prevent police misconduct or take action against it; however, reform administrators and "honest" police officers must maintain a standard of transparency for reform to occur (Ward and McCormack, 1979).

Textbox 3.1. River Cops Scandal

There was a major police-corruption scandal in Miami, Florida, commonly referred to as the River Cops Scandal. The former chief of police for the Miami Police Department requested that the US Department of Justice examine the causes of and potential remedies for American police corruption. The Department of Justice asked the International Association of Chiefs of Police to conduct the study. The 128-page monograph is the result of that seminal study.

Police Sexual Misconduct: The Sleazy Blue Line

PSM is the optimum example of police misconduct or rule violation that is a crime with a human victim (Barker, 2020a). This form of police misconduct is ubiquitous in police work, worldwide, and is best described by Barker (2020a) as the "sleazy blue line." PSM is any form of proscribed sexual contact engaged in by a sworn police officer. Its practice is pervasive and has a long history in US police agencies. PSM can occur whenever there is an intersection of an opportunity—a person of the same sex or the opposite sex comes into contact with a sworn police officer—with an inclination on the part of that officer to engage in consensual or forced sexual contact with that person. Typically, the nature and extent of PSM depends on the real or perceived risk of the disclosure and/or punishment of the act. The occurrence of PSM is best understood as a rational causal equation:

> Causal Equation: Opportunity + Inclination + Low Risk = Police Sexual Misconduct

I receive daily reports of worldwide accounts of PSM from the alerts I have set up and from official press releases. The number and nature of the acts are overwhelming, particularly in the United States and the United Kingdom. As I write this chapter, a shocking police sexual-assault scandal is unfolding in Kansas City, Kansas (Berger, December 12, 2022). A thirty-five-year retired detective, a sexual predator, who worked low-income, predominantly black neighborhoods is alleged to have brutally abused and sexually assaulted multiple black women during his time with the Kansas City Police Department. One allegation claims that the "bad to the bone" (BTTB) detective protected drug dealers who forced women to work as prostitutes. In return, the detective was allowed to rape the women. This example is appalling and atypical of most PSM violations. However, there are other notifications I received in the last two weeks. On December 13, 2023, a police detective and a former *school resource officer* with the police department in Rock Hill, South Carolina, was indicted and charged with twelve counts of distributing child-sexual-abuse materials and six counts of receipt of child-sexual-abuse materials (US Attorney's Office, District of South Carolina, Department of Justice, December 13, 2023). A deputy sheriff in Camden County, Missouri, who was also a school resource officer, was arrested and charged on December 18, 2023, with fourteen felony counts of the possession and distribution of child-sexual-abuse materials (Fuchs, December 18, 2023). Putting police sexual predators in schools is akin to putting a fox in a hen house. It has disastrous results. On December 21, 2023, a police lieutenant with the police department in Longview, Texas, was sentenced to eleven months in federal prison for attempting to entice an eleven-year-old child to engage in sexual activity (US Attorney's Office, Middle District of Florida, Department of Justice, December 21, 2023). He was caught during an FBI sting as part of Operation Safe Childhood, a nationwide initiative against child sexual exploitation. There are other egregious examples of PSM cited in this book, including sexually motivated murders by police assailants. Sexual aggressors wearing badges exist in the law-enforcement occupation, worldwide. Sexual aggressors in blue are present at all levels of American law-enforcement agencies—from local to federal (Barker, 2020a).

PSM can be a violation of the organization's policies, rules, and regulations, although not all agencies have specific sexual-misconduct policies. PSM can also be a violation of the law, ranging from being a misdemeanor to being a felony. Therefore, PSM ranges from workplace harassment and consensual sex to forcible touching and violent acts, such as rape and murder. Police work, as an occupation, shares certain characteristics that increase the likelihood of sexual misconduct in the workplace setting.

POLICE WORK IS A SEXUAL-ABUSE-PRONE OCCUPATION

Sexual abuse is most likely to occur in occupations in which there is an unequal distribution of power; this differential produces opportunity for those with more power to perpetrate sexual abuse and makes those with less power more likely to be victims of sexual abuse (Calhoun and Coleman, 2002). In effect, the unequal power relationship increases the likelihood of improper sexual relationships. If the sexual predator selects targets from a vulnerable pool, he or she is safe from exposure. The existence of occupational sexual misconduct is no secret. States pass laws that prohibit sexual relationships between workers and clients in recognized sexual-abuse-prone occupations. Examples of such categories of workers that readily come to mind are priests and other clergy, coaches, doctors and other medical workers, schoolteachers, and university or college professors. The #METOO movement expanded the list of sexual-abuse-prone occupations exponentially. Elected officials were added to the list. The political occupation may have the most instances of sexual abuse and cover-up, based on exposure in the social media.

Those in criminal-justice-related occupations—police officers, corrections officers, judges, probation officers—are exemplars of workplace sexual misconduct. The victim or recipient of the sexual advance in an abuse-prone criminal-justice occupation has less authority or status than the perpetrator, a government official who is backed by the state. The police-work setting and its unsupervised, clandestine police–citizen encounters exacerbate the occurrence of police sexual abuse. Sexual aggressors in blue at the local level have the largest vulnerable pool (Barker, 2020a). The supposed "blue wall of secrecy" assures that all but the most heinous acts will not be reported and acted on by many police officers. However, PSM has a workplace basis and occurs in all policing settings, worldwide. Selected examples in other countries buttress the occupational nature of police-work-related sexual deviance.

Australia

Australia has a long history of police corruption and police sexual abuse (Chan, 1997). The Independent Broad-based Anti-corruption Commission (the IBAC) for the state of Victoria defined police predatory behavior as "a police officer or Protective Services Officer [who] misuses their authority to commence or attempt to commence an emotional and/or sexual relationship with a person they have met in the course of their duties" or " a police officer or PSO misuses their authority to sexually assault, stalk, harass, or groom a person they have met in the course of their duties" (IBAC, 2022). IBAC found that, from 2018 to 2022, there were twenty-seven incidents of predatory behavior engaged in by Victoria police officers. The incidents involved officers of all ranks and from all police regions.

The careful selection of victims is a factor in the occurrence of PSM in Australia. Australian aboriginal girls are targets for rape, custodial sexual abuse, and other forms of sexual violence. The Australian police brotherhood exacerbates the sexual-abuse problem, as such brotherhoods do worldwide. A recent study of Australian police found that a minority of police officers—4 to 6 percent—would not report fellow officers for thefts, perjury, and sexual assault (Porter and Prenzler, 2016).

Police misconduct that goes unreported and unpunished, based on extraneous factors such as race and ethnicity, extends to other areas of workplace crime among Australian police officers. A recent inquiry into Aboriginal in-custody deaths since 1991 found that thirty-three Aboriginal persons—Aboriginal persons are Australia's largest minority—had died, but no Victoria police member had been investigated or punished for any of the deaths (Clarke, May 8, 2023). The inquiry also found that there were 175 complaints of Victoria police officers engaging in racist behavior; however, only one officer had been sacked for alleged racism. The chief commissioner of the Victoria police said that "[the Victoria police] has caused harm in the past and unfortunately continues to do so in the present." He issued the following apology, "As a result of systematic racism, racist attitudes and discriminatory actions of police have gone undetected, unpunished, or without appropriate sanctions and have caused significant harm across generations of Aboriginal families" (Clarke, May 8, 2023).

Canada

Our neighbors to the north, in Canada, have a sordid history of PSM, including rape and murder, in their police agencies—federal (Royal Canadian Mounted Police [RCMP]), provincial, and local. A 2013 Human Rights Watch report documents firsthand reports of rapes and other sexual assaults of indigenous women and girls in Northern British Columbia, Canada, assaults that had gone on for decades. Forcible rapes and the sodomy of young girls were common police practices (Human Rights Watch, 2013). Some of these incidents are graphically described—too graphically to present here—in the report. The most sexual atrocities occur in British Columbia's communities along Highway 16, which is known as the "Highway of Tears." The report made three recommendations that dealt specifically with PSM:

- The British Columbia provincial government should expand the mandate of the Independent Investigations Office to include authority to investigate allegations of sexual assault by police;
- The RCMP, in cooperation with indigenous communities, should expand training and monitoring of training for police officers to counter racism and sexism in the treatment of indigenous women and girls in custody and to improve police responses to violence against women and girls in indigenous communities; and
- The RCMP should eliminate searches and monitoring of women and girls by male police officers in all but extraordinary circumstances and require documentation and review of any such searches by supervisors and commanders. It should prohibit cross-gender strip searches under all circumstances.

> In addition to this report, in 2020, there were thirty-eight ongoing investigations of alleged sexual

misconduct complaints against members of the Toronto Police Service (Trinh and Baksh, November 26, 2020). One allegation was a sexual-harassment complaint filed by a female officer who had intervened to stop another officer from using unjustified force against a black suspect. She was branded a liar and a rat and subjected to sexual harassment. Other PSM complaints were reported to the Ontario police services in recent years (Puddister and McNabb, March 16, 2021).

United Kingdom (England and Wales)

Police misconduct and crime began as an occupational/workplace problem in the United Kingdom. The police occupation, as a recognized line of work, began with the 1829 London Metropolitan Police model, and the Met model was replicated by many local American police agencies in the early nineteenth century. The abuse of power in the form of sexual misconduct came with the occupation. That tradition continues in both countries. In March 2021, Sarah Everard a thirty-three-year-old marketing executive was kidnapped, raped, and murdered by a Metropolitan police officer, Wayne Couzens. He will be included in the discussion of "killer cops." She was walking home from a friend's house in south London when she was abducted. Ms. Everard was a random victim, but Couzens was a repeat sex offender. Also, another serving Met officer has been charged with two rapes—one in August 2022 and the second in September 2022 (Ross, September 9, 2022). Both women in the latter rapes, one a fellow Met police officer, were intoxicated when the sexual assaults occurred. Sexual assaults appear to be common in complaints against British police officers. The Independent Office for Police Conduct (IOPC), which investigates complaints against the police in England and Wales, reports that abuse of power for a sexual purpose (APSP) is the most frequent form of police corruption (Anon, October 26, 2021).

A 2021 UK report found that there were 750 allegations of sexual misconduct against officers in forty-three police forces in England and Wales and against officers in Police Scotland and the British Transport Police between 2016 and 2020. The Met—the United Kingdom's largest police force—recorded 530 sexual allegations. The Greater Manchester Police agency had 158 allegations—130 against male officers, eleven against female officers, and seventeen in which the officer's gender was unknown (Wolfe-Robinson, October 11, 2021). Sweeting, Arabaci-Hills, and Cole (2021) conducted a quantitative analysis of police-misconduct hearings about which information was posted on the public websites of police forces in England and Wales in November 2018 and April 2019. They found 155 cases that clearly identified PSM in thirty UK police agencies. They recognized that all police forces in England and Wales posted such information and that the amount varied by agency. The cases were ranked in order into seven categories: 1) sex with victims; 2) inappropriate sexual behavior directed toward staff; 3) sexual contact with a member of the public; 4) sex with juveniles; 5) sex while on duty; 6) voyeurism; 7) and pornography-related behavior. Nearly one third of the cases involved sexual relationships with victims, witnesses, and other vulnerable people. Victims of domestic abuse, rape, and sexual abuse predominated. Evidence of mental issues and substance abuse among victims was present in many cases, evidence that such victims were especially vulnerable targets for police sexual predators.

Most of the perpetrators were male police constables; such officers would most likely encounter these victims. The second largest category of victims was colleagues. Officers at the level of sergeant or above were seven times more likely to be involved in this sexual misconduct. Supervisors' nonconsensual touching and speech were directed toward those of a lower rank; there was a power differential in these cases. Detective constables were 1.8 times more likely to target offenders than to target police constables. All eight of the female sexual predators had sexual relationships with offenders. The latter category had the highest risk of exposure and harsh discipline. All the female offenders were dismissed. There was evidence to suggest that some sexual deviants, especially those who targeted children, joined the police service because of the opportunities for sexual misconduct. Others had succumbed to the morally corrupt police-work setting. It was evident that the risk of sanction for prohibited sexual behaviors varied by police agency, indicating the peer group and social setting provided definitions of accepted and discouraged PSM.

Scotland

The outgoing chief constable of Police Scotland made an astonishing admission that the Scotland police force is "institutionally racist and discriminatory" (Smith, May 25, 2023). He said that the admission was necessary to become anti-racist. His exact words were, "It is right for me, the right thing for me to do as chief constable, to clearly state that institutional racism, sexism, misogyny, and discrimination exist." It appears that he was right on target. Sexism and misogyny complaints from female officers with Police Scotland—the central police agency—led to the appointment of a special working group (Sex Equality and Tackling Misogyny Working Group) to investigate the sexual misconduct issue in 2021 (Smith, June 1, 2023). The first report from the working group was damning.

An online survey—with 529 responses—found that sexism and misogyny were an issue in Police Scotland and 86 percent of the female officers had experienced or witnessed it. The respondents reported that women who were promoted were characterized as unqualified "tokens." Any woman who complained or reported unwanted sexual advances was ostracized and labeled as a "grass"—the English term for rat—or as not being able to take a joke. One respondent wrote, "We're conditioned not to make complaints as police officers generally [common to police groups worldwide], and I think women feel this when it comes to sexism. Things are written off as 'banter' and you don't fit in if you challenge that, you're a trouble maker."

The 2023 report was greeted with surprise, but it should not have been. The seventeen-thousand-officer agency was created in 2013 when the eight regional Scottish police forces were combined into one force—Police Scotland. The regional forces had a long history of discriminating against what the English call BAME groups and communities—meaning black, Asian, and minority ethnic (Gordon, November 11, 2020). A 2018 damning report found that the "canteen culture" of the Scottish police forces was racist, misogynistic, and emotionally damaging to BAME members and women. The report made eighty-one recommendations that were never implemented. The report suggested that BAME members and female recruits were being driven out of the police forces within three to five years. It remains to be seen what effect the latest report has on Police Scotland.

Typology of American Police Sexual Misconduct

The Sweeting et al. study results, by showing that different opportunities and outcomes occur based on the nature of the American police workplace setting, points to a need for a typology of American PSM. PSM is a complex phenomenon, ranging from consensual sex to homicide, including murder. Some PSM acts arise from the officer's occupational arrest powers, and some do not. There is violence in some acts and not others. The nature of some acts and the identity of some actors are truly surprising; perpetrators range from federal to local police officers. For example, the last known American serial killer was a US border patrol agent who killed four women in twelve days (Hastings, December 15, 2022). Sex aggressors serving as local police officers include a former member of the New Orleans Police Department who pleaded guilty to sexually assaulting a fifteen-year-old crime victim (Office of Public Affairs, Department of Justice, November 17, 2022). Many instances of PSM, such as those involving viewing and possessing child pornography, do not involve contact with a victim.

A former Philadelphia police officer was sentenced to five years and ten months in prison for receiving and possessing child pornography (US Attorney's Office, Eastern District of Pennsylvania, Department of Justice, December 16, 2022). Sometimes victims are unaware of their victimization, as in pornography crimes. A Baltimore Police Department SWAT officer was sentenced to twenty-five years in federal prison for exploiting a child to produce child pornography. He hid a spy camera in a bathroom and recorded minors, whose ages ranged from three to sixteen, using the bathroom (US Attorney's Office, District of Columbia, Department of Justice, December 15, 2022). In some cases, such as those involving minors or prisoners, victims may have appeared to give consent; however, their consents were invalid because of their status, and the acts were illegal. The diversity in acts and aggressors led to creation of a PSM typology.

BARKER'S POLICE SEXUAL MISCONDUCT TYPOLOGY

Barker's PSM typology identifies different acts along the following dimensions: aggressors, victims, peer-group support, risk, frequency of occurrence, and suggested preventive actions (Barker, 2020a). This typology is based on real-life occurrences, not on ideal types of police sexual experiences. It is grounded on Barker's "on the job" encounters and forty plus years of research and structured and semi-structured interviews with police officers at all levels of government. Creation of this typology was a first step toward understanding, explaining, and eliminating PSM (see Textbox 3.2).

Textbox 3.2. Typology of Police Sexual Misconduct

1. Sex-related criminal homicide
   Two categories
      A. Serial sexual murder
      B. Rape or sexual assault plus murder
2. Serial rape and sexual predation
3. Sexual extortion, also known as sexual shakedown
4. Betrayal of trust
5. Consensual sex while on duty
6. Custodial sexual misconduct
7. Harassment/discrimination in the police workplace
8. Child molestation
9. Child pornography
10. Sexual exploitation in joint school- and community-sponsored programs

---

1. *Sex-Related Criminal Homicide*

First Category: Police serial sexual murderers.
Acts: This rare behavior is committed by mentally disturbed police officers.

Gerard John Schaefer Jr. was the epitome of a seriously disturbed police officer who was a sexual serial killer. In the early 1970s, in Martin County, Florida, this deputy sheriff, a college graduate, was described by a psychiatrist as an "anti-social personality, which is manifested by sexual deviation, and erotic sadism" (Mason, 2008). He tortured and killed his young female victims in twos and threes because it was more fun. He believed that the victims were whores or intended to be whores, as he suspected his mother had been. This disturbed individual should never have been hired as a police officer. A perfunctory background check would have revealed his prior psychological problems; but the Martin County sheriff hired Schaefer without doing a background check. It was a desperation hiring that the sheriff soon regretted.

The newly elected sheriff needed personnel, and Schaefer was a college graduate and a former police officer. He was a "gypsy" or "wandering cop." Prior to the licensing or certification of police officers in Florida, it was possible to get in trouble in one police agency and easily move to another agency. It is still possible today in some states, but it is becoming harder to do it. We will discuss these dangerous "gypsy" or "wandering cops" fully in later chapters.

Schaefer was fired from his previous police employment for bizarre behavior and moved to another police agency. Schaefer, at his new agency, began kidnapping young girls, usually hitchhikers, in groups of two or three. He would take his victims to secluded spots, handcuff them, put nooses around their necks, and tie them to the branches of trees. Then he would torture them and sexually abuse them before filleting them like a fish (Barker, 2020a). Schaefer was convicted of two murders and sentenced to death; however, he was killed in prison by another inmate. His actual body count is unknown, although he is linked to many other murders.

David Middleton, also known as the "cable guy killer" or the "prince of darkness," maybe because he was black, was first identified as a disturbed sexual predator during his eight years with the police department in Miami, Florida. It appears that he began his career in murder while serving as a Miami police officer. In 1990, he was sentenced to two five-year sentences in connection with sex-related false imprisonment and sexual aggravated battery. The original charges were kidnapping and sexual assault of two prostitutes, which he did while on duty. He learned from this conviction to kill his victims. He was known by his police peers as a "bad cop"—a real "sick puppy" according to several cops who worked with him. After leaving police work, he continued to commit sexual murders. He was convicted of two murders in 1998. Both sexual murders involved sadistic tortures. Middleton is suspected of other murders.

Another police officer who was a serial sexual killer, Anthony "Jack" Sully, was an eight-year veteran of the police department in Millbrae, California, before he quit and established his own business. The evidence suggests that Sully murdered prostitutes while he was with the police department. After leaving the department, he tortured and murdered six people in six months in 1982. According to court documents, Sully reportedly told a coconspirator in the murders, "the only difference between killing someone now and killing someone as a policeman was that the police had permission to do it" (Barker, 2020, p. 127). His known victims were four prostitutes, a pimp, and a drug dealer. Sully's police experience facilitated his bizarre murders. This former police officer is on California's death row, awaiting execution.

The police officers who were most recently identified as serial sex murderers are enigmas. They, like Gerard Schaefer Jr., have college degrees and were considered good candidates for law-enforcement positions. Joseph DeAngelo, known as the "Golden State killer," served in Vietnam in the US Navy. DeAngelo has an associate of arts degree in police science and a bachelor's degree in criminal justice. College degrees, particularly in criminal justice, are seen by many as the silver bullet for police reform. Nonetheless, this professional-appearing police officer, of police serial killers, is the most prolific in American history. DeAngelo is responsible for at least thirteen murders, fifty rapes, and 120 burglaries, committed from 1974 to 1986, while he was a police officer in Exeter, California. (As an aside, Sergeant Joe Bangs, of the Massachusetts Metropolitan District Commission Police, is a convicted bank burglar, robber, drug dealer, and drug addict. Bangs, considered the most corrupt and criminal cop in Massachusetts police history, has a bachelor's degree and a master's degree in criminal justice [Flowers and Deaver, 2014].)

Numerous errors and missteps in investigating DeAngelo's crimes resulted in his long reign of terror. The best narrative on DeAngelo is the chilling book written by the late Michelle McNamara, *I'll Be Gone in the Dark* (McNamara, 2018). Her decades of research contributed to the final resolution of DeAngelo's crimes and his conviction. DeAngelo, like most serial killers, was hiding in plain sight. The law-enforcement officer who was most recently identified as a serial killer is a career federal agent. Juan David Ortiz was a ten-year veteran supervisory agent with the US border patrol, with a bachelor's degree and a master's degree, when he was arrested for and confessed to the murders of four prostitutes. He was arrested after his fifth victim escaped and reported him. He is incarcerated while awaiting trial. Therefore, many of the details of his crimes are not available at this time.

Second Category: Rape or sexual assault plus murder.

Acts: Generally, no psychiatric personality problems are evident in the perpetrators in these cases. The commission of murder in these incidents is a situational and instrumental act to avoid detection and is common in aggressive sexual assaults, especially when the victim knows the perpetrator. The victims are killed to eliminate a witness, reducing the possibility of the sexual aggressor being identified, or is killed while resisting the sexual assault. The murders are best described as "rape plus murder" incidents (Healey, Beauregard, Beech, and Vettor, 2014). The sexual aggressors discussed below were known law-enforcement officers who were identified and prosecuted. Personal "on the job" experiences and fifty years of research on police crime leads me to suspect that this category of police crime is underreported.

The first known cases of police "rape plus murder" to be reported and prosecuted were those of California Highway Patrol officers in 1982 and 1986. In both cases, the officers made pretext stops of young women—trolling for victims. Then, the officers raped the women and killed them when they threatened to report the sexual assaults. These officers' crimes could possibly have been prevented by prior agency action. Both officers were known sexual predators. The police peer group knew that these officers were stopping women and coercing them into sex but overlooked their behavior. Both officers were highly productive ticket writers and good at making DUI arrests. According to court testimony, trolling for sex was common in the California Highway Patrol, and it is in many police departments.

In 1990, a Florida highway patrol officer, a known sexual predator and a skirt chaser, admitted that he pulled over a woman, the mother of a six-year-old child, drove her to a secluded area, and slowly strangled her as she pleaded for her life. This officer was also a "gypsy cop" who should never have been hired by the Florida highway patrol. Other examples of known killer cop sexual predators include an officer in Monroe, North Carolina, with a reputation for trolling for sex, who stopped a cocktail waitress going home after her shift. He knew the woman and became enraged when she turned down his sexual advances and mocked him. He threw her to the ground and stomped her to death. Lastly, an officer from Amarillo, Texas, died in prison waiting for his execution for the 2002 rape plus murder of the daughter of a Texas state representative (Barker, 2020). He killed her because she saw his face.

Dimensions:

- **Aggressors**—only male officers, no female police officers identified in the literature
- **Victims**—male, female, and transgender (victims may be of the same sex as the officer)
- **Peer-group support**—little peer-group support when the incident results in murder yet low-to-moderate support for the underlying sexual misconduct

- Risk—a high-risk behavior if a murder results from a police sexual assault
- Frequency of occurrence in police agencies—rare and episodic
- Preventive action—proper background checks, psychological testing, internal discipline and decertification systems

2. Serial Rape and Sexual Predation

First Category: Serial Rape. The police officers who commit serial rape are true outliers and are considered rogue or BTTB even in corrupt police departments. These impulsive and violent men could have been or might at some other time be involved in incidents of rape plus murder. The worst appeared to be Michael Pena, a three-year NYPD veteran, who had gotten off his shift and spent the night drinking with his buddies. He went looking for sex. He approached a petite twenty-five-year-old woman waiting for a bus to take her to her first day as a teacher. Pena grabbed the woman and dragged her into an alley between two apartment buildings and began sodomizing her. Her screams alerted eyewitnesses in the building. One screamed for him to stop, and Pena yelled back, "I'm almost done." The witness called 911. When the police arrived, Pena told them he was "on the job" and showed his NYPD identification, expecting to be turned loose. He was arrested and, at the station, appealed to a lieutenant for some leniency and whined about his handcuffs being too tight. Later, it was discovered that this brutal rape was not a one-time event (Barker, 2020a). In 2012, Pena was sentenced to serve from seventy-five years to life in prison.

In 2001, a police officer in Hartford, Connecticut, Julio J. Camacho, pleaded guilty to raping two known prostitutes while he was on duty and in uniform. In both cases, he handcuffed the women, pushed them into his patrol car, drove to a secluded area, and raped them. He pleaded guilty on the condition that the government would not pursue charges of rape made by four other women. Camacho was a problem officer during his entire time with the Hartford Police Department and is a suspect in the murder and disappearance of his four-year-old daughter and her mother, his estranged wife (Barker, 2020).

A Florida state prosecutor admitted that a three-year veteran of the Miami Police Department, Michael Ragusa, was a serial rapist who misused his police position on numerous occasions (Barker, 2020a, p. 123). The rapes he committed should never have happened. The city's psychologist had warned, "This is not somebody you would want to hire." Four Florida police departments had already rejected him, based on his sordid past and personality defects. Why was he hired? The Miami background investigator had a worse background than Ragusa did. The background investigator was considered to be the most disciplined officer in the Miami Police Department's history. He was "shit canned" to his background investigator's position to keep him away from the public and off the street. In the end, Ragusa was sentenced to serve ten years in prison after pleading guilty to sexual battery, kidnapping, and kidnapping with a weapon. Following his guilty plea, four other rape charges were dropped.

Dimensions:

- **Aggressors**—at this time, only male officers are known to be involved
- **Victims**—female victims
- **Peer-group support**—varies with the extent of police occupational/workplace deviance in the police agency (in police agencies where all types and patterns of deviance are present, one would expect the peer group to give direct or implicit support and that is an empirical research question)
- **Risk**—varies by agency
- **Preventive action**—the type of agency and its history will determine the best course of preventive action varying from the identification of individual rapist

Second Category: Sexual Predation. Sexual predators are violent men who commit repetitive sexual assaults with coercion, including the threat of violence. However, there is always the possibility of violence because of the unequal power relationship between the police and citizens. And the sexual aggressor is visibly armed. Further research may reveal little difference between category one, serial rape, and category two, sexual predation. However, for now, we maintain that there is a difference and that police sexual predators in this category *hunt for and select* their victims from a pool of vulnerable persons with credibility problems. One particularly BTTB police sexual predator stands out. A white Oklahoma City police officer was arrested and charged with sexually assaulting fourteen black women in a five-month period from February 2014 to June 2014 (Barker, 2020a). The victims ranged in age from thirty-four to fifty-eight and included a grandmother. All but the grandmother had credibility issues, such as having outstanding warrants or a prostitution background. The officer was convicted of eighteen counts of sexual battery, rape, and other offenses and sentenced to 263 years in prison.

A five-year veteran of the police department in West Sacramento, California, was arrested and tried for sexually assaulting six women between October 2011 and September 2012 (Barker, 2020a). Most of the women victims were known prostitutes. He was sentenced to 205 years in prison. An openly gay former "employee of the year" in the sheriff's department in Broward County, Florida, was stalking and stopping illegal male immigrants from El Salvador and Mexico (Barker, 2020a). He performed oral sex on them and got their contact information for later liaisons. There is an inherently unequal power relationship between special agents with the US Department of Homeland Security and undocumented women. ICE agent John Jacob Olivas used this imbalance in power in an extortionate manner for sexual purposes (US Attorney's Office, Central District of California, Department of Justice, December 21, 2022). He was convicted of three counts of deprivation of civil rights under color of law for sexual purposes. He showed his victims his credentials and his weapon and threatened to make them "disappear" if they didn't have sex with him.

Dimensions:

- **Aggressors**—at this time, all male officers
- **Victims**—marginalized female victims or marginalized male (same sex) victims
- **Peer-group support**—peer-group support appears to vary (more research is needed to make definitive claims)
- **Frequency of occurrence in police agencies**—no official or scientifically accurate estimates exist of this type of sexual misconduct yet knowledgeable experts estimate that from 5 to 25 percent of officers in any police agency are sexual predators (Barker, 2020a; Stamper, 2016)
- **Preventive action**—proper background checks, internal discipline, decertification systems, early warning systems

3. Sexual Extortion, also known as Sexual Shakedown

During routine proactive activities, such as traffic and citizen stops, police officers who are inclined toward sexual misconduct engage in quid pro quo sexual shakedown. The events are typically opportunistic, and not the trolling or hunting behavior found in sexual predators, although both types of officers who engage in PSM use pretextual stops. Pretextual stops are commonly used in aggressive police strategies known as "zero tolerance," "stop and frisk," and "quality of life" policing. These stops cause recurrent complaints in overpoliced minority communities. Supposedly, pretextual stops are based on reasonable suspicion to suspect a crime has occurred or will occur; however, the real reason is usually the police officer's bias, based on race, ethnicity, or another inappropriate factor. Sometimes such stops are based on the police officer's intent to create an opportunity for PSM. This deviant behavior of making pretextual stops to create an opportunity for PSM can become systematic in rogue police departments where BTTB officers dominate. One California police department is often identified as a rogue police department.

 Irwindale, California—Sexual Shakedown in a Rogue Police Department. In 2013, this twenty-four-person police department was known as a rogue police agency (Barker, 2020a). From 2013 to 2015, there were fourteen incidents in which PSM was alleged, and three officers were on administrative leave for multiple complaints of sexual shakedown of women during traffic stops. One egregious incident involved a sergeant being charged with five felonies, including kidnapping to commit another crime, oral copulation under color of authority, and sexual battery by restraint. All the charges related to his actions during a traffic stop of a female newspaper-delivery person. He pleaded guilty to one charge of oral copulation under color of authority and one charge of sexual battery by restraint and was sentenced to nine years in prison. The city paid the victim $400,000 to settle her multimillion-dollar civil suit. In most incidents of sexual shakedown, one officer acts alone.

Wayne State University Campus Police Officer. In 2011, a Wayne State University police officer stopped to assist a young woman who had a flat tire. He discovered that she had been drinking. That made her vulnerable to his sexual plans. This campus police officer drove her to the campus, accessed a locked building, and took her to a lounge. He told her that he was taking her to a holding cell and that, if she would give him oral sex, he would forget about the drinking, change her tire, and let her go. She complied. The young woman called the Detroit police when she got home and reported the incident. The campus officer was arrested, charged, and convicted of sexual assault. He was sentenced to sixteen to thirty years in prison.

San Antonio, Texas. In 2010, a six-year veteran of the police department in San Antonio, Texas, stopped a transgender woman prostitute. He handcuffed her, put her in his patrol car, and drove her to a secluded area where she performed oral sex on him. The officer let the transgender woman go, and she reported the incident (Barker, 2020a). The officer pleaded guilty to a misdemeanor charge of official oppression and received a one-year sentence.

Denver, Colorado. A Denver police officer stopped a heroin user with a long rap sheet; she was a vulnerable woman with credibility problems. He ran a warrants check and found an outstanding warrant of false reporting to a pawnbroker. The four-year veteran officer drove the woman to an isolated area and offered to let her go in exchange for engaging in oral sex. She complied and then reported the officer. He was convicted of sexual assault and kidnapping and sentenced to serve eight years in prison followed by ten years to life of sexual-offender probation (Barker, 2020a).

A bizarre 2021 PSM incident demonstrates the need for reform to end the phenomenon of "gypsy" or "wandering" police officers. A campus police officer working at the University of Massachusetts, Dartmouth, resigned during an investigation of allegations that he sexually groped a female student. The same officer was then hired as a school resource officer at a nearby regional public-school district. His new duties included investigating sexual assaults and working with students who had been sexually abused (Cheung, 2021). The latest information, as of December 20, 2022, is that he is no longer the school's resource officer. However, the hiring of problematic officers who have been let go from other departments is a major issue in American policing.

Dimensions:

- **Aggressors**—male and female (victims may be of the same sex as the officer)
- **Victims**—male, female, transgender (victims may be of the same sex as the officer)

- **Peer-group support**—peer-group support depends on the victim's identity, age, and social status (some police peer groups view sex with marginalized persons as a perk of the job)
- **Frequency of occurrence**—this PSM type is probably the second-most common type of police misconduct—brutality is first—in police agencies worldwide
- **Preventive action**—a departmental zero-tolerance stance, improved administrative rule-making, and early warning systems that identify potential sexual offenders

4. Betrayal of Trust

These acts of PSM result from reactive police strategies. Generally, they do not involve quid pro qua interactions. Rather, the police officer takes advantage of vulnerable persons and perverts the motto "To Serve and Protect." In a typical incident, a citizen is a victim of a crime or observes some disturbance and trusts the police to help in some manner. The citizen dials 911, expecting help, and the "help" turns out to be a nightmare. "Officer friendly" arrives, sees the citizen as a sex object, and engages in PSM.

Dial 911, Get a Rapist. "I called 911 for help," the nineteen-year-old mother of two said to the court. "I didn't call 911 to be the victim" (Daley, January 29, 2012). This young women was enrolled in the University of Wisconsin, Milwaukee, majoring in criminal justice to fulfill her ambition to be a police officer. She called 911 and asked for a Milwaukee police officer to come and help her with some unruly teenagers who were cursing her and throwing bricks through her windows. When the responding officer left, the young mother of two was a severely depressed former college student contemplating suicide.

The responding officer, a thirteen-year veteran of the Milwaukee Police Department with an extensive discipline record, including three complaints of sexual abuse, sodomized and raped her. When other officers came on the scene, she reported the sexual abuse and was jailed for two days for making a false claim against a police officer. The prosecutor refused to charge the officer. The victim was released and retained an attorney who convinced an assistant US attorney to file charges of civil-rights violations against her police attacker. The civil-rights trial lasted for three days. The federal jury found the Milwaukee police officer guilty of sexually assaulting the victim, and the judge sentenced the former officer to serve twenty-four years in prison (Barker, 2020a).

Shooting Fish in a Barrel. A deputy sheriff in Iredell County, North Carolina, Richard "Ben" Jenkins, likened finding sexual opportunities among women making complaints of domestic violence to shooting fish in a barrel (Barker, 2020a). Jenkins was the sheriff's department's domestic-violence investigator. Women who came to him to file charges against their husbands or to seek protection from domestic violence were subjected to lewd comments and constant sexual propositions. He stalked them while he was on and off duty and treated them as his special cache of sex partners. He wasn't by himself. A federal judge in a civil suit said that it was the custom in the sheriff's department to "sexually harass females over whom they had power." There were multiple victims. Deputy Jenkins was immediately fired after a court set a $425,000 judgment against the sheriff's department, and the sheriff announced that he would not seek reelection.

Nude Pictures of Victims. In 2011, a deputy sheriff in Hickman County, Tennessee, somehow persuaded domestic-violence victims to allow him to take nude pictures of them, including of their private parts, as "evidence." He was sentenced to serve twenty-four months in prison.

Rape of Stroke Victim. A twenty-two-year veteran of the police department in Sacramento, California, was sentenced to serve sixty-three years to life for four sexual assaults of a seventy-five-year-old stroke victim recovering in a senior living complex. He was charged with nine counts, including rape, forcible oral copulation, and sexual battery. The sexual assaults took place in 2010 and 2012 (Barker, 2020a).

Sex with Victim. In March 2021, a Chicago Police Department detective was assigned to investigate an attack of a victim of sex trafficking who was living in a homeless shelter. He was accused of having sex with her on several occasions when he was on duty. He gave her $100 on two occasions. It is alleged that he repeatedly threatened the woman, telling her, "You are going to jail for being a whore." Following the investigation of her complaint, the Civilian Office of Police Accountability recommended that he be fired. The police department said the detective planned to retire in light of the allegations. The detective was never criminally charged, and he no longer works for the police department (Anon, December 20, 2022).

Dimensions:

- **Aggressors**—male and female (the victim may be of the same sex as the officer)
- **Victims**—male and female (the victim may be of the same sex as the officer)
- **Peer-group support**—more research is needed in this area but it appears that peer-group support is low to medium, depending on the peer group's definition of consent, and that exposure of the acts creates scandals
- **Risk**—varies by setting and the victim's age and disability
- **Frequency of occurrence**—More research is needed to make definitive statement but episodic incidents occur in the United States and the United Kingdom
- **Preventive actions**—administrative rulemaking, internal discipline, and frequent audit ("disturbed" individuals have been identified, indicating improper vetting)

5. Consensual Sex on Duty

This appears to be the most numerous act of PSM. Consensual on-duty sex is present, and always has been, in police agencies, worldwide. Nevertheless, it is unethical, often coerced, and criminal in some settings and circumstances. Since the founding of the police-work occupation in 1829, women "of the night" and of "loose virtue" service the boys in blue. Sex with willing partners is viewed as a perk of the job in many police agencies.

One police chief described patrol cars as "traveling bedrooms" because of the amount of sex and sleeping that took place in them (Ahern, 1972). This biased and sexist view allowed a male-dominated culture to develop and continue in the police-work occupation. This biased and sexist view demeans women and perpetuates a "good ole boys" defense to coerced sex with less-than-willing victims. Later examination of incidents reveals that many apparently willing partners had succumbed to real and perceived pressure.

In 2013, a police sex scandal that rocked the police department in Lakeland, Florida, revealed an organizational systematic culture of police on-duty sex involving supervisors and other sworn officers (Barker, 2020a). Sex while on duty was the norm for the entire department. Two women crime analysists admitted to having sex with multiple sworn officers and being subjected to repeated sexual harassment. A Florida state attorney's report noted that, from 2006 to 2013, at least ten sworn officers had sex with a civilian employee of the police force. The on-duty sex acts took place at the Lakeland Police Department, at other Lakeland municipal buildings, in patrol cars, and in city parks. Seven sworn officers admitted to the illicit sex acts. One sex act occurred in a patrol car in a church parking lot while a funeral for a slain departmental officer was taking place. Although no criminal charges were brought against any sworn officer—due to the statute of limitations and evidence issues—numerous officers, including two sergeants, were fired, and several other officers, including a captain and the chief, retired. A female sergeant was charged with neglect of duty for not reporting known violations. She resigned in lieu of being fired. A female crime analyst, who was a main target in these incidents, was fired, although she claimed whistleblower status.

Oklahoma Sex Scandal. A man entered a convenience store in the family-oriented community of Yukon, Oklahoma (population, 25,000), and observed the twenty-three-year-old female clerk orally copulating a uniformed Yukon police officer. The perplexed man backed toward the door, repeating, "I didn't see nothing. I didn't see nothing." He called the store owner and told him what he saw. The storeowner confronted the young clerk, and she gave a tearful confession. He called the police, and the sordid details of a yearlong series of sexual encounters came out (Barker, 2020a). The clerk said one officer would introduce her to another officer, and she felt compelled to have sex with each one. They all warned her that, if she told anyone, she would get in trouble and get fired. Three officers admitted to sexual misconduct and resigned. One refused to resign and was fired. The police department directed that all officers receive ethical training, and the department established an early warning system to identify problem officers. The female clerk wasn't fired, but she left town.

Love Nest in a Storage Unit. In 2013, bizarre incidents of consensual on-duty sex occurred, involving the chief of police in Cleveland, Tennessee, and the executive director of Mainstream Cleveland—a nonprofit organization (Barker, 2020a). During their working hours, they would rendezvous in a specially equipped (with a blanket and a pillow) storage unit for sex. Upon exposure of this practice, the married chief retired.

Dimensions:

- **Aggressors**—male, female, transgender (the victim may be of the same sex as the officer)
- **Victims**—male, female, transgender (the victim may be of the same sex as the officer)
- **Peer-group support**—high peer-group support, often looked on as a perk of the job (police work is one of many sexual-abuse-prone occupations)
- **Risk**—low risk
- **Frequency of occurrence**—occurs in all police agencies and the frequency and amount depend on the agency's informal culture

Preventive actions are administrative rule-making and a departmental zero-tolerance stance.

6. Custodial Sexual Misconduct

Custodial and detention workers who are classified as law-enforcement officers work at detention facilities at all levels of government (Barker, 2020a). Municipal law-enforcement agencies have jails and lockups. Sheriffs and their deputies, jailors, and detention staff are defined by statute as law-enforcement officers. The federal government defines any government official engaged in detention duties as a law-enforcement officer. Custodial and detention officers, however defined, have narrow or limited arrest powers. Sexual abuse by these officers is a major PSM problem. The "on the job" sexual misconduct occurs in a setting where the sexual aggressor has a captive pool of vulnerable victims with legally defined credibility problems. Potential victims can't walk away, run, or summon help. Often, they cry for help; but help never comes. Custodial and detention workers with the inclination for sexual misconduct have a captive pool of vulnerable targets with credibility problems, having been charged with crimes—providing opportunity. The environment—a lockup, jail, or prison—is a low- or no-risk setting. Some of the most egregious examples of PSM and excessive use of force occur in custodial settings (Barker, 2020a).

Custodial Sex in a Jail in Custer County, Oklahoma. A sheriff who was with the jail in Custer County for twelve years ran a sex-slave operation from his jail (Barker, 2020a). In 2008, he was arrested and charged with fourteen counts of second-degree rape and seven counts of forcible oral sodomy on jail inmates and participants in the county drug court. He was convicted of five counts of second-degree rape and three counts of bribery by a public official—accepting sex in exchange for influence is bribery. The judge sentenced the former sheriff to serve seventy-nine years among the sodomites. Fourteen of his victims sued the county and received a judgment of $10 million.

But We Love Each Other. This was the justification that a young female federal corrections officer at the Metropolitan Detention Center in Brooklyn, New York, gave for having an affair with an inmate. The inmate was a Bloods gang member charged with the murders of two NYPD officers. She became pregnant and had the baby before she was sentenced to one year in prison (Barker, 2020a).

Sexual Rape of a Transvestite. A black male detention officer at the Orleans Parish Prison in Louisiana removed a male transvestite prisoner from his cell, handcuffed him, and forced him to perform oral sex in a closet. The guard was arrested and charged with second-degree kidnapping and sexual malfeasance in prison. The guard claimed the sex was consensual; however, in Louisiana, sex between a prisoner and any member of detention personnel, under any circumstances, is illegal (Barker, 2020a).

Recent Examples.

May 18, 2022—A former federal corrections officer at the Federal Medical Center, Carswell, in Fort Worth, Texas, pleaded guilty to sexually abusing multiple female inmates at the facility (DOJ, May 18, 2022). The facility is an administrative security federal prison that serves female prisoners with specialized medical and mental-health needs.

May 24, 2022—A former federal corrections officer at the Metropolitan Detention Center in Los Angeles pleaded guilty to one felony count of deprivation of civil rights under color of law for sexually assaulting a woman in custody in December 2020 (Office of Public Affairs, Department of Justice, May 24, 2022). He allegedly entered the cell of a woman who was in COVID-19 isolation to bring her breakfast. He sexually assaulted the woman, causing her pain and putting her in fear of physical harm.

July 2022—A female corrections officer with the Douglas County, Georgia, sheriff's office was arrested and charged with allegedly having sexual relations with a male inmate (Van de Riet, July 14, 2022). According to the news account, another inmate sent a letter to the sheriff, alleging that the officer was having sex with inmates. She allegedly admitted that she had kissed and performed oral sodomy on an inmate.

December 8, 2022—A federal jury convicted the former warden of the Federal Correctional Institute in Dublin, California, of sexually abusing three female inmates and fostering a culture of abuse at the all-female low-security correctional institution (Office of Public Affairs, Department of Justice, December 8, 2022). The sexual assaults occurred between December 2019 and July 2021. Five other correctional officers at this facility were charged with and convicted of sexual abuse.

The sexual abuse of inmates can involve persons who are not correctional staff members. In 2008, a Roman Catholic priest at the Federal Medical Center, Carswell, in Fort Worth, Texas, was arrested and was charged with and pleaded guilty to two counts of sexual abuse of a female inmate (Office of Public Affairs, Department of Justice, May 5, 2008). The victim was his assigned clerk for the religious services department. The priest, a naturalized American citizen from Nigeria, was sentenced to four years in prison. In 2013, a male prison doctor was sentenced to twenty-five months in prison and two years of supervised release after pleading guilty to sexually abusing three inmates at the United States Penitentiary Atlanta in Atlanta, Georgia, and another inmate at the District of Columbia jail (February 7, 2021). The sex acts included oral and anal sex. He was a physician at the penitentiary from January 2011 to July 2012.

Dimensions:

- **Aggressors**—male and female (victims may be of the same sex as the officer)
- **Victims**—male, female, transgender (victims may be of the same sex as the officer)
- **Peer-group support**—varies with the victim's identity and the institution's culture
- **Risk**—low to no risk
- **Frequency of occurrence**—widespread
- **Preventive action**—administrative rule-making, vetting of personnel, and zero tolerance for violations

7. Harassment or Discrimination in the Police Workplace

Sexual harassment or discrimination can be one of, or a combination of, the following acts: gender discrimination, unwanted sexual attention, and sexual coercion. The Equal Employment Opportunity Commission says that sexual harassment occurs in a variety of circumstances (Barker, 2020a):

- The victim as well as the harasser may be a man or a woman. The victim does not have to be of the opposite sex.

- The harasser can be the victim's supervisor, an agent of the employer, a supervisor in another area, a coworker, or even a nonemployee.
- The victim does not have to be the person harassed but could be anyone affected by the offensive conduct.
- Unlawful sexual harassment may occur without economic injury to or discharge of the victim.
- The harasser's conduct must be *unwelcome* (italics added).

There are three categories of sexual harassment (Collins, 2004; Barker, 2020a):

Gender harassment: This includes a range of verbal and nonverbal behaviors that convey insulting, hostile, and degrading attitudes about gender, including sexual epithets, slurs, taunts, the display of obscene or pornographic materials, and other threatening or hostile acts.

Unwanted sexual attention: Verbal and nonverbal behavior that is offensive, unwanted, and unreciprocated, such as being stared at, leered at, touched, or constantly asked for sex.

Sexual Coercion: This is the classic quid pro quo form of sexual harassment: trading sex for job-related benefits.

California Police Chief Sexually Harasses Her Male Officers. In 2012, the first female police chief of Paso Robles, California, was accused of sexually assaulting her male officers (Anon, March 21, 2012; Barker, 2020a). The chief, a twenty-four-year veteran of the Paso Robles Police Department was a poster child for the advancement of women in American police work. She moved up the ranks as the department's first woman sergeant, lieutenant, and captain before being appointed chief in 2007. There were numerous allegations lodged against her: a long list of sexual assaults against male officers, including a number in front of witnesses; and repeated sexual affairs with subordinates, including one that resulted in a child. One officer claimed she grabbed his penis while he sat in her car. The city hired an investigator to examine the allegations. In March 2012, the chief abruptly resigned after signing a separation-and-release agreement. Under the agreement, the city gave her $250,000, and both parties agreed not to sue. The city would not confirm or deny that an investigation of the allegations had been conducted.

A Pattern of Sexual Harassment. In the New Britain, Connecticut, police department, a female officer—a nine-year veteran—alleged that the head of the internal affairs unit had engaged in numerous acts of sexual and gender discrimination because she rejected his sexual advances. She was also passed over for promotion, special assignments, and extra-duty jobs because of her sex and rebuffing his sexual advances (Stacom, April 21, 2011; Barker, 2020a). She claimed that offensive comments and advances were a "a routine culture of the New Britain Police Department"—a 140-person department with twelve female officers. The longtime chief and the internal affairs unit commander retired; the complainant received a $60,000 payout on her civil suit. During the next year she was promoted to sergeant.

Sexual Harassment and Gender and Religious Discrimination. In Philadelphia, Pennsylvania, a black female police captain—a twenty-three-year veteran—who was Muslim, alleged that the deputy police commissioner had engaged in a three-year (from 2008 to 2011) pattern of treating her differently, based on her race, gender, and religion (Peacock, April 20, 2012; Gambacorta, May 1, 2012; Barker, 2020a). He had created a hostile work environment. In 2013, the internal affairs unit head was moved to lower administrative duties, and the city of Philadelphia paid a settlement of $45,000 to the complainant.

Sexual Harassment of Male Police Officers. Three former officers with the police department in Bangor, Michigan, alleged in a federal lawsuit that the male city manager and police chief—the same person—made sexually provocative comments to them, racially discriminated against a black officer who threatened to file a complaint, and asked them to have sex with him (Kark, July 4, 2021). The chief shared explicit and inappropriate details of his homosexual relationships with other persons, including police officers. The black officer claimed racial discrimination and sexual harassment because he was demoted and fired after threatening to file a sexual-harassment complaint.

Bisexual Officer Filed Suit. A female bisexual officer with the police department in Greenburg, New York, filed suit against the department, alleging that she was continually sexually harassed by other officers (Cooper, October 20, 2021). She also accused her nightshift partner of sexually assaulting her while they were on duty.

Dimensions:

- **Aggressors**—all sexes and sexual orientations
- **Victims**—all sexes and sexual orientations
- **Peer group support**—medium to high, depending on the agency's culture
- **Risk**—low to medium
- **Frequency of occurrence**—widespread
- **Preventive action**—administrative rule-making and a zero-tolerance discipline system

8. Child Molestation: Police Victimization of Children while On Duty

Sexual contacts with a child are defined by law as criminal acts. Consent is not possible. In the United States, a child or minor is defined by state statute. However, the Office of Juvenile Justice and Delinquency Prevention (OJJDP) defines a child as "someone who has not reached his/her 18th birthday (OJJPD, 2010, p. 13). Therefore, any law-enforcement officer who engages in any sexual activity with a child (anyone younger than eighteen) of any gender is a child molester. The sexual abuse of a child is always a criminal act; consensual sex with a child is not possible. Child molesters are often referred to as pedophiles. That may not be accurate. Pedophilia is a psychiatric disease requiring treatment. Child molestation is a serious crime of violence requiring punishment. Pedophiles have a specific preference for children and have sexual fantasies and erotic imagery focusing on children (OJJDP, 2010). Pedophiles can indulge in their sexual fantasies legally through thought or (private) masturbation. When a pedophile acts on his or her sexual preferences and molests a child, he or she is a child molester and is subject to punishment, not treatment. Identifying and punishing child molesters should be a high priority for all law-enforcement agencies. Unfortunately, that doesn't happen when the child molester carries a badge.

Child Molester: Multiple Male Victims. A Pittsburgh public-school police officer was arrested and charged in 2012 with twenty-three offenses, including involuntary deviate sexual intercourse, corruption of minors, endangering the welfare of children, and indecent assault (Barker, 2020a). The criminal complaint listed four male victims who were about thirteen at the time of victimization. The incidents went back to 1998. The victims all attended the school system's alternative program for problem children (juvenile delinquents). In other words, they were perfect victims for a police child molester. At trial, he was found guilty on thirteen charges and sentenced to thirty-two to sixty-four years in prison.

Child Molester: Multiple Female Victims. A nine-year veteran with the police department in Long Beach, California, was charged in 2012 with twenty-four felony child-molestation charges: sexual penetration by a foreign object of a person under eighteen; oral copulation of a person under eighteen; unlawful sexual intercourse; using a minor for sex acts; and meeting a minor for sex purposes (Van Dyke, May 11, 2012). In 2013, he pleaded guilty to seven felony counts and was sentenced to eleven years and eight months in prison.

Is This Justice? A ten-year veteran of the sheriff's office in Pocahontas County, West Virgina, was first indicted on nineteen counts of child sexual abuse of four children. Then, some months later, he was indicted again on forty-seven counts of alleged sexual abuse of minor girls and women. In all, sixty-six incidents took place over fifteen years, from 1995 to 2010 (Smith, November 14, 2012). He was allowed to plead guilty to one count of a crime against a seventeen-year-old girl and was sentenced to not less than ten nor more than twenty years in prison.

Decades of Child Molestation and Sexual Assault. A former police sergeant who had retired from the police department in Flint, Michigan, was arrested for raping two children under thirteen years of age in 2014 (Mitchell, September 6, 2014). They were the daughters of a woman he was in a relationship with. The investigation revealed that the retired sergeant had assaulted at least fifty women and children during his police career. The assaults took place inside the police station, in police vehicles, and on city property. In 2016, the retired officer pleaded guilty to sixteen counts of first-degree criminal sexual conduct that included victims under thirteen years of age (Acosta, November 16, 2016). One of the young victims described the acts performed at police headquarters and in patrol cars. She said other police officers knew what was happening. He was sentenced to fifteen to twenty-five years in prison.

Dimensions:

- **Aggressors**—male and female (victims can be of the same sex as the officer)
- **Victims**—male and female minors
- **Peer-group support**—generally frowned upon by the majority of police officers yet, in some departments, there is a tendency to not publicly condemn molesters of teenagers, which creates a perceived safe setting
- **Risk**—high risk except if the victim is a teenager
- Frequency of occurrences—rare against victims who are younger than thirteen yet a surprisingly high number of police officers have sexual contact with thirteen- to seventeen-year-old male and female homeless and runaway minors (more research is needed)
- **Prevention actions**—improved vetting including psychological testing, a strictly enforced zero-tolerance policing, raising the punishment for engaging in or knowing of this crime and not stopping or reporting it

9. Child Pornography

Police officers viewing or possessing *adult* pornography while on duty is typically not a crime. It might be a violation of the department's policies, procedures, or rules. Therefore, police officers engaging in such activity with *adult* pornography may be subject to administrative sanction, including dismissal.

On the other hand, the production, possession, viewing, or transmission of child pornography is a crime. In particular, the possession of child pornography by any person is a criminal offense, and persons engaging in this offense are subject to administrative and criminal penalties.

The non-job-related possession, transmission, or viewing of child pornography by a law-enforcement officer, whether on or off duty, is a serious crime. The production of child pornography—child molestation—involves a victim and an aggressor; however, possessing, viewing, or transmission of already produced material does not require victim contact and is not viewed as a violent crime. That rationalization is often used to justify the act of viewing or possessing; however, it is not successful.

A veil of respectability hid the sordid truth about Anthony Mangione, who was a federal law-enforcement officer for twenty-seven years. He was the head of the US Immigration and Customs Agency (ICE) for South Florida. He supervised 450 federal law-enforcement officers in nine countries as they investigated drug smuggling, money laundering and financial crimes, commercial fraud, national security, and cybercrimes. The cybercrimes that he and his agents investigated included the transportation, receipt, and possession of child pornography as part of the government's effort for Project Safe Childhood (Barker, 2020a). Mangione also collected child pornography and transported it to other collectors. According to the FBI, Mangione received and transported visual depictions of minors engaged in sexually explicit acts from March 2010 to September 2010. He also possessed electronically stored messages that included child pornography (Federal Bureau of Investigation, Minneapolis Division, September 28, 2011). The disgraced federal officer entered into a plea agreement and admitted to sending ten emails containing child pornography. He was sentenced to forty months in prison followed by twenty years on supervised release.

The largest collection of child pornography in Connecticut history (22,282 images and 4,064 videos) was seized from a police captain with the Granby, Connecticut, police department (FBI, February 10, 2012). He pleaded guilty and was sentenced to ten years in prison.

Operation Predator. The US Department of Homeland Security conducts Operation Predator, which is a national and international effort to identify, investigate, and charge child predators who possess, trade, and produce child pornography. In 2011, one of its operations discovered that a South Carolina highway patrol officer was involved in possession and transmission of child pornography (Barker, 2020a). He pleaded guilty and was sentenced to three years in prison.

Child Pornography Chat Room. A Baltimore police officer set up at least seven different chat rooms that allowed users to message, video chat, watch videos and images, share files, and discuss the sexual exploitation of children (US Attorney's Office, District of Maryland, Department of Justice, July 21, 2020). He pleaded guilty to the possession of child pornography and was sentenced to four years in prison.

Police Chief Distributes Child Porn. The former police chief in East Helena, Montana, pleaded guilty to distributing child pornography on social media in 2019 (US Attorney's Office, District of Montana, Department of Justice, December 7, 2021).

Philadelphia Police Officer. A Philadelphia police officer pleaded guilty to receiving and possessing a collection of hundreds of images of child pornography (US Attorney's Office, Eastern District of Pennsylvania, Department of Justice, July 22, 2022).

Sharing on Social Media. A Perryton, Texas, police officer was sentenced to seventeen years in prison after pleading guilty to using Kik, a popular social media app, to share child pornography. He shared one image of an adult male engaged in sex acts with a blindfolded child (US Attorney's Office, Northern District of Texas, Department of Justice, March 21, 2022).

Part of Criminal Group. A thirty-year-old female Gwinnett County, Georgia, police officer who had returned to full-time police duty from military duty was one of four people arrested for child exploitation—the production and distribution of child pornography (Turner, May 30, 2023). Her employment was terminated immediately after her arrest.

New Jersey County Sheriff's Officer Arrested. A county sheriff was arrested after a long investigation into child sex-abuse material being stored on an online file storage server (Lissner, June 8, 2023). He was placed on an unpaid administrative status until his trial date. The sheriff expressed that he was mortified by the arrest and added that such conduct did not reflect the values of the sheriff's office. One would hope that is true. However, the number of law-enforcement officers involved in the possession, distribution, and production of child pornography, worldwide, is disturbing (Barker, 2020a).

Child Sex Abuse in the United Kingdom. Barker (2020a) identified numerous examples of PSM in the United Kingdom, including incidents involving child molestation and child pornography. Baroness Casey, in her report on the London Metropolitan Police—the largest UK police agency—concluded that women and children have been failed by the London Metropolitan Police, with racism, misogyny, and homophobia at the heart of the force (Mackintosh and Manning, March 21, 2023). Among the report's recommendations was better protection of children, especially black children.

The British police have a history of child exploitation. In 2002, fifty British police officers were arrested in a crackdown on US websites for paid access to child pornography, some of it involving children as young as five (Anon, December 17, 2002). In 2003, a Cambridgeshire police constable, married and the father of two children, six years and fourteen months of age, respectively, admitted having three hundred indecent images of girls, some as young as four (Press Association, March 28, 2003). More recent examples include a West Yorkshire police officer who had more than one hundred images of children as young as three being sexual abused (Anon, April 27, 2022); and a Sussex police officer who downloaded child porn from Twitter while on duty (Barlow, April 19, 2023). The most bizarre case was that of three former Met officers, one serving and two retired, who were accused of engaging in a child sex-abuse image conspiracy (Home Office, January 19, 2023). The serving officer was a well-known and respected chief inspector who committed suicide before he could be charged. The chief inspector had a secret room behind a trap door, holding child pornography, sex toys, and children's clothing (Davis, January 18, 2023).

Dimensions:

- **Aggressors**—male BTTB officers with some female officers in supporting roles
- **Victims**—male and female minors (under eighteen)

- **Peer-group support**—no agency support, but small groups of like-minded deviants are possible
- **Risk**—high
- **Frequency of occurrence**—occurs worldwide and may be the most organized form of PSM
- **Prevention tactics**—zero tolerance and increased risk

10. Sexual Exploitation in Joint School- and Community-Sponsored Programs

PSM may occur in schools or in police–community programs working with minors. A 2013 study by a noted criminologist revealed a disturbing pattern of police sexual abuse of teenage girls who were enrolled in police-sponsored Explorer programs (Walker and Tribeck, 2013). The national exposure generated attention to all such programs and revealed a flood of complaints of PSM incidents in such programs, PSM that continues unabated (Barker, 2020a).

Barker's Study. Barker's study of newspaper articles from 2009 to 2015 of PSM of teenage boys and girls in community-sponsored programs found seventy-two incidents. The programs were sponsored by local, state, and federal law-enforcement agencies throughout the United States (Barker, 2020a). Thirty-one of the reported incidents occurred in Explorer programs. This program is designed for police ride-alongs involving fourteen to twenty youths. The dark side of these community- or police-sponsored programs expands the pool of vulnerable victims for police sexual aggressors.

Most Egregious Example. In 2000, an openly gay deputy who had been with the Los Angeles Police Department (LAPD) for twenty-five years, David Kalish, became a finalist for the open LAPD chief of police position. Past allegations against him of engaging in PSM while he supervised the LAPD's Explorer program became public (Winton and Blackstein, March 26, 2003; Barker, 2020a). A California man alleged that Kalish had sexually molested him when he was in the 1970s Explorer program. Then two more men made allegations. One said that Kalish had sexually molested, harassed, assaulted, fondled, and coerced him from 1974 to 1979, when he was in the Explorer program. Kalish was not selected as chief, and the new chief put him on paid leave and asked for an investigation of the allegations. Five months later, the Los Angeles district attorney issued a three-page memorandum, saying that there was sufficient evidence to charge Kalish with child molestation, but the legal deadline for prosecution had passed. The memo said, "Kalish engaged in oral copulation and masturbation with an Explorer scout in the LAPD Devonshire Division Explorer Program when the victim aged 15–17" (Winton and Blackstein, November 7, 2003).

School Resource Officer. The reports of PSM by school resource officers are numerous. Selected examples include the following: In 2014, a school resource officer in Dothan, Alabama, was convicted of having sex with a student and sentenced to ten years in prison (WSFA 12, news staff, July 21, 2014). A Cottage Grove, Illinois, school resource officer is facing seven counts of sexual misconduct with students (Sepic, February 3, 2020). A Moncks County, South Carolina, school resource officer is facing charges for sexually abusing a fifteen-year-old female student (Przetak, June 10, 2021). Finally, two school resource officers, one male and one female, in Goose Creek, South Carolina, were arrested and charged with sexual exploitation of a child and misconduct in the office for inappropriate relations with a seventeen-year-old student (Phillips, August 4, 2022).

Dimensions:

- **Aggressors**—male and female (the victim may be of the same sex as the officer)
- **Victims**—male and female (the victim may be of the same sex as the officer and most are not legally of the age of consent)
- **Peer-group support**—depends on the agency, with sexual opportunities being considered a perk in some agencies (more research is needed)
- **Frequency of occurrence**—widespread in US police agencies
- **Prevention action**—zero tolerance and internal auditing

Conclusion

Police work is a morally dangerous and sexual-abuse-prone occupation. PSM is one pattern of police occupational/workplace deviant behavior. PSM is not confined to the United States. The behaviors that encompass the types and categories of PSM vary in the identity of the aggressors and victims, the level of peer-group support, the incidence of PSM, and possible preventive actions. This chapter provided selected, not exhaustive, examples of each type. PSM fits into a causal equation in which inclination plus opportunity and real or perceived low risk are responsible for the nature and extent of police occupational/workplace misconduct and crime. Police lying, which the next chapter addresses, also plays a significant role.

Discussion Questions

1. How does PSM fit into the larger paradigm of occupational misconduct and crime? Your answer should include a comparison of at least one criminal-justice agency with one entity that is not a social service agency.

2. Were you surprised to learn that some American police officers were serial sexual killers? Why or why not?
3. Why do some police sexual predators have long careers of sex crime? Read the case study below before you answer.
4. Is the term "the sleazy blue line" an apt description of the American policing occupation? This is not a yes or no question. Support your answer.

CASE STUDY OF A POLICE SERIAL SEXUAL PREDATOR

Todd Allen graduated from Emporia State University in Emporia, Kansas, in May 1994, with a bachelor's degree in sociology. Several months later—on October 3, 1994—he joined the Hutchinson City Police Department in Hutchinson, Kansas (Mannetta, October 20, 2022). Hutchinson is a city of about forty thousand, located about fifty miles from Wichita. Allen worked as an officer with a Drug Abuse Resistance Education program from 1996 to 2001 before becoming a school resource officer (Miller, August 19, 2022). He had a good reputation and received no disciplinary actions during his police career. Officer Allen was known among his neighbors and coworkers as a family man who used all his vacation time to go to his two boys' school and sporting events. The congenial family man was active in his church. He retired from the police department in 2019 and took a job as a security officer at a local hospital. That is all in the rearview mirror now. Currently, this former police officer is free on a $250,000 bond and is wearing a GPS ankle monitor. He is charged with five counts of rape, two counts of kidnapping, nine counts of aggravated sexual battery, one count of indecent liberties with a child, and five counts of breach of privacy and eavesdropping (being a "peeping Tom") (Ladden-Hall, August 18, 2022). The charges are related to a spree of unsolved sexual assaults that took place in Hutchinson parks between October 2012 and November 2018, while Allen was a police officer, and a string of prowler reports from May 2019 through June 2022, while Allen was a security officer. The ages of his alleged victims were between fifteen and eighteen, and the sexual assaults were done using the same method of operation.

It is alleged that Allen would approach the victims as they sat in their cars and shine a light in their face to blind them. He would identify himself as a cop or security officer, tell them to get out of the car, and then sexually assault them. Allen was caught in one of his "peeping Tom" episodes, and his involvement in the previous crimes came to light. He is currently awaiting trial.

CHAPTER 4

Police Misconduct

POLICE LYING

Key Terms:

Perjury

Verballing

Accepted and necessary lies

Procedural lies

Whoops raids

War theory of crime control

Testilying

Brady cops

Chapter Objectives:

After reading this chapter, the reader should be able to do the following:

- Describe police lying as a form of police occupational/workplace deviance
- Outline and discuss the various categories of police lying
- Provide the timeline for the development of police perjury
- Examine a reform strategy for dealing with lying cops

Textbox 4.1. Justice Game

The following was overheard in a southern courtroom as the convicted prisoners were being led away:

"You lied. You lying motherfucker. Ain't no way you could see me drop that dope," the angry man now in handcuffs yelled to his arresting officer.

> The veteran cop glared at him. The other cops in the courtroom squirmed in their seats. They knew this dirtbag didn't know the rules of the game he was playing.
>
> Another handcuffed prisoner in line yelled, "You fuckin fool. You can't out lie the po-leece. You can't out shit the bullshitters."
>
> The courtroom burst into laughter. Order was restored. The games were renewed. The judge signaled for the next players to approach. The officer and the suspect had engaged in *the justice game* to see who the better liar was, and the suspect lost (see Hunt and Manning, 1991). The police are the grand masters in the criminal-justice circus of lies.

Lies are "speech acts" that the speaker knows are misleading or false and that are intended to deceive (Hunt and Manning, 1991). There are good lies, and there are bad lies. Lying is a part of most occupations, legal and illegal. We expect politicians to lie. We expect salespersons to lie. Lying is part of the sales occupational culture, worldwide. Doctors, nurses, medical workers, and first responders lie and give hope to the very sick and dying. We expect them to. Lying is a part of the police-work occupational culture, worldwide. We don't expect that, but it happens continuously.

Police lying is an example of police misconduct that does not always involve personal profit; however, it can. In these cases, it is a technique to accomplish organizational goals and facilitate patterns of police corruption and crime. Ask a law-enforcement officer if he tells lies, and he will answer, "Of course not" (Dunkle, 2021). But that is a lie. And the officer knows it. Former LAPD chief Daryl Gates allegedly said that, first and foremost, a good cop is a con man. And Chief Gates was an exceptional con man when dealing with the public and social media. For years, he convinced the public that the Rampart police scandal was the result of a few bad apples and was not an LAPD organizational issue. He told that lie with a straight face for years.

Police Lying Is Normal Police Behavior

Lying is normal behavior among officers fulfilling police occupational duties, depending on the work setting. Police lying is required and accepted in undercover assignments in which deception is the name of the game the police play. One can make a good argument that police public relations is good police lying and mostly smoke and mirrors. On the other hand, some police lying is a crime or a means to commit a crime, such as perjury, as presented in the opening vignette. DNA analysis proved that some were wrongly convicted due to police lies. DNA evidence proved that some police officers gave false and misleading testimony; this topic is more fully discussed in the next chapter.

Career criminals and repeat offenders know it's hard to out lie the cops when the police believe the end, obtaining a conviction of a "bad guy," is more important than the means. Unfortunately, on occasion, police lies get "the innocent."

Police Lying in Its Historical Context

Lying among police officers has been a sordid tradition since the 1829 founding of the police occupation in London. An early British journalist in 1838 said that the English policeman who wanted to exert his power and didn't have a charge to arrest would invent one (Miller, 1973). American cops are still doing that. Arrests for "invented" charges was then and is now a police workplace problem affecting the London poor and marginalized classes. For example, disorderly conduct or suspicious activity was a vague charge used by British police to stop, search for weapons, or interrogate hapless victims who were poor and without political power. These members of what the British social elites termed the "dangerous classes" were subject to stop and frisk on sight. The controversial stop and frisk practices of the police didn't start in New York City.

Furthermore, police lying in court (perjury) is not a new phenomenon. As a British police expert said, the "*modus operandi* of corrupt officers' changes little; wrinkles are just added from time to time" (Morton, 1993, p. 96). In 1846, several British police constables admitted that they had lied in court to convict an innocent man who was suspected of killing a police officer (Morton, 1993). The tradition continued in England. Years later, in 1987, a judge, when sentencing four constables for lying about a police assault, said, "You behaved like vicious hooligans and lied like common criminals" (Morton, 1993, p. 169). In 1989, the chairperson of a police complaint committee said, "Obviously there is a nucleus of officers there [Scotland Yard] willing to misbehave in order to secure convictions which they probably think are justified" (Morton, 1993, p. 174).

Police lying is a part of the UK police argot. In the United Kingdom, police lying to convict is called "fitting up" a person, and it includes fabricating evidence, planting evidence, and committing perjury in court to secure a conviction. In the United Kingdom, a police officer "fits up" a suspect by "verballing"—saying that the suspect made a statement that he didn't make—or planting evidence (Morton, 1993). Sometimes, the officer honestly believes that the person is guilty, and the officer thinks that the law needs a little help to ensure the conviction.

This British police "verballing" practice would be "discovered" and labeled "testilying" by American police officers. American police experts and scholars refer to these long-standing police-misconduct practices by the misnomer "noble cause corruption," which is not noble, although, in most cases, it doesn't involve a personal gain.

Police lying in the forms of testilying and noble cause corruption came to the United States with the adoptions of the London Metropolitan Police model, although some argue that police lying was a result of the 1961 US Supreme Court decision in *Mapp v. Ohio.*

American Policing and Police Lying

The body of America literature on police lying focuses on testilying, which supposedly began in response to the restrictions on American policing coming out of the Warren Supreme Court decision in *Mapp v. Ohio.* This 1961 decision introduced the exclusionary rule to state police agencies. This decision set off a debate as to whether the exclusionary rule led to police lying in court to bypass the rule. The Mapp decision made the Fourth Amendment's exclusionary rule applicable to state proceedings, therefore, supposedly forcing state police officers to lie. The claim that police lying started after the 1961 Mapp decision lacks foundation (Dorfman, 1999). This is a myth embraced by historically challenged scholars.

As stated, police lying was a routine police workplace problem long before 1961 in England. Police lying, as an occupational and workplace problem, was transported to the United States along with the London Metropolitan Police model. Dunkle (2021) and Barker (2011) argue that police lying is like police violence and other forms of the police misconduct that is endemic to the police function and occupation. Dunkle calls for the abolition of policing because of these inherent occupational/workplace problems and their inherent racial bias. That conclusion goes a *bridge too far.* He is correct in his belief that police lying, including perjury; police violence; PSM; and other types of police occupational deviance are endemic in police work; however, the solution is not abolishing the police. Abolition of the police is an overreaction and not practical. We need improvement and reform rather than abolition. Police lying, in all its forms, is a regularly occurring police practice; a brief examination of Dunkle's study supports the argument that police lying in the form of perjury is, in fact, a persistent American police problem. However, police perjury can be minimized and controlled.

POLICE PERJURY IS A PERSISTENT AMERICAN POLICE PROBLEM: DUNKLE

Dunkle's study examined early American newspapers and commissions that were appointed to investigate police misconduct. He found hundreds of cases of manufactured charges, which the police used to justify the clubbing and beating of citizens in the late nineteenth century. In 1894, in New York state, the Lexow commission found numerous accounts of police perjury being used to cover up the rampant brutality and corruption, leading the chair of the committee, Clarence Lexow, to remark, "the air was blue with perjury" (Dunkle, 2021). He was correct. Police officers in the burgeoning nineteenth-century American urban centers felt compelled to exaggerate or invent the "facts" when they testified—to "gild the lily," so to speak. In New York City, the first vice officers falsely accused poor women of being prostitutes. The practices of planting of evidence and then giving perjured testimony to ensure guilty verdicts were common in American police history. In 1911, the New York legislature passed the Sullivan Law, which made carrying a concealed weapon a crime carrying a mandatory seven-year sentence in prison. The hoodlums of the time sewed up the pockets on their coats to prevent the police from planting a gun (Reppetto, 1978). In 1930 and 1931, NYPD vice officers were convicted of using "unmitigated perjury" to obtain false convictions for prostitution in twenty-seven cases involving poor black and immigrant women.

EARLY AMERICAN NATIONAL COMMISSIONS FOUND POLICE PERJURY

The Wickersham committee, established by President Hoover in 1929, was the first national commission to study the US criminal-justice system. The commission found substantial evidence of American police perjury. The commission found that perjury—lying in court—and third-degree police tactics were intertwined. The bruised and battered suspects who, according to the police, had confessed were said to have "fallen down the stairs." A bloody suspect sometimes was said to have "become unruly and been beaten by his cellmate," or it was said that a "drunk prisoner fell off the bench and hit his head on the concrete floor." The same excuses were still being used in the 1960s,'70s, '80s, '90s, and today (personal experience).

Wickersham investigators found that traffic accidents between white and black drivers always ended up being deemed the black driver's fault because of police lies (Dunkle, 2021). The police officers would manufacture the evidence if necessary. The commission found numerous instances of "evidence" against blacks that was manufactured and massaged by the police in the South during the Jim Crow era. According to the Wickersham commission, the justification (rationalization) for police unlawful practices was the "war theory of crime control"—according to this theory, policing was a no-holds-barred attack against the enemy: criminals.

Textbox 4.2. The War Theory of Crime Control

"[U]nlawful police work come[s] down in the end to the phrase: 'This is war.' . . . The criminal is the enemy; he is to be defeated by being quelled. Being the enemy, he has no rights worthy of the name. He is to be met by the weapons of war. Individual rights, including those of non-combatants, are subject to invasion like the rights of non-combatants in wartime. The policeman is a peacetime soldier. If bullets go astray, if civilians are inconvenienced, if civil rights are suspended, those are accidents inherent in a warfare that is waged in crowded cities. Criminologists of the humanitarian class are to be scorned, because they are the pacifists in this war. Defense attorneys are to be frustrated and outwitted because they are the enemy's diplomatic corps. Citizens who would make objection to the excess of authority are giving aid and comfort to the enemy."

Source: Hopkins, 1931.

WAR THEORY OF CRIME CONTROL IN ACTION

The rhetoric of the *war theory of crime control* equates controlling crime with being in a state of emergency that justifies unacceptable and illegal strategies against the criminal enemy. Those who don't support the police aid the enemy, the theory goes. Vestiges of the war rhetoric are present in today's conservative social media. History also shows there is a price to pay in a free society that abandons civil liberties in the name of crime control. That price includes police brutality, convictions of innocent persons, and creation of distrust in the fairness and legitimacy of the police. In a free society, we trust our agents of social control to act in a fair and equitable manner. Sometimes they don't. However, not all police lies are deviant lies. There are categories of police lies.

Categories of Police Lies

CATEGORY: ACCEPTED POLICE LIES

Good and Bad Lies?

In what appears to be an oxymoron, lies are sometimes accepted as a necessary, although controversial, police technique. Accepted police lies are told to accomplish a defined law-enforcement mission. One police scholar opines that these "good lies" expose the truth about criminal conduct (Wilson 2010). She writes that there are two types of good lies: 1) lies necessary for undercover operations, and 2) lies told by the police to persuade the guilty to confess. The police use the second type to their advantage. Cops know that there is no honor among thieves, so, if there is more than one criminal, one will "rat" out the other. So, the first thing the police do is separate them and claim that the other is talking. This technique works most of the time, even against the supposed brotherhood of cops. However, many of these lies and deceptive practices result in wrongful convictions that belie the "good lie" label (the next chapter discusses this topic further).

The second type of "good lies"—those used to persuade the guilty to confess—must be carefully regulated so that the police don't pressure the innocent to confess. Professor Saul Kassin, who has studied false confessions for over forty years, cautions that presenting false information to a susceptible person or a young person can alter the person's memory of events and lead to a false confession (Kassin, January 30, 2021). In any report—verbal or written—the police officer must truthfully admit to any lies told. Transparency of police actions in instances involving police lying dictates that all interviews and interrogations be videotaped and that the officers testify as to what lies were told and for what purpose. The purpose would be letting the jury decide if the police officer's conduct was acceptable beyond a reasonable doubt.

Good Lies: Undercover Operations

The first type of accepted "good lie" is the most obvious example of lies told by undercover and plainclothes officers. Such law-enforcement officers must conceal their identity and talk, act, and dress according to the environment they are in to prevent exposure or death (Barker, 2011). However, even these good lies have their problems. The behavior becomes evil when the officer engages in criminal behavior. Police officers, while undercover, directly or indirectly participate in smuggling drugs into prisons, laundering money, fencing stolen goods, printing counterfeit money, and committing perjury. These acts, unless performed by a criminal police officer, are generally considered necessary—within limits—and are an accepted part of covert policing, especially in deep-cover operations. These lies are deemed to be acceptable, because such lying is thought to be a means to achieving the end of justice.

Undercover Operations

There are some remarkable examples of federal police officers who "went deep cover" in organized-crime criminal enterprises. FBI special agent Joe Pistone infiltrated a New York crime family for six years (see Textbox 4.3). Billy Queen—an agent with the Bureau of Alcohol, Tobacco, Firearms and Explosives (ATF)—rode with the Mongols Motorcycle gang. He was even elected to the office of secretary/treasurer in a chapter. ATF agent Jay Dobyins rode for two years with the Hells Angels in Arizona (Barker, 2018). Secret operations such as these cannot be performed without deceptive practices. However, even deep-cover officers may not engage in unjustified criminality. They cannot legally take narcotics or commit serious crimes, such as gang rapes, murders, and assaults, while engaging in undercover assignments. For example, police officers cannot engage in gang rapes to join an outlaw motorcycle gang. An undercover officer cannot murder a snitch to become a made member of the Mafia. Organized criminal groups know this, and this leads to staged crimes to satisfy the initiation requirements (personal experience).

Textbox 4.3. Still Undercover: Joe Pistone

Joe Pistone, the former undercover FBI agent who was responsible for the successful prosecution of three Mafia crime families (the Bonanno family in New York City, the Ballistrieri family in Milwaukee, and the Trafficanti family in Florida) in the late 1970s, still believes he has a half-million-dollar contract on his head (Jacobson, July 27, 2021). Pistone, better known as Donny Brasco, his Mafia nom de guerre, still lives undercover. He has changed his name several times. Pistone does not live in one place for a long period, having relocated five or six times since 1981. His neighbors never know who he really is. He was the first FBI agent to go undercover with the Mafia in 1975. His assignment ended in 1981 after his mob bosses ordered him to kill a rival gangster in order to become a "made" man in the Mafia. The pretend burglar and jewel thief grew up in an all-Italian neighborhood and was familiar with the mob and its members' behavior patterns so he was a "natural" for this assignment. However, no one ever expected that it would be so successful and last so long. Pistone was thirty-two, married, and the father of two daughters when he began his undercover assignment. He had to live completely away from them for years. His autobiography, *Donnie Brasco: My Undercover Life in the Mafia*, became a national bestseller and then a movie starring Johnny Depp as Donnie Brasco.

There is a personal cost to becoming a professional liar. Undercover law-enforcement officers who spend too much time with the "bad" guys come to see them as friends and suffer what a UK fourteen-year veteran detective sergeant described as "moral injury." He was diagnosed with severe post-traumatic stress disorder because of his sense of guilt for deceiving people who thought he was their friend (Livadeas, November 10, 2020). Anyone who has worked undercover can relate to this "moral injury." No longer involved in drug work, Livadeas advocates for the decriminalization of drugs. Several undercover officers went "native" in their motorcycle gang assignments and became more biker than cop (personal experience). Undercover operations can result in unintended and lasting social costs.

In most countries, including the United States, undercover agents must not engage in sexual relations with members of the infiltrated group. There have been exceptions to this rule, which led to a bizarre outcome. The College of Policing Guidelines, which provide standards and rules for UK police officers, at one time allowed engaging in sexual relationships to protect the undercover officer's cover. However, this practice resulted in unintended consequences. The College of Policing said, "[T]he activity [sexual relationships] will be restricted to the minimum conduct necessary to mitigate the [immediate] threat" (Livadeas, November 10, 2020). The officer must not start the normally prohibited behavior, and it must not be repetitive or become an intimate sexual relationship. As common sense would predict, the practice became a convoluted nightmare when one undercover officer pushed the envelope to its limits.

Worst-Case Scenario

Sexual contact between a law-enforcement officer and a citizen is seldom considered to be consensual because of the imbalance of power between them. For that matter, sex is never truly consensual, no matter the status of the partners, when engaging in it is based on lies and deceptive practices. This is especially true when one of the participants is a professional liar—an undercover law-enforcement officer. Allowing undercover officers to engage in on-duty sex when it is necessary to accomplish a police objective or prevent revealing the officer's identity can be a nightmare of gigantic proportions. A good example of this is a strange odyssey that began in London, England, in 1987, and ended in Sydney, Australia, in 2016 (Farrell and Evans, March 9, 2016).

In 1987, British undercover officer John Dines took the name and identity of John Barker, an eight-year-old boy who had died of leukemia. Dines became a member of a secret London Metropolitan Police unit, the Special Demonstration Squad, that spied on political groups. Using the name John Barker, Dines posed as an anticapitalist activist for five years and infiltrated environmental activist groups. He met a social-justice activist, Helen Steel, and they began a two-year relationship, even considering marriage. Dines attempted to break off the relationship. In 1991, Dines complained of the onset of a mental breakdown and disappeared the next year, telling Steel that he was going to South Africa because he could not handle things anymore. Steel was devastated and feared that Dines could kill himself in his depressed mental state.

Unbeknownst to Steel at the time, Dines went to work at Met headquarters before leaving in 1994. Dines then moved to New Zealand, and, later, the Met moved him to Australia. While Dines was in Australia, the British police learned that Steel was searching for him. In 2010, Steel finally learned Dines's identity and that he had been an undercover police officer. In the same year, the Australian graduate school of policing and security at Charles Sturt University hired Dines.

Six years later, Steel flew to Australia and confronted Dines at the Sydney Airport while he was greeting a party of Indian police coming for training. Dines's emailed comment on that meeting was, "I gave her a personal and unreserved apology for all and any hurt that she may have suffered. I do not intend to make any other comment."

Steel became a throwaway lover and collateral damage to a police operation in which the means were less important than the ends.

The typical undercover or plainclothes assignments performed by local police agencies are not generally as dangerous or as long-lasting as those with organized-crime groups that cross local and state boundaries. Local, county, and state agencies' plainclothes operations are predominately vice operations addressing prostitution, gambling, and narcotics. These assignments, especially in narcotics operations, can be dangerous. There are potentially serious legal problems with using undercover or plainclothes officers and other deceptive practices, particularly in vice operations. If the officer goes beyond determining if the suspect broke the law and induces him or her into committing a crime, the officer has entrapped the suspect. Entrapment is commonly raised as a defense, and it does happen.

Cops at all government levels do entrap suspects and lie to cover it up. In 1989, the sheriff's department in Broward County, Florida, produced $20,000 worth of cocaine (Barker, 2011). They sold cocaine and arrested people who bought it. The resulting bad publicity forced the department to stop this practice. Was it entrapment? Possibly. However, more commonly, police misconduct occurs at the local-police level, where there is long-term association between officers and criminals, which increases the number of possibilities for corruption. Police professional organizations, such as the IACP have recommended that such assignments be subject to strict supervision and audit and limited to one-year assignments (see Bureau of Justice Assistance, September 1989).

CATEGORY: LIES TOLD TO THE MEDIA AND THE PUBLIC

Most lies that are told to the media and the public are lawful because the police must control and conceal certain information about cases, individuals, suspects, and victims. Law-enforcement officers and the public generally agree that, within limits, it is acceptable for law-enforcement officers to lie to the media or not divulge information that would disrupt an ongoing investigation. The standard FBI response to media questions is, "We won't confirm or deny an investigation." Local agencies frequently get in a bind by talking to the media. Withholding the names of suspects or victims is acceptable, but "planting" or spreading misinformation is not, except under extreme emergencies. In this category, police lie often from the top down.

Often the police chief must lie or manage the truth or else he or she must explain police discretionary decision-making. That opens Pandora's box. The police chief is loath to tell the truth about the lies that he or she and their officers tell. How does the police chief explain that officers can decide whom to stop and where to stop them, what questions to ask them, and when to search their person or vehicle? Would the police chief explain that the presumption of innocence is a legal fiction that stops at the interview room? Certainly not. That is why the true nature of police practices is denied and is a secret kept from outsiders whenever possible.

But the twenty-first-century police executive has a problem. Technology, bystander journalism (video and audio recordings), the Internet, and 24/7 media coverage have made police lying much more difficult. Police officers know that the bromide that "The truth will set you free" is BS. In police work, the truth gets you fired or put in jail in many instances. The truth is a dangerous thing in the wrong hands—that is, nonpolice hands.

CATEGORY: NECESSARY EVIL LIES? LEGAL?

Some police lies are rationalized by the police as "necessary evils" in the fight against crime. Detectives are judged by their case clearance rates, and confessions provide evidence of a cleared case. Therefore, detectives are under a lot of pressure to not accept "no" for an answer, and determined officers keep pushing even if they must resort to psychological or physical coercion. Law-enforcement officers are trained to lie or embellish the "facts" during interrogations. They may say that they have evidence when they don't or claim that a witness or accomplice has identified the suspect as the perpetrator. Inventing evidence and distorting facts are perceived as necessary evils. Following a polygraph examination, officers may falsely tell the suspect that he has failed the "lie detector" exam. The interrogator promises or suggests that a lesser punishment or a reduction in the number or type of charges will result from a confession. This tactic is often successful when capital punishment is a sentencing option. However, in many instances, the officer is consumed by tunnel vision. The officer feels he knows the "lied to person" is guilty and wonders "Why won't he admit it?" Maybe, it's because he is innocent?

The overzealous officer believes that the suspect is guilty of the crime and proceeds to document his belief. This is a dangerous practice used by police officers to induce false confessions. A polygraph examiner with the Department of the Army Criminal Investigation Division told me, "I know the bastard is guilty, and now I am going to go in there and prove it." I lost all confidence in polygraph examinations after that. Since then, I have learned that my conclusion was premature. The polygraph is a valuable investigative tool in the hands of a trained, ethical examiner searching for truth and justice. However, the ethical examiner must be neutral and not for or against the examinee.

Nevertheless, there are polygraph examiners who lie and deceive and champion the cause of their public or private employer. These examiners do not comply with the standards promoted by their professional associations, such as the American Polygraph Association. Even under the best circumstances, there are chances of false-positive or false-negative results. It is not possible to always identify the deceptive or the truthful. However, the examiner must never deliberately tip the scale. There are reported cases in which polygraph examiners gave false reports that subjects failed the examinations. One such incident is cited in the 2013 US Supreme Court decision, *Billy Wayne Cope v. State of South Carolina*. In this case, the defendant confessed to killing his daughter after he was falsely told that he failed the polygraph examination. Several months later, DNA analysis from saliva and semen revealed that a serial burglar and rapist had committed the crime. In effect, any confession without corroborating evidence is suspect. False confessions will be discussed more fully later.

Police lies do not always result in deaths and injuries. However, the "Dirty Harry" problem exists in police work because the ends—convictions—are deemed to be more important than the means—flawed or illegal practices—to attain them (Klockers, 1985). Law-enforcement officers fabricate evidence, falsify police reports, and lie in court or during internal proceedings because they believe that these practices are necessary evils. This misconduct can be an individual, group, or systematic. A 2013 publication in *The Washington University Law Review* examined the 1997 Ramparts scandal and the 2003 Tulia scandal, two police scandals in Texas, to document systematic and widespread criminal lying by bad cops (Covey, 2013). Some cops, like the LAPD officers involved in the 1997 Ramparts scandal, were engaged in criminal lying as a unit. The 2003 Tulia scandal involved one rogue officer lying against multiple persons.

The activities of a specialized gang intelligence unit of the LAPD, called Community Resources against Street Hoodlums (CRASH), produced one of the largest police scandals in United States history, the 1997 Ramparts scandal. The resulting investigation implicated numerous police officers in murder, other violence, theft, and drug dealing. LAPD CRASH officers planted drugs or contraband on suspects, forced confessions, and gave perjured testimony in court. The investigation resulted in the invalidation of approximately 156 felony convictions. CRASH officers' supervision of the special unit was lax or nonexistent. It was routine to conduct illegal searches, beat and shoot people, and plant evidence. No one checked on the behavior. It appears that the same sorts of behavior, without supervision, occurred in Memphis, resulting in the "murder" of Tyre Nichols.

In Tulia, Texas, one undercover agent serving on a drug task force falsely arrested 20 percent of the adult black residents of the city for the possession or sale of powdered cocaine. His perjured testimony resulted in the wrongful conviction of thirty-five people. The governor later pardoned the defendants. A Texas state judge said that the agent engaged in blatant perjury and "was the most devious, nonresponsive law enforcement witness this court has witnessed in twenty-five years on the bench in Texas." The agent's prior theft arrest, employment problems, mental-health problems, and unpaid debts should have precluded his employment (Blakeslee, 2005).

The Tulia and Ramparts scandals are but two of the seventeen scandals involving group exonerations since 1989. These group exonerations vacated the convictions of 2,500 wrongfully convicted persons, ranging from a low of 6 to 1,116 overly black persons per scandal, which will be examined fully in Chapter 5.

CATEGORY: COVER-UP LIES

Cover-up lies are those told to conceal a crime committed by an officer in the course of fulfilling his or her normal duties. These types of lies most often occur after the use of excessive force. The following story about a departmental disciplinary hearing story was told to me by a working police officer. According to the officer, the chief said the following after the hearing, "Officer X, I can't prove you lied. Therefore, I can't fire you. But, I am going to transfer you to a walking beat on the graveyard shift and put a written note in your file that you are a liar." The officer, after he told me the story, turned to me and said, "That's shit. He can't prove it but I'm still getting punished. That's bullshit." "Are you going to appeal his decision?" I asked. "Hell no. I'm guilty as hell. I lied like a motherfucker. I got lucky."

CATEGORY: PROCEDURAL POLICE LYING

Procedural lying occurs when the officer lies in a "court" setting about such topics as consent searches; probable cause; and custodial interrogations (i.e., lies about whether he complied with requirements set in *Miranda v. Arizona*). These lies are criminal perjury, committed to ensure that the evidence obtained, although legally flawed, is not excluded from the prosecution phase. The officer is ensuring the conviction of someone whom he feels he knows is a criminal. Some would justify it as an instrumental adjustment to meet overly restrictive rules. In these instances of police perjury, officers "fluff up" the evidence on a factually guilty person at a preliminary or suppression hearing. However, if an officer lies at a hearing, he or she will have to lie in court, which is committing perjury, to ensure a conviction. For example, an officer makes an illegal search and discovers drugs. In court, the officer testifies that he saw the defendant "drop" the dope or contraband as he approached—i.e., that it was an in-sight dropsy case. In-sight and abandoned evidence is admissible in court.

The incidence of "dropsy cases" exploded in my department after the Mapp decision. It is a well-known secret in today's law-enforcement community that officers are encouraged to say that suspects get slippery fingers when police approach and drop their drugs and guns. Slippery drugs and drug drops do happen but not to the extent that police officers allege in their testimony. There is a real US police problem of law-enforcement officers deciding that convictions are more important than the truth.

Law-enforcement officers often "sanitize" consent searches of residences or cars to meet constitutional requirements. Typically, they do not have a profit motive; rather, they lie to engage in police malfeasance, which will be discussed later. For example, the officer testifies that the subject gave consent to have his vehicle searched, when he did not, to justify a shakedown. Procedural lies occur often in weapons and drug cases. Official misconduct, brutality, and criminal behavior are common police workplace occurrences, and so are police lies to cover up these deviant behaviors (Dorfman, 1999).

Police lying is an example of procedural lies that can, and often do, lead to police-caused homicides that include murder and manslaughter.

Procedural Lies: Deadly Raids

Procedural lies—criminal perjury—told to secure drug-search-and-seizure warrants have resulted in the worst examples of police malfeasance and murder due to the militarization of police actions—the "war theory of crime control" in practice. According to criminologist Peter Kraska, in the 1980s, military-style and armed SWAT teams became the primary method in urban areas to deal with armed groups and serious threats to public order (Kraska, 2007). The American civilian police drew from and patterned themselves around the tenets of militarism and the military model. The resulting militarization morphed into overzealous black-clad ninja police engaged in "dynamic entries" during the "war on drugs." By 1995, 89 percent of US police departments serving populations of fifty thousand or more had a tactical or SWAT team.

There is an unintended consequence of the militarization of the American police. The warrior cops, dressed in black "battle dress uniforms," bloused over their steel-toed boots, execute no-knock dynamic-entry raids during the night-time that leave innocent suspects or others present on the premises dead or seriously injured. The "shock and awe" no-knock technique is overused and dangerous. Between 2010 and 2016, ninety-four people died during the execution of no-knock search warrants (Dolen, 2019). That figure includes thirteen dead police officers. Innocent parties startled by the police crashing through their doors, fire on the police or arm themselves because they reasonably think they are the victims of a home invasion. The invading police fire when they are fired upon or see something in an innocent person's hand. Many of these deaths are the result of police error—the police have entered the wrong house or targeted the wrong person—with no intent to kill or injure an innocent person.

Narcotics officers are the worst abusers of procedural lies as they carry their "save the world" righteous banners into battle in the "war on drugs." To them, statistics and seizures are more important than the truth. This is painfully demonstrated in what is known as a "whoops raid," a raid executed on the wrong house or person. No-knock search warrants are issued when officers' lives are in danger if notice is given. "Whoops raids," whose authorizing warrants are issued on the basis of lies, can result in disaster, such as the 2006 death of Kathryn Johnston in Atlanta; several deaths in 1919 in Houston, Texas; and the 2020 death of Breonna Taylor in Louisville, Kentucky.

Kathryn Johnston, Atlanta, Georgia, 2006. The innocent eighty-two-year-old great grandmother was killed in a botched "no-knock raid" based on falsified information. The narcs lied about the danger and falsely swore that an informant had bought drugs at the residence. When the cops broke down her door, the startled women, thinking she was being robbed, met them with an ancient weapon and was shot repeatedly. The wild ninja warriors in blue then planted drugs in the house when none were found. To defend the murder of the eighty-two-year-old grandmother, one officer had to lie to defend two other officers who had lied to obtain the search warrant. Three undercover officers were tried and convicted of manslaughter and sent to prison.

Houston, Texas, 2019. Although the death of Ms. Johnston was tragic and the result of police lies, a recent Texas case is a textbook case of the disastrous consequences to the public and the police when police officers engage in criminal behavior based on lies.

On January 28, 2019, at approximately 5 p.m., nine Houston, Texas, undercover narcotics detectives, backed up by six uniformed officers, executed a no-knock search warrant at an address in southeast Houston (Florian, 2019). The no-knock search warrant stated that, "Affiant [the lead narcotics officer] has established sufficient reason to believe that to knock and announce their purpose by the officers executing this search warrant would be futile, dangerous and otherwise inhibit the effective investigation of the offense or offenses related to the purposes of this warrant." According to the swearing detective, a confidential and reliable informant bought heroin in the residence and saw a semi-automatic handgun in the house. The informant also saw other bags of heroin in the house. A second narcotics officer swore that he witnessed the purchase of black tar heroin by the informant. The allegations of heroin purchases and the presence of other heroin in the residence, if correct, constituted probable cause to believe that the occupants were drug dealers. The allegation of the presence of a semiautomatic handgun in the residence, if correct, constituted probable cause of dangerous conditions. Then, as the popular saying goes, the sh—t hit the fan.

The dynamic entry went wrong, resulting in the deaths of two people in the residence, the injury of four officers, and the death of a family dog. Public and police reaction was swift. The chief of police, the mayor, and the president of the Houston Police Officers Union angrily defended the police and denounced the shooting of police officers and blamed it on citizens who are critical of the police. The chief was quoted as saying, "We are sick and tired of having a target on our backs." The chief said that a pit bull dog attacked the first officer through the door, and he shot and killed the vicious dog. The male homeowner then shot that officer in the shoulder. The officer fell on a couch. The homeowner's wife allegedly made a move to pick up the downed officer's shotgun and was shot and killed by another officer. The continuing shootout resulted in deaths and injuries.

Approximately two weeks after the raid, the official version of the scenario and its justification collapsed. The search warrant return inventory did not support the claim of a major drug bust. The document listed eighteen grams of marijuana, 1.5 grams of cocaine, two shotguns, and two rifles. There was no heroin and no semiautomatic handgun. The finding of a limited amount of drugs substantiated what the neighbors told the police after the "made for TV" raid. The two dead civilians were occasional recreational drug users, not drug dealers. Their occasional drug use was well known. An internal investigation in the police department revealed that the confidential informant who the lead detective said bought heroin at the residence denied ever being at the residence. The informant added that he had never bought heroin from either the dead man or his wife. The lead detective was accused of lying to obtain the no-knock search warrant. His police partner later told the investigators that he did not observe the drug buy as he previously testified. Currently, the lead narcotics detective is charged with two counts of felony murder. His partner is charged with tampering with a government document for lying on the offense report.

Breonna Taylor, 2020.

Just before midnight on March 13, 2020, seven out-of-uniform Louisville, Kentucky, police officers in military gear executed a no-knock search warrant on the apartment of Breonna Taylor. Taylor, who was a black woman and a twenty-six-year-old emergency-room technician, was in bed with her boyfriend, Kenneth Walker, when the plainclothes police officers knocked on the door without identifying themselves and then used a battering ram to knock down the door. In the brouhaha that followed, the police fired thirty-two shots. Five of those shots struck and killed Taylor, an innocent woman. There never was any evidence that Breonna Taylor was ever involved in drug dealing. She had no criminal record.

The original suspect, the target of multiple raids done that night—the Taylor raid was one of five raids pertaining to a drug-trafficking conspiracy—testified that Taylor was not involved. It is incumbent on police officers to specify the particularities of each raid to establish probable cause to obtain a search warrant. This was not done. In the justification for the search of Taylor's apartment, no one said that he had seen her with drugs or seen drugs in her apartment. On the Taylor warrant, the officer offered false statements to connect her to the target. He said that Taylor's apartment was a stash house for drug deliveries. The officer said a postal inspector had told him that suspicious packages were being delivered to the apartment from the target drug dealer. The postal inspector denied that outright. The entry and the subsequent events were without legal justification and were based on police lies. The unconstitutional boiler-plate justifications for the other four search warrants never mentioned Taylor. In effect, an unconstitutional search warrant, sworn to by a lying police officer, led to Breonna Taylor's police-caused homicide. This is another incident of police-caused murder, which will be discussed in the "killer cops" chapter.

The police left Ms. Taylor on the floor, bleeding out for twenty minutes, as they searched her apartment. It was customary and a part of Louisville Metro Police Department procedure to have an ambulance stand by when executing a no-knock search warrant in which violence is a possibility, but the raid supervisor had dismissed the waiting ambulance. This action belies one of the stated rationales for a no-knock warrant. That is only one example of the lies or misstatement of facts that are the "framework" of this tainted police action that led to the reckless and preventable death of Breonna Taylor. The raid should never have happened, and the police found no drugs, guns, cash, or contraband in their ninja raid.

The city of Louisville settled with the Breonna Taylor family for $12 million and made historic changes to police policies. Now, commanders must sign search warrants; no-knock search warrants are banned; and dynamic-entry raids must be videotaped. No-knock search warrants should be banned nationwide, and video-taping of all raids should be required. A multilayered approval system is the norm in federal agencies and should be the norm in all American police agencies (Balko, September 24, 2020; Cook, 2022; "Breonna Taylor," July 18, 2023).

False Swearing or Testilying: Procedural Lying

Police perjury in a court setting is an egregious form of police procedural lying. It is also a persistent police problem with a long history. Cops testify in court as part of their official duties all the time. They do it for a living. However, false swearing by officers is a serious crime, often leading to wrongful convictions and wrongfully long prison sentences. These lying officers don't just "fluff up" the evidence; they create the evidence. Some officers have framed innocent people. Law-enforcement officers' deceptive tactics, combined with their creative writing skills, are the lynchpins of false swearing and what is now known in the popular media as testilying. As we saw, this practice has a very long history in the police-work occupation. However, only twenty-five years ago, the term "testilying" was identified by the Mollen Commission in New York in 1992, as a part of NYPD police culture and as a tool used to convict suspects, regardless of guilt.

Police false swearing expands outside the courtroom. Creative false swearing can and does include the following, at a minimum: 1) creating informants to obtain a search warrant, 2) justifying a warrantless search during a stop and frisk, 3) covering up a mistake, and 4) planting evidence (called "flaking"). However, police officers have been "fudging up the case," "fiddling with evidence," "fluffing up the evidence," "shading the facts," "making things better," or "testilying" to stick it to the bad guys for good purposes since the beginning of the police-work occupation. The behavior just didn't have a popular label in America until the 1990s.

My sergeant in the 1960s made that clear to me: "A good cop is half rabbit [slang for crook]. Strictly follow the rules and you don't get shit done. The dirtbags must know they can't out lie a good cop." At that time, the practice in my department was known as "fluffing up the evidence." At first, most officers feel bad about taking an oath to tell the truth, with God as their witness, and then telling a lie to ensure that some dirtbag received his just punishment. Their fellow officers convince these officers that it isn't a lie. It just wasn't the complete truth. And everybody does it. It is easier to go along to get along so most went along.

At the time in my department, it was common practice for senior carmen to carry small stacks of signed search warrants in their "war bags." Rather than swear before a magistrate, the officer would fill in the empty spaces as needed. Again, everyone did it, and everyone knew about it. This practice was, and is, rare. As I made clear in the 1970s, "the largest percentage of [police lying] occur through the overzealous and misguided efforts of well-intentioned officers who believe that 'good' crime control requires some misrepresentations of the facts" (Barker, 1977).

I am told that Scottish police call testilying "pious perjury." According to legend, the term "pious perjury" derived from the sixteen centuries when the death penalty existed for certain property offenses. Police officers would reduce the value of the property to lessen the sentence for some, not all (Hosteller, November 22, 2011). I suspect that some Scottish officers increased the value to get rid of a repeat offender.

Furthermore, false swearing or testilying is one of the worst-kept criminal-justice secrets. Criminal-justice professionals are aware of the deceptive practice. This is a reluctantly kept—wink, wink—secret in the closed community of criminal-justice practitioners. In a bizarre 2005 case in Inkster, Illinois, two police officers and the head of the Wayne County drug unit pleaded guilty to giving and allowing perjured testimony in court against two drug defendants. The judge admitted that she knew of the perjured testimony, but she was not tried (Oosting, January 9, 2009).

Selected Examples of Police Lying. The following examples of police officers being charged or convicted of lying or perjury are taken from my newspaper and a Google alert search list from 2009 to 2021. This is an illustrative, not exhaustive, list.

- A veteran NYPD sergeant admitted in court that he perjured himself when he testified in court against an alleged marijuana dealer. He bent the rules only to get a bad guy off the street, he explained to the judge. He was training other cops just out of the police academy when he gave the perjured testimony. He was sentenced to twenty-four days at Rikers Island and had to quit the job and lose his pension (Melissa Grace, June 27, 2011).
- The judge in a Texas drug case said that the in-court testimony of two highly respected police officers in Dallas, Texas, was not credible. The officers were charged with fabricating physical evidence and aggravated perjury. Sixty of their convictions were dismissed (Lita Beck, March 1, 2013).
- A Tulsa, Oklahoma, police officer, who was in prison for his conviction on six counts of perjury and two counts of civil-rights violations, was held in contempt and had time added to his sentence when it was discovered that he gave false testimony about an alleged informant (Jarrel Wade, February 28, 2013).
- In Sacramento, California, seventy-nine DUI convictions were reversed when it was revealed that the police officer in these cases had falsified drunk-driving reports and had lied at state department-of-vehicles administrative hearings. He was sentenced to a year in the county jail. His lawyer said he didn't act with malice. His intentions were good—getting drunk drivers off the streets (Anon, April 19, 2013).
- An NYPD officer known for making a lot of arrests was sentenced to six months in prison when he was convicted on ten counts of filing a false instrument. He testified that he arrested a man for making a drug arrest he had witnessed. However, video surveillance arrest showed the man was innocent (Russ Buettner, July 12, 2013).
- Two NYPD detectives in Yonkers, New York, were fired and faced perjury charges after it was revealed that an informant whom they had used to obtain a falsified search warrant was in prison in another state at the time (Jonathan Bandler, January 13, 2015).

- In 2017, the now-defunct Chicago Police Board recommended the officers' employment be terminated for violating police policy and lying about the circumstances of and justification for the shooting. The police commissioner also filed departmental charges and recommended that the officers be fired. They were suspended instead, prompting a civil suit.
- Two Chicago police officers assigned to the gang unit allegedly submitted false affidavits to search suspected drug dealers' properties and then stole cash and drugs from the properties (US Attorney's Office, Northern District of Illinois, Department of Justice, May 10, 2018).
- A retired Kansas highway patrol officer was found guilty of lying to the FBI during an investigation of illegal gambling in Wichita, Kansas. He was filmed playing in an illegal cash poker game in 2014, when he was still a trooper. The site where he was filmed had poker tables, a cabinet for valuables and poker chips, video-surveillance equipment, liquor, and snacks. The illegal casino had dealers, food servers, and waitresses giving massages to the players (January 28, 2019).
- Thirteen Springfield, Massachusetts, police officers were indicted on assault charges. The underlying incidents involved four victims, filing false reports, and lying to conceal their misconduct (March 27, 2019).
- Two Trenton, New Jersey, police officers were charged with the use of excessive force on a compliant driver after a police chase and lying to cover up the assault (April 23, 2019).
- In Franklin Township, Franklin County, Ohio, a police officer was sentenced to twelve months and one day in prison for deprivation of civil rights under the color of law. He kicked an arrestee in the head while the victim was lying on the ground, handcuffed. The officer then lied and filed false reports to conceal his misconduct (June 19, 2019).
- A Hadley, Massachusetts, police officer was sentenced to fourteen months in prison after he was found guilty of using unreasonable force and filing a false report to conceal the incident. He struck an arrestee sitting on a bench multiple times in the face. The beating fractured the arrestee's nose and required surgery to repair the damage (June 30, 2019).
- A twenty-five-year veteran federal probation officer was sentenced to thirty months in prison for lying to the FBI about his sexual exploitation of male probationers. The judge described his behavior as "loathsome and disgusting" (August 13, 2019).
- A Patterson, New Jersey, police officer was part of a drug-dealer robbery gang (this will be further discussed later) and admitted that he filed false reports and lied to cover up this activity (September 9, 2019).
- A Department of Homeland Security supervisor was convicted of lying to the FBI to conceal that he was providing official information from

law-enforcement databases to be used in a scam directed at immigrants (October 4, 2019).

- A Pittsburgh, Pennsylvania, police officer was sentenced to one year of probation with ninety days of home detention for lying to FBI special agents during the investigation of a robbery. The officer denied knowing the identity of the robber, who was the son of a woman he had been in a seven-year romantic relationship with (October 28, 2019).
- A twenty-two-year veteran Chicago police officer, who was facing charges relating to lying before the Chicago Police Board, resigned. Allegedly, he lied about seeing the 2014 fatal shooting of a fellow police officer. His body camera revealed that he could not have seen what happened during the shooting (Gorner and Hinkle, March 26, 2021).

There will be numerous examples of cover-up lies in the chapters that follow.

Dealing with Cops with Known Credibility Problems

That police officers lie and that their employment generally is not terminated for lying that falls short of perjury for profit are well-known and condoned facts in police work; officials struggle with how to deal with deviant police liars. Some officers are known as liars with credibility problems. For example, many urban departments put known liars on what is known as a "Brady list," which is named after a 1963 US Supreme Court decision—*Brady v. Maryland*. The defendant, Brady, was arrested for and convicted of murder. However, Brady said that he had been present but that another man had committed the murder. Brady said that he had had no intention of committing a murder. Unbeknownst to Brady, the other man admitted to being solely responsible for the murder; the prosecutor did not reveal the exculpatory information. In many states with the felony-murder rule, the fact would not have been exculpatory. However, this Supreme Court decision says that prosecutors must disclose any exculpatory information that shows or indicates the innocence of the defendant. In the context of police lying, this rule would include any evidence that an officer involved in a case has credibility problems; for example, an officer may have been sanctioned administratively for lying on a report or to a supervisor, and such information would have to be disclosed to the defendant.

There is no one national official list of police officers with credibility problems, but many—the exact number is unknown—states and cities are keeping such "Brady lists" and making this information public. An officer does not have to be convicted of a crime or fired to wind up on the list. If you are a cop, you don't want to be on a Brady list.

In general, an officer who is on a Brady list at some time has committed an act of dishonesty. They are not credible witnesses because their character is in question. The infraction may have been an administrative decision, such as filing a deceptive report or lying to a supervisor. In other words, there are objective and subjective reasons for ending up on the "credibility issues" list.

Brief examples are presented below. A more detailed analysis will appear later.

Arizona, 2020—An Arizona news network, ABC 15, was able, through public record requests, to publish the first searchable Brady list in Arizona, which led to the creation of a public list. All but two counties provided data (Biscobing, February 2020). The year-long project of compiling the county attorney's list, using supportive information dating from the late 1990s through the time of compilation, resulted in a list of 1,400 officers. Of the 1,400 officers on the list, 220 were still on the job. The largest police agency in Arizona—the Phoenix Police Department—had 390 officers on the list, with 106 of them remaining active at the time. Several dozen of the officers were correctional officers or other personnel who were not sworn, such as evidence technicians. Most of the officers who are currently on the Arizona list have been placed on it since 2010. There was and is a lot of information missing from Arizona's Brady list because Arizona's method of compilation relies on police departments to investigate and self-report problem officers to county attorneys' offices.

Oregon, 2020—A recent survey (Woodworth and Kanik, July 13, 2020) of Oregon's thirty-six counties found that, after a 2013 Oregon State Committee on Judiciary required district attorneys to disclose any information favorable to the defendant, the counties responded in a variety of ways. The general findings revealed the following:

- Most officers, though not all, who are on a Brady list lose their jobs, either for their offense or because they can no longer testify for the prosecution.
- Some counties let officers appeal their Brady listing, but most don't have a process for appeal.
- Excessive use of force, not just dishonesty, can land an Oregon officer on a Brady list.

More than two hundred Oregon officers were on the list. Among the offenses that led to being put on the list were tampering with evidence, demonstrated incompetence, lying during internal affairs investigations, failing to report crimes, and committing crimes themselves.

Suffolk County, Massachusetts, 2020—The district attorney's office of Suffolk County, Massachusetts—whose jurisdiction covers Boston, Chelsea, Revere, and Winthrop—released a list of 136 law-enforcement officers on a

"Law Enforcement Automatic Discovery" list (Wuthmann and Jarmanning, September 27, 2020). The list included seventy state troopers, fifty-four Boston police officers, and officers from Chelsea, Revere, Massachusetts Bay Transportation Authority police, and a special police officer. To be included on the list, the officer must be subject to criminal charges or allegations of discrimination, investigated for lack of truthfulness or integrity, or subject to any finding that the officer isn't credible.

Proposed Kansas Police Credibility Checklist, 2022—The new district attorney for Douglas County, Kansas, has proposed a controversial eleven-item checklist to be filled out for each police officer in the county (Clark, April 26, 2022; see textbox 4.4). The proposed list has prompted a debate among the police agencies and the district attorney's office.

Textbox 4.4. Douglas County, Kansas, Law-Enforcement Checklist

1. Does this officer have a juvenile adjudication on his/her record?
2. Does this officer have an arrest or conviction on his/her record?
3. Any agency/department finding of misconduct reflecting on trustfulness, credibility, or integrity?
4. Any agency/department investigations of this officer for misconduct reflecting on truthfulness, credibility, or integrity?
5. Any allegations or complaints of bias against a target, subject, defendant, or group of individuals?
6. Has this officer provided any prior inconsistent statements on material issues in a case?
7. Are there any present allegations or complaints of misconduct against this officer?
8. Have there been any allegations or complaints against this officer regarding specific instances of misconduct going to truthfulness, credibility, veracity, use of force, inaccurate reporting, mishandling of evidence, false documentation, and/or failure to follow procedure in handling of a confidential informant or source of information?
9. Has anyone in your agency/department or other agency/office/department expressed an opinion/reputation concerning his/her truthfulness, credibility or veracity?
10. Has this officer failed to report a use of force?
11. Do you understand that you have a duty to update the checklist if new information arises in the future or if an answer to any previous question would change?

Conclusion

Police deviant lying is a major American police misconduct problem. As stated, the "war theory of crime control" and the warrior ideology were the dominant guide for American policing well into the twenty-first century and were used to justify many police abuses, including police perjury. This police culture was in place long before the 1961 decision in the Mapp case, which supposedly had a direct effect on police lying, making the ends more important than the means. However, as Dorfman (1999), my personal experiences, and research make clear, American police officers were lying in court, on warrant applications, to hide corruption and crime, to defend brutality, to cover up murders, and to punish dirtbags long before the Mapp decision.

Police officers learn to lie and learn when lying is or is not acceptable through the workplace socialization process. In the academy, they learn police ethics, departmental rules and regulations, and definitions of criminal behavior. Next come "on the job" experiences through which they learn what is acceptable and unacceptable behavior in their workplace setting. Finally, they observe the behavior of the veterans who translate talk into action (Barker, 2011).

Discussion Questions

1. Why is it important to know the history of police perjury?
2. Why will police lying never be entirely eradicated?
3. Does the Douglas County district attorney's checklist create overreaction to possible police perjury? What would you add to or delete from the checklist?
4. Discuss police undercover operations with English officer John Dines in mind. What are the moral implications of operations that are similar to his?
5. Read the true instance of police lying below, and discuss its implications. Why would police officers engage in this behavior? Do you agree or disagree with the officers' behavior? If not, what should be their punishment, if any?

NOBLE CAUSE INJUSTICE: TREE TOP'S SAGA

The following account of true events was told to me in the summer of 2018. I have heard similar stories, set in multiple locations, from different individuals. The individuals involved in these narratives shared the same social and economic characteristics—they were persons of color with credibility issues, living in poverty in high-crime areas. The unnamed city is a large metropolitan urban area in the Southwest. The anti-gang task force in this city has the reputation of "flaking"—planting evidence on real and suspected dealers. The task force has also been involved in several questionable shootings. Incidents like the one described occur throughout the United States and the United Kingdom as police officers engage in police corruption for the job (the United Kingdom) or "noble cause injustice" (the United States).

Adrian X turned eighteen last Wednesday. His official birthday celebration ends tonight. A full moon lights up the stoop of Adrian's Section 8 row house. Adrian, also known as Tree Top, six-five and rail-thin minus his black-and-red bandana and dreadlocks, sits listening to his boom box and eating pizza. Tree Top is a member of the Black Original Gangsters and has a long record of juvenile arrests for possessing drugs and has had no detention stays. The anti-gang task force is pissed at Adrian. They are determined to bust him somehow for distribution—a felony that will send him to prison. The ninja black-clad gang cops better hurry. Adrian is maturing out of gang life. He and Joanie have a little boy. Adrian just started trade school and promised his mama that he would give up the gang life. She is skeptical but hopeful. However, she has heard these promises before. So have the gang cops. "I'm leaving the Black Originals and going back to school," Adrian always tells them and the juvie judges before they send him back to the streets.

Adrian looks up as a black unmarked police car pulls to the curb. He knows the officers. He knows the car. The same anti-gang cops had tossed him and his homies for years. The gangbangers sold drugs on the open market but never held more than two bags on their person—the limit for possession. Possession got the holder some brief time in the juvie institution. Over three bags was a prima facie case of intent to distribute—resulting in prison time for an adult (eighteen or older) or a long stay in juvie for a minor. Undeterred, the gang cops kept stopping and searching the gangbangers and flaking those who pissed them off.

"Get your black ass down here," Officer Davis yelled. He was a stocky little guy—about five-six with a buffed-out frame. His Marine buzz cut was getting a little thin on top. Most gangbangers talked about the mean stare he had, especially for people who were taller than he was, like Tree Top.

Adrian came down the stairs and walked to the front of the car. He took off his hoodie and laid it on the car's hood. He knew the drill. Spread-eagled, Adrian assumed the search position and waited for the pat-down.

"You turned eighteen last week, didn't you?" Davis asked. Adrian nodded.

"Happy Birthday, nigger, you done graduated to the big time. No more juvie for you, Tree Top. You're going to prison now." His white teeth flashed in a sardonic smile.

"For what I ain't done nothing. I ain't got nothing on me."

"What's this in your hoodie pocket," said Davis's partner, Officer Howard. The six-foot burly, buffed-up, bully gang cop had his left hand resting on the hoodie's right pocket spread out on the car's hood.

"There ain't nothing in that pocket, Officer Howard. I ain't got shit on me."

"Then reach in there and hand whatever is in there to me," Howard said.

Tree Top reached in the pocket and pulled out six small, clear, plastic packets, and said, "That shit ain't mine. You flaked me, you asshole. That ain't right."

"Flaked you. Who's gonna believe that shit? I bet your fingerprints are on those packets, not ours. Tell it to the judge." Both officers laughed as Davis put on the handcuffs.

"Man, I've been fucked," a sad Adrian said.

"You sure have. But wait till you get to prison and become some bad dude's bitch. A handsome homey like you is going to be in demand," Howard said with a wicked smile.

"You're under arrest for possession of heroin with intent to distribute. That's good for fifteen years. Bye bye, Tree Top."

Tree Top took a plea deal for five years. He complained to the public defender that the cops were lying. All the public defender said was, "What do you want me to do? You know you can't out lie the cops. Take the five and move on."

That's what Tree Top did.

CHAPTER 5

Wrongful Convictions

FALSE CONFESSIONS AND OFFICIAL MISCONDUCT

Key Terms:
Factually innocent
Procedural error
Probable cause
Tunnel vision
Hold back details
Appropriate adults (United Kingdom)
National Registry of Exonerations
Anthony Ray Hinton
Trial penalty

Chapter Objectives:
After reading this chapter, the reader should be able to do the following:

1. Define and describe false confessions and wrongful convictions
2. Describe the nexus between false confessions and wrongful convictions
3. Describe the development and importance of the National Registry of Exonerations
4. Draw attention to the danger of presumptive guilt

The chapter is divided into two segments: first, it discusses false confessions, and then it segues into wrongful convictions. False confessions are a major contributing factor in wrongful convictions. False confessions are an anomaly in the American criminal-justice system for those observers who are unfamiliar with police practices. The question that such observers most often ask is, "Why would a person confess to a crime that he or she did not or could not have committed?" Their next question is, "How can the police get someone to confess to a crime that he or she didn't commit?" Such observers feel that it just doesn't make sense and that it is not rational behavior. However, maybe it is.

Some falsely confess or make incriminating statements because at the time they were physically or psychologically coerced, threatened, or frightened. Others were drunk, or stoned. These examples make some sense. Then what happens if the person comes to their senses, sobers up and recants? That is not the end. Usually, no one believes that the confession was false. Now it's their word against the officer's. In most cases their lawyer, an overworked public defender, hasn't got time to listen to the new version of the event. The public defender is just a small player in the American system of assembly-line justice. Play your part in the justice game, the public defender cautions. They advise that the false confessor take the deal and move on or suffer worse consequences. Recall "Tree Top's Saga" from the previous chapter.

What if the false confessor is mentally impaired or young or was lied to? Well, in nonlegal terms, the false confessor is screwed. Others say that what was just described are rare events and ask, "Why the fuss?" Are false confessions rare events? Is there some problems with the way the American police "produce" confessions, false or true? There may be. Maybe the suspect was tortured by the police. The cry goes up that that doesn't happen in the United States anymore. Yes, it does.

False Confessions Resulting from Police Torture

Beatings of blacks and others without power were common in the 1960s and early 1970s in many American police agencies (personal experience and early research). One very successful robbery detective described his "aluminum chair technique" to me in the late 1960s. He said you put a suspect in a room with two aluminum chairs. The suspect sits in one chair and the detective in the other. Whenever the detective suspected the "n__" was lying, the detective got up and hit him on the head with his aluminum chair. I never saw him in action, but others told me they had, and his success was legendary. Other victims and officers told me of cattle prods and plyers on the fingers or up the noses of suspects.

In the 1970s and 1980s, at least 150, maybe more, black Americans were tortured by at least fifteen white Chicago police officers in Area 2 of Chicago's south side under the command of Lieutenant Jon Burge (Taylor, 2019). Torture worked in some cases to elicit true confessions. The horrendous physical techniques elicited confessions from guilty persons. That was the stated purpose of the torture. However, evidence shows that an unknown number of the victims made false confessions and served long prison sentences prior to being exonerated. In Chicago's Area 2, torture was normalized as an interrogation technique and it was well known by others in the prosecutors' and public defenders' offices. But, if the targets were black males with credibility problems, no one cared (Riebam, 2016). What went on behind closed doors was tolerated as long as it stayed secret from the public. It didn't. A public scandal took place, and, in 2003, the Illinois governor pardoned four black men on death row who had been tortured by Burge and his crew. Civil suits and exoneration hearings are still ongoing. How could this happen in a country that prides itself on the common-law presumption of innocence and in which the state must prove guilt beyond a reasonable doubt?

PRESUMPTION OF INNOCENCE: TRUE OR LEGAL FICTION?

False confessions make sense to those who believe, as many do, that the presumption of innocence is often a legal fiction that the police and many of the criminal-justice officials only give lip service to when it is convenient to do so. An unknown number of American law-enforcement officers, when they identify a "person of interest," assume the person is guilty and seek to get a confession rather than gather the facts. Then, once they have a confession that proves them right, the investigation is over. Unfortunately, some American police officers believe that the end, a signed confession, is worth any means to get it.

Intentionally or unintentionally, the police interrogation techniques used by lazy, incompetent, and BTTB police officers result in false confessions being provided by people who are innocent or not guilty as charged. These BTTB detectives and investigators are in the minority, but, if you judge their behavior by lives lost, families ruined, and other social consequences, they may be the apex of police occupational/workplace deviance. Only God knows how many innocent persons were sent to their deaths by these malefactors. Students of police occupational deviance saw the connection between occupational deviance and wrongful convictions in the early twenty-first century.

A 2003 report from the Center on Wrongful Convictions at the Northwestern University School of Law (Warden, May 12, 2003) created new interest in these false confessions and wrongful convictions. The report said that, since 1970, forty-three wrongful murder convictions had been documented in Illinois. Twenty-five of those wrongful convictions were due in whole or in part to false confessions produced by police interrogations. The report went on to say that this figure was not the true picture. The report said no one knows how many false confessions resulted in wrongful convictions. We still don't know. Furthermore, how many of those unknown false confessions are the result of police misconduct or coercion is also unknown.

WHAT ARE FALSE CONFESSIONS?

There are three categories of false confessions: 1) voluntary false confessions are rare occurrences that occur without any police coercion; the subject confesses to a crime to protect someone else (a person may confess to a crime to protect a loved one, such as a wife or a child); 2) coerced-compliant false confessions appear to be the most common type; the subject falsely confesses to a crime during an interrogation marked by external physical or psychological coercion; however, the confessor knows that the subject is innocent; and 3) coerced-internalized false confessions in which the vulnerable subject is coerced into thinking that he or she committed the crime (Gubi-Kelm, Grolig, Strobel, Ohlig, and Schmidt, 2020). The second type, coerced-compliant false confession, is the most likely to be elicited by the common accusatory model of interrogation in use by American police detectives. Why would a person falsely confess? When I first asked myself that question, the answer, the trial penalty, popped into my head. Most cops have seen or suspected that some pleaded guilty to crimes they didn't commit to escape the well-known trial penalty.

THE TRIAL PENALTY AND FALSE CONFESSIONS

There is a trial penalty for those who turn down plea bargains or refuse to confess and, instead, go to trial. The trial penalty is explicit in the operation of the criminal-justice system. Our criminal-justice system is one of "assembly line" justice, with all actors—law-enforcement officers, prosecutors, attorneys, and judges—involved to some degree in the "speed things along" bargaining process. Guilty pleas are the desired outcome. The latest Bureau of Justice statistics reveal that guilty pleas resolve over 97 percent of federal cases. An unknown number of these defendants are innocent of the offense or are not guilty as charged. Former and current criminal-justice workers know this. Anyone that has gone through the criminal-justice system as a defendant—guilty or not—knows this. There are several reasons for their rational decisions to plead guilty. Sentence leniency or charge reductions result from guilty pleas.

A prominent Innocence Project attorney described why he advised his innocent client to plead guilty. His client, a young black man whose case was being tried by an overwhelmingly white jury in Texas, was offered one year in prison if he pleaded guilty to a crime he didn't commit. He was advised to plead guilty to avoid a much longer sentence if he was convicted (Swarns, June 1, 2023). The Sixth Amendment enshrines the right to a trial for anyone accused of a crime, yet, in the United States today, less than 3 percent of criminal cases go to trial because of the trial penalty. The trial penalty is the practice of offering more lenient sentences in exchange for a guilty plea before trial and promising a longer sentence if the suspect is convicted after trial. In effect, that means that fighting for one's innocence means risking spending decades in prison. Innocent people can and do plead guilty under these circumstances (Swarns, June 1, 2023).

In Tulia, Texas (discussed earlier in Chapter 4), those who falsely pleaded guilty received an average sentence of four years in prison. Those who went to trial and were convicted were sentenced to an average of 51.2 years. According to the author of the Ramparts-Tulia study, the trial sentence was from four to thirteen times longer than plea sentences. The study cites the case of an innocent man who was offered a five-year sentence for a crime that carried a maximum twenty-year sentence. Because he was innocent, his father told him to turn the deal down. He did and was convicted and sentenced to twenty years. What would be a more compelling example of why an innocent person may plead guilty?

Furthermore, it takes money and power to play the justice game in the United States. Most persons who come in contact with the criminal-justice system are poor and without power. The same statement is true for those playing the justice game in other countries. The House of Lords 2019 report, cited in Chapter 1, writes of a defendant who could not get funding for a DNA expert from the authorities or the legal aid agency (House of Lords, 1, May 2019, p. 31). She contacted the author of a textbook on DNA, who agreed to do it for nothing. Our system of justice operates on the idea that confessing or pleading guilty moves things along. The American accusatory system of interrogation is the best example of this.

Textbox 5.1. Legal Fiction

"Innocent until Proven Guilty" is a legal fiction.

"The law holds that it is better that 10 guilty persons escape than that 1 innocent person be convicted" (Blackstone, 1769). This is NOT TRUE; it is a legal fiction.

A legal fiction is defined as an assumption accepted as fact by the courts but applied quite differently in action by practitioners. It sounds good, but it is not how things work. The assumption of guilt often results in wrongful convictions. The American accusatory injustice system assumes the suspect is guilty and sets out to secure a confession to prove it.

How the Accusatory System Works

1. The cops identify the "obviously" guilty person, but he could be in fact innocent. The first step to obtaining a false confession is to identify an innocent person as the suspect, using tunnel vision.

2. They interrogate him, and he confesses but is in fact innocent. The second step to obtaining a wrongful conviction is obtaining a psychologically coerced confession.
3. The prosecutor NOW has a "slam dunk" case. Confessions are the "queen of proof." Confessions should be the beginning of the investigation; however, they are the end. Confessions trump everything, even evidence.
4. The cops have a terminal case. The investigation is over. Move on.
5. The jury disregards the recanting of the conviction. Cops don't lie to suspects. Psychological torture is a crock. People don't admit to murders they didn't do.
6. Fifteen years later, DNA analysis identifies the real murderer.

The state says that it can't issue a certificate of innocence because he confessed, but they won't try him again. Sorry. The cops say they did nothing wrong.

The American accusatory system of interrogation, as illustrated above, is a cynical but accurate depiction of the predominate accusatory model of interrogation that is guilt-presumptive and confession focused. It is a good model for producing true and false confessions. The questions for this system are standard for any police interrogation practice. Do the police tactics and practices in the accusatory interrogation model minimize or increase public harm and promote or lessen police legitimacy? Are wrongful convictions due to false confessions a persistent police problem? Can false confessions elicited by the police be minimized? Do other criminal-justice officials wrongly convict factually innocent persons? How many factually innocent persons have been wrongly convicted? From an evidence-based perspective, the answers to these questions require a thorough examination of American police practices and tactics.

As Sherman said in his seminal work on evidence-based policing (EBP) in 1998, "evidence-based policing simply says that police practices should be based upon scientific evidence about what works best" (American Society of Evidence Based Policing, http://www.americansebp.org). As we saw in the early American police professional movement, this critical idea of police tactics being based on nothing more than common sense has always been a part of police reform.

The American Accusatory Interrogation System: Through the Guilt-Presumptive Lens

The current accusatory approach to interrogation used by most US law-enforcement officers is the Reid technique of interrogation (a detailed explanation follows later). It was developed by a former Chicago cop turned polygraph examiner and formalized in 1963 (Meissner, Surmon-Bohr, Oleszkiewiez, and Alison, 2017; Trainum, 2016 and 2021; French, 2019). This practitioner-oriented approach was a welcome change from the third-degree methods and intuitive interrogation methods used by streetwise police veterans who received praise for their ability to solve cases and elicit confessions. At first, the accusatory approach had no scientific basis to support its basic tenets, but it worked. Or the police community thought it worked. For decades the American police have used the "nonphysical" accusatory approach to interrogations. But physical coercive tactics did not stop entirely. Innocent and guilty suspects were subjected to physical pain and torture to extract confessions.

Flint Taylor's seminal work, *The Torture Machine: Racism and Police Violence in Chicago*, chronicles the depravity that occurred in Chicago in the 1980s and early 1990s as hundreds of black men were tortured into giving true and false confessions. The "new" accusatory interrogation approach was intended to end physical torture, but its psychological terror and misuse produced true and false confessions.

The guilt-presumptive accusatory approach assumes the suspect is guilty and "helps" the subject justify his or her actions and finally admit them. The goal is a confession, and the technique is very good at producing confessions—true and false. The confrontational guilt-presumptive approach is designed to make accusations and refuse to accept denials. The interrogator confronts the suspects with evidence of their guilt even if the evidence is false. An officer might say, "your accomplice ratted you out" or "your fingerprints or DNA were found at the scene," even if this is not true. Lying or "massaging the truth" is a common interrogator technique. Remember "you can't out lie a cop." Certain groups, like the young or the mentally deficient, are especially vulnerable to these tactics, resulting in wrongful convictions after giving false confessions. Situational factors, such as the isolation and length of the interrogation session, affect the interrogators' ability to learn the truth. Many of these techniques are not allowed in other countries.

For example, England, France, Germany, Spain, New Zealand, Australia, Japan, Taiwan, and all of Scandinavia will not allow lying to subjects (Kassin in Snook et al., 2021). The United States, China, and Israel do allow the interrogator to lie to the suspects. That fact should raise a red flag. In 2014, the American Psychological Association passed a resolution that recognized that giving false evidence to an interrogation suspect increased the risk of a false confession (Snook et al., 2021). The Chicago Police Department stands out as an American police prototype for false confessions and wrongful convictions obtained while using the accusatory model of interrogation.

CHICAGO POLICE DEPARTMENT AND FALSE CONFESSIONS

As mentioned above, Taylor's work, *The Torture Machine: Racism and Police Violence in Chicago*, describes how Chicago police officers in the 1980s and early

1990s tortured hundreds of black men into giving true and false confessions. The Chicago Police Department is once again being rocked by another coerced false-confession scandal. In 1973, former Chicago police commander Jon Burge first used his "nigger box"—a hand-cranked electrical device with wires attached to alligator clamps—to torture suspects into false confessions. In 1983, Burge and his crew were still using the "nigger box" and other torture techniques. There were other Chicago officers using torture techniques, such as applying cattle prods to the genitals of suspects. In December 2020, a man who had been wrongly convicted after giving a false confession after torture by Burge and his crew and misconduct by the prosecutor was declared innocent and freed from prison after thirty years (Crepeau, December 20, 2020). He was freed after his third retrial, when it was discovered that the prosecutor had lied on the stand during the retrial.

In the 1990s, a black sergeant and his drug crew terrorized blacks in Chicago's Ida A. Wells housing project, extracting false confessions and falsely testifying against those whom they couldn't shake down. Nearly one hundred convictions have been overturned (Hauck, February 11, 2020).

The latest Chicago Police Department officer to be exposed is Detective Reynaldo Guevara who was, for twenty years (from the 1980s to early 2000), one of the most successful detectives at solving cases through confessions. The secret to his success was revealed in lawsuits and exonerations. In April 2023, Guevara was alleged to have framed fifty black and Latino men by coercing false confessions (Hope, March 21, 2023). So far there have been thirty-nine exonerations. One of those exonerations was of a twenty-one-year-old woman wrongly convicted of murder in 1993 and sentenced to death and later commuted to life without parole. Nineteen years later, in 2022, her conviction was vacated, and her case was dismissed (Registry, 2022). There have been eleven federal lawsuits filed against the former detective, who has retired and left the city of Chicago.

When testifying in one federal civil lawsuit brought against him for framing an innocent suspect for murder, the former police detective took the Fifth Amendment privilege two hundred times to prevent prosecution for perjury (Meisner, June 6, 2022). Guevara was refusing to answer questions about running a corruption racket in a Hispanic neighborhood; his activities included pinning false murder cases on suspects, shaking down drug dealers for protection money, and taking money from gang members to rig police lineups.

CERTAIN GROUPS ARE OVERREPRESENTED IN FALSE CONFESSIONS

Justice Souter, of the US Supreme Court, in a 2009 case, *Corley v. United States*, wrote that custodial police interrogations could "induce a frighteningly high percentage of people to confess to crimes they never committed." He was correct. The empirical evidence from numerous studies shows that persons accused of a crime can be, and are, frightened into pleading to a crime they did not commit; at particular risk are those who are poor, powerless, mentally disabled, intellectually disabled, or too young or immature to understand what is going on (Trainum, 2016). Exoneration studies show that, from 1985 to 2003, 44 percent of those exonerated were juveniles who falsely confessed. Studies suggest that juveniles are more likely to make false confessions and are less likely to understand their Miranda rights to remain silent or request counsel.

The Miranda warning does not ensure that false confessions will not occur. Innocent persons are most likely to waive their Miranda rights. The suspects want to convince the officer that they are not guilty. Police officers are trained to convince people to waive their rights and they do a good job of it (Trainum, 2016). The suspect may want to know what is happening, and the officer won't tell him or her until the suspect waives his or her rights. Furthermore, some persons—juveniles, persons with a low IQ, mentally challenged persons, or otherwise disabled persons—under stressful and frightening circumstances, cave under psychological coercion. Some confess and implicate other innocent persons. They "rat" out others in exchange for reduced sentences.

A criminal lawyer, writing in the winter 2020 issue of *Juvenile Justice Update*, describes her first false-confession case and provides a strong critique of the accusatory interrogation method and the Reid method and their effect on juveniles (Gee, 2020). Her client was fifteen years old and was held in police custody, denied access to his family, and handcuffed to a table for sixteen hours. He was only let out to go to the bathroom. The family was not notified he was in police custody. His stepmother reported him missing. Every time the juvenile asked for his family, he was told he could see them after he confessed. During the interrogation the officers alluded to nonexistent evidence and nonexistent witnesses. They supplied the fifteen-year-old with true facts—"hold back facts"—that only the perpetrator would know. Finally, in the early morning hours, the sleep-deprived youngster confessed, using essentially what the persistent detectives had dictated. In the interim period before his court appearance, the attorney's investigator identified the real perpetrator and got a statement exonerating her client. The hearing judge found that the police had coerced the fifteen-year-old into making a false confession.

Gee opines that her juvenile client's false confession is not an anomaly. In support of her argument, she cites the following statistics from a 2019 Innocent Project report: 63 percent of false confessors were under twenty-five; 32 percent were under eighteen; 22 percent were mentally retarded; and 10 percent were mentally ill (DNA Exonerations in the United States, cited in Gee, 2020). Gee provides a critique of the popular Reid method of interrogation and how it contributes to false confessions from juveniles.

REID TECHNIQUE

As stated, the current American accusatory method and the Reid technique assume guilt, and their goal is a confession. The Reid technique consists of nine steps (Gee, 2020, p. 19; Cabell, Moody, and Yang, 2020). French (2019) divides the nine steps into three components: 1) tell the subject you—the interrogator—know they are guilty and encourage them to confess; rebuff any attempts to deny guilt; 2) offer the suspect several scenarios for how he or she committed the crime; suggest the suspect choose the least culpable or morally justifiable reason—minimization; 3) overstate the strength of the evidence. The interrogator begins lying to the suspect—saying things like, "We have a witness that saw you commit the crime." Lying is legally permitted. The interrogator then impresses on the subject that he or she will be convicted whether or not he or she confesses.

The problem with these seemingly innocent techniques is that they are psychological coercion and manipulative and successful in eliciting confessions—true and false. The accusatory method relies on the interrogator to gain control over the subject as soon as possible, presume guilt, and use close-ended sentences as confrontational tactics to elicit a confession. An alternative method that is popular in the United Kingdom and the rest of Europe and that is practiced in some American police agencies is the "information gathering" or "planning and preparation, explain, account, closure, and evaluation" (PEACE) model, which allows the subject to give the details of the incident without interruption—the goal being to gather as much information as possible. According to many experts, this technique produces more true confessions and fewer false confessions because of the rapport between the subject and the interrogator. The keys to its success, according to Cabell et al. (2020) are the techniques used by the interrogator. The Reid techniques are classified as corruption-prone techniques because they increase the likelihood of a confession to incriminate the guilty.

Cabell et al. (2020) concluded that the majority of methods used in the accusatory method of interrogation are confession-prone techniques used under stressful social settings. Isolating the subject increases stress and immediate negative outcomes to denial for guilty and innocent persons. The constant contradiction of the suspect's innocence convinces the innocent suspect that he or she cannot get the interrogator to believe him or her. Appealing to the person's emotions presents confession as a good thing to innocent and guilty subjects. Interrupting denials demonstrates the futility of not confessing and induces fear of a prolonged period of high stress. Minimizing the effects of a confession downplays the consequences of pleading guilty to a crime the suspect didn't commit. Presenting details from the crime increases the probability of conviction. A confession might lessen the sentence. These psychologically coercive methods, which can go on for hours, will have a devastating effect on an isolated young person who cannot seek help from his family. Juveniles are especially likely to end a lengthy and stressful interrogation to earn a reward of sleep and food and to be reunited with their parents or other loved ones.

In the United Kingdom, in using the fact-gathering method, law-enforcement officers are not allowed to lie to a suspect (Gee, 2020). In the special cases of suspects under seventeen, the police must notify the parents immediately. Minors in the United Kingdom must have a parent or an "appropriate adult" present during any interrogation. If no available "appropriate adult" can be found, the police must call the National Appropriate Adult Network to have a trained person be appointed prior to any interrogation of a minor (Gee, 2020). The United Kingdom requires appropriate adults for minors but recognizes that others need help when dealing with the police (see Textbox 5.2).

Textbox 5.2. When an Appropriate Adult Is Required

Police must secure an appropriate adult (AA) when they detain, question, or strip search (exposing intimate body parts) a child or another person who may be vulnerable. A vulnerable person is someone whom there is reason to suspect any of the following:

- May have difficulty understanding the full implications, or communicating effectively, about their arrest, detention, interview, rights or entitlements; or
- Does not appear to understand the significance of what they are told, questions they are asked, or their replies; or
- Appears particularly prone to confusion, suggestibility, compliance, or providing unintentionally unreliable, misleading or self-incriminating information (Home Office 2019, 2022).

Relevant factors include learning disability, mental-health conditions (e.g., schizophrenia, bipolar disorder, post-traumatic stress disorder, neurodivergence [e.g., autism, ADHD], and physical conditions [e.g., brain injury, dementia]).

- The Role of an Appropriate Adult
- The AA safeguards a person's interests (including the person's rights, entitlements, and welfare) by doing the following:
- Providing them with support, advice and assistance and helping them to understand their rights

- Assisting them with communication, while supporting and respecting their right to silence
- Observing whether police are acting properly and fairly toward them
- Intervening to ensure their rights are protected and respected (Home Office 2019).

OTHER FACTORS OR POLICE TECHNIQUES THAT INFLUENCE FALSE CONFESSIONS

In the absence of real or circumstantial evidence of guilt, a confession acquired by deceit, false statements, false promises, trickery, or physical abuse is considered by some police officers to be absolute proof of guilt. A confession is the most damaging evidence against a defendant. Police officers know that the average juror erroneously believes that an innocent person would not admit guilt, and these jurors accept a confession as proof of guilt. After all, common sense dictates that an innocent person would not confess to a crime he or she didn't commit. Post-conviction DNA tests have debunked that myth. In sum, the improper or illegal practices of law-enforcement officers using with tunnel vision often lead to false confessions, and these techniques include false testimony; false promises of leniency; denying the person's needs—for water, sleep, or bathroom breaks; excessive use of force, including torture; illegal searches; and other questionable practices, such as psychological coercion and physical violence (Trainum, 2016).

Wrongful Convictions

Chicago, for the fifth year in a row, has been named the US wrongful conviction capital by the National Registry of Exoneration (Cherone, May 16, 2023). Over one-half of US exonerations occur in Chicago (see table 5.1). One-hundred and forty-two exonerations of wrongful convictions were recorded in Cook County in 2022. All but two of those exonerations involved Chicago police officers. Chicago has a troubled history when it comes to persistent police problems. For almost five years, the Chicago Police Department has been under investigation by the US Department of Justice Civil Rights Division, following the 2014 murder of seventeen-year-old Laquan McDonald and its cover-up (Schilke, June 27, 2023). Since the Department of Justice investigation began, the Chicago Police Department's internal affairs unit has opened up eleven thousand police-misconduct investigations. The monetary and social costs of this police misconduct are horrific.

If you measure the social costs of false confessions by time, the case against the Chicago Police Department is overwhelming. Thirty-six Chicago men and

Table 5.1.   2022 Exonerations by Major Theme and Crime

Executive Summary and Major Themes:
- Exonerations—233 exonerations in 2022
- Years lost to wrongful imprisonment—233 wrongly convicted persons lost an average of 9.6 years—2,245 years in total
- Official misconduct—192 cases of the 233 cases involve official misconduct; sixty-three cases or 78 percent of the murder cases were due to official misconduct
- The importance of professional exonerators—innocence organizations and conviction integrity units were responsible for 171 exonerations—74 percent of the total
- No-crime cases—59 percent of the 233 cases were cases in which no crime occurred—allegations were of drug possession, murder, and child abuse

	Type of Crime		Number of Cases
Violent Crimes	Homicide	Murder	80
		Manslaughter	1
	Sex crimes	Adult sexual assault	4
		Child sex abuse	12
Other Violent Crimes	Robbery		11
	Attempted murder		4
	Assault		2
	Other		3
Nonviolent Crimes	Drug crimes		100
	Weapons possession/sale		3
	Conspiracy		3
	Other		10
Total			233

Source: The National Registry of Exonerations 2022 Annual Report.

women served twenty-five years before they were exonerated (National Registry of Exonerations, 2022; see Table 5.2). Two men were in prison for over forty years for crimes they did not commit. No amount of money can right that wrong. The Registry lists 228 men and women who have been incarcerated for over twenty-five years. In 2022, eighty-one wrongly convicted persons were exonerated of homicide—eighty for murder and one for manslaughter (see Table 5.2). Chicago taxpayers paid $9 million in 2022 to a man who spent twenty-five years in prison for a murder he didn't commit as a result of Detective Guevara's official misconduct (Cherone, May 16, 2023). One man who spent decades in prison for a murder he didn't commit said he hoped the publicity and lawsuit will ensure, "That this never happens again" (Gunderson, April 29, 2023). I am not optimistic. However, Chicago is not alone in the wrongful convictions due to official misconduct.

Table 5.2.   Risk Factors: Wrongful Convictions Not Related to False Confessions to Police

Wrongful Conviction	Number
Perjury or false accusation	756
Official misconduct other than eliciting a false confession	561
Inadequate legal defense	341
Mistaken witness identification	316
False or misleading forensic evidence (based on unreliable or unproven methods, expressed with exaggerated and misleading confidence, or fraudulent)	257

Source: Scherr & Normile, 2022.

The longest-serving person before exoneration was a black man from Louisianna. He served forty-four years in prison for the rape of twin fourteen-year-old white girls. The rapes never happened. Simmons's attorney was never given the medical records and witness statements undercutting the girls' perjured testimony. He was exonerated in 2022 (Dunn, June 5, 2023).

POLICE OFFICERS AND WRONGFUL CONVICTIONS: WORLDWIDE

Deviant police officers are the major criminal-justice officials leading to false confessions, resulting in erroneous convictions worldwide. This is supported by a report authored by Bruce MacFarlane—special counsel to the Canadian General Counsel on Organized Crime. His 2005 report, *Convicting the Innocent—A Triple Failure of the Justice System*, makes this clear. The MacFarlane report documented false confessions to law-enforcement officers occurring in Australia, Canada, the United Kingdom, New Zealand, and the United States. The report concludes that the major predisposing circumstance for wrongful convictions worldwide is the police's "noble cause corruption." This vigilante-justice ideology posits that the end justifies the means and that improper practices are justifiable to ensure a conviction, because the suspect committed the crime (MacFarlane, December 18, 2005).

CAUSES OF WRONGFUL CONVICTIONS

Although it is impossible to list every possible cause of wrongful convictions, there is general agreement that there are six common causes of wrongful convictions: 1) eyewitness misidentification, 2) junk science—forensic science methods without proper scientific validation, 3) false confessions, 4) official misconduct—on the part of prosecutors, police officers, and forensic science analysts, 5) false testimony from jailhouse snitches, and 6) inadequate counsel—bad lawyering. One source attributed 80 percent of the initial wrongful convictions in DNA exoneration cases to eyewitness misidentification (Krieger, summer 2011). The 80 percent figure may be debatable; however, the available evidence demonstrates that eyewitness misidentification is the major cause of wrongful conviction, and law-enforcement officers can and do manipulate eyewitness identification. This statement holds true for live lineups, photo arrays, and shows—identification at the scene. These police techniques are vulnerable to official misconduct by police officers (personal experience and expert-witness consultations).

Wrongful Convictions: Law Enforcement

Wrongful convictions result from false confessions to law-enforcement officers. From 20 to 25 percent of wrongful convictions are estimated to come from false confessions elicited by rogue or lazy police officers (Krieger, summer 2011). In these cases, the officer wrongly assumes that the suspect is guilty or has some venal reason to elicit a confession by any means. "Reasonable suspicion" to interrogate is often due to bias based on race, gender, ethnicity, or another personal basis for bias. The officer may think, *X is a thief because all people like X are thieves.*

CATEGORIES OF WRONGFUL CONVICTIONS

According to the National Institute of Justice, there are two ways to classify wrongful convictions:

Category 1: The convicted person is in fact innocent of the charges. He or she did not commit the crime as charged. How do we know a person has been wrongfully convicted, especially if the person has confessed to the crime? This is usually established through post-conviction DNA testing. The first US exoneration due to DNA analysis occurred in 1989. Since then, there have been at least 375 DNA-based exonerations. However, DNA analysis is not the silver bullet to forever prevent wrongful convictions. There are rogue forensic scientists. Sixteen convictions based on DNA evidence, from 1980 to 1991, were found to be attributable to forensic charlatans who presented false results (Laporte, April 2018). An examination of a discredited forensic analysis found that seven of the ten bite-mark examinations cases from 1985 to 1996 involved official misconduct (Laporte, April 2018).

Category 2: A second source of wrongful convictions is procedural error. Procedural errors violate the person's civil rights and can be used to reverse the conviction of a person who is in fact guilty of the charges. As we saw in the last chapter, police officers lie to prevent this from happening. Lies about fabricated confidential informants are the most common procedural lies told by police officers to obtain search warrants (Neely and Cillo, 2019). Therefore, procedural error refers to mistakes of omission or commission, where the criminal-justice official failed to follow or adhere to the legal process, such as the officer failed to give the Miranda warning (an omission error). Or the officer failed to follow some accepted legal standard (i.e., did a stop without reasonable suspicion or did a search without a warrant), leading to a conviction being overturned. Generally, this is a mistake, not an intentional act. However, intentional acts of police misconduct by law-enforcement officers can and do result in wrongful convictions.

In intentional acts of police misconduct, the officer knows that he or she is violating the person's civil and human rights but doesn't care. The ends are more important than the means. A recent Texas case is an example of a wrongful conviction due to procedural error (Harris, March 10, 2021). The Dallas County district attorney's office recommended that the 1987 conviction of a man who has spent over thirty years in prison be vacated. The district attorney's conviction integrity unit found that his conviction was based on prosecutorial misconduct. The prosecutor withheld exculpatory evidence. In this case, the eyewitness lied when he denied that he received a reward, and a jailhouse informant falsely testified that the alleged perpetrator confessed to him. The jury might have come to a different verdict if they had known these facts.

In the American criminal-justice process, confessions are *terminal* evidence of guilt. Following the suspect's confession, the police officer halts the investigation and gives the case to the prosecutor. Unfortunately, the existence of a false confession virtually assures a guilty verdict or a guilty plea (Scherr and Normile, 2022). Only 10 percent of appeals of murder convictions are successful (Scherr and Normile, 2022). And these successful challenges are the result of procedural errors, not factual errors—a lack of culpable evidence. "He said he did it" suffices. Cops know that. Cops also know that a person claiming his conviction is based on a false confession must overcome the burden that he is responsible for his confession and his subsequent conviction. This is not an easy task, especially when the false confession is buttressed by perjured testimony (on the part of a forensic analyst, a police officer, a jailhouse snitch or a coerced eyewitness).

Common sense says a person does not act contrary to his or her own self-interest. The nexus between official criminal-justice misconduct—among prosecutors, police, forensic analysts—and wrongful convictions and possible racial bias remained a well-known dirty secret hiding on the dark side of the police-work occupation until DNA testing shined the light on it. That light is brighter today. The recent "turn to innocence" in the death-penalty discussion, spurred on by DNA testing, has created the most successful death-penalty reform and concurrent examination of wrongful convictions in American history (Aronson and Simon, 2009).

DNA Testing

The first DNA testing used in criminal cases occurred in the United Kingdom in 1986 and was made public in a nonfiction work by a fourteen-year LAPD detective turned author. Joseph Wambaugh, in *The Blooding*, describes the largest manhunt in British crime history and the use of a new scientific breakthrough—DNA analysis—as a forensic crime-fighting tool. Two young English girls were brutally murdered, four years apart. The British police took blood samples from four thousand men living in or around the village where the murders occurred and compared them to the DNA found in blood on the victims. The testing continued until a DNA match was found. The subject was arrested, and he confessed, proving the value of the new scientific technique (Wambaugh, 1989).

DNA testing began in the United States in 1988, when the DNA of Gary Dotson, a convicted rapist, was tested. He was the first American prisoner to be exonerated by post-conviction DNA analysis (Aronson and Simon, 2009). Dotson had been convicted in 1979 and sentenced to twenty-five to fifty years in prison. However, his "victim" had a "come to Jesus moment" and became a born-again Christian in 1985. She recanted the accusation on national television. Dotson had been convicted on questionable forensic evidence, including hair analysis and blood typing, and on the false testimony of the victim. Dotson's DNA analysis excluded him as the perpetrator and, in 1989, his conviction was vacated.

Following the release of hundreds of innocent persons after Dotson's exoneration, wrongful convictions due to civil-rights violations became a social-justice issue. DNA testing is a double-edged sword and *could* provide conclusive proof of guilt or innocence. A wave of exonerations followed the 1988 introduction of DNA testing. By 1996, sixty-five people had been exonerated by post-conviction DNA analysis. The wave of police and criminal-justice reform issues sparked by the exonerations wave continues, spurred on by a new database.

NATIONAL REGISTRY OF EXONERATIONS

In the past, the media, fueled by dubious information from suspect sources or blockbuster memoirs from wronged persons, provided the only available information on allegations of wrongful convictions and possible racial-bias indicators. No official government sources existed. That has not changed, but there is a new data source. A nongovernmental source—the National Registry of

Exonerations—publishes accurate information on known exonerations. The data comes from official court records, supplemented by news reports and attorney interviews. In 2022, there were 228 exonerations in twenty-six state court systems and in the District of Columbia system and five in federal court. The top states, with five or more exonerations, were Illinois, with 176 exonerations; followed by Michigan, with sixteen; Texas, with eleven; Louisianna, with nine; New York, with nine; Ohio, with seven; Pennsylvania, with six; Virgina, with six; California, with five; and Tennessee, with five. Five states—Florida, Indiana, Massachusetts, North Carolina, and Wisconsin—had three exonerations; ten states—Alabama, Arkansas, Connecticut, Delaware, the District of Columbia, Georgia, Kansas, Missouri, Oregon, and Rhode Island—reported one exoneration (2022 Registry Annual Report, p. 5).

The National Registry of Exonerations is a joint project of the Newkirk Center for Science and Society at the University of California, Irvine; the University of Michigan Law School; and the Michigan State University College of Law (Gross, Possley, Roll, Stephens, September 1, 2020). The registry was founded in 2012 in conjunction with the Center on Wrongful Convictions at Northwestern University School of Law. Their 2022 annual report puts the total list of known US exonerations from 2012 to 2022 at 3,284 (The National Registry of Exonerations, 2022). To be included on the list, a person must have been convicted of a crime and then officially and completely cleared, based on new evidence, not a legal technicality—factual errors, not procedural errors. The 2022 report was limited to 2,400 cases in which official misconduct—malfeasance—distorted the evidence used to determine guilt or innocence. In plain English, that means, "misconduct that produces unreliable, misleading or false evidence of guilt, or that conceals, distorts or undercuts true evidence of guilt" (p. iii).

The criminal cases in the Registry are arranged in chronological order of misconduct, from initial investigation to conviction to wit: witness tampering, misconduct in interrogations of suspects, fabricating evidence, concealing exculpatory evidence, and, finally, misconduct at trial. Official misconduct was the major cause of the convictions of innocent defendants. The data reveal that police officers committed misconduct in 35 percent of the known cases and committed most of the witness tampering, interrogation misconduct, and fabricating of evidence.

Criminal Justice Officials

When the National Registry of Exonerations published its report on exonerations from 1989 to 2019, it was documented that American police officers and other criminal-justice officials engaged in questionable and racially biased practices that led to wrongful convictions. According to the Registry report, the evidence suggests that an unknown number of American officers and other criminal-justice personnel deliberately framed innocent persons. Law-enforcement officers engaged in physical and psychological coercion that led to manifest injustice. Law-enforcement officers tampered with witnesses and perjured themselves in court. Some prosecutors withheld evidence and allowed perjured testimony. Forensic analysts falsified findings and gave perjured testimony. On occasion, a combination of one or more of these criminal-justice officials was involved in the wrongful conviction of innocent persons.

Police Officers' Misconduct

Thirty-five percent of the 2,400 exoneration cases listed and examined were the result of police-officer official misconduct. The Registry broadly defined police officers as any sworn peace officer of a police agency, ranging from those serving in a one-person local police department to federal special agents. Police officers were responsible for most of the witness tampering, misconduct in interrogations, and fabricating evidence reported. Police officers also concealed exculpatory evidence and committed perjury in court. At least thirty police officers identified in the Registry were convicted of crimes related to their misconduct. The most common form of police misconduct leading to wrongful conviction occurred when the police coerced a false confession from an innocent defendant. As stated, identifying an innocent person as a suspect is the first step to obtaining a false confession and a wrongful conviction. The Registry defined false confession as a false statement offered to a law-enforcement officer at any point during the proceedings that was interpreted as an admission to a crime. Scherr and Normile (2022) identified 230 cases in this category.

There were other risk factors found by Scherr and Normile that contributed to exonerations and that were not due to false confessions to police (Table 5.2). As stated, cops know that a confession is the gold standard of evidence. Most people assume that an innocent person would never admit to crimes that never happened or crimes that he or she didn't commit. Not true. Some do. It happens. The registry provides numerous examples of innocent persons confessing or pleading to crimes they did not commit. Since 2006, 149 Harris County, Texas, defendants who pleaded guilty to drug possession have been exonerated after pleading guilty. They were arrested after police field tests came back positive for illegal drugs. The alleged drugs were tested in the crime lab, sometimes weeks, months, or years later, and were found not to be illegal drugs. The disturbing results were found because Harris County tests the material seized from drug defendants' event after they plead guilty (Samuels, March 7, 2017). The district attorney says that Harris County does so to ensure the integrity of convictions. According to the results, most of those exonerated were African American.

Prosecutors' Misconduct

Prosecutors were responsible for 30 percent of the misconduct found in the Registry data. Their misconduct was mostly concealing exculpatory evidence and some witness tampering. The following illustrative, not exhaustive, examples come from the Registry.

- The 1976 convictions of four black males known as The Ford Heights Four were vacated and the men exonerated in 1996, when it was discovered that the prosecutor had allowed perjured testimony in court. Their lawsuit was settled for $36 million in 1999.
- In 1983, Ellen Reasonover, a black female, was convicted of murder in St. Louis, Missouri, and sentenced to life. She was exonerated and set free in 1999, when it was shown that the prosecutor withheld exculpatory information that would have shown her innocence. She settled a lawsuit for $7.5 million.
- A Wisconsin white man was convicted of sexually abusing a family friend's fourteen-year-old daughter and sentenced to seventeen years in prison in 1998. He was exonerated in 2007, when it was revealed that the prosecutor had concealed that the stepfather had been charged with sexually abusing the child during the same period. The prosecutor and the stepfather had negotiated a no-charge deal if he would testify against the family friend.
- A 2001 Virginia murder trial of a fifteen-year-old white boy ended with his conviction and life parole sentence. His conviction was vacated in 2012, when it was discovered that the prosecutor withheld exculpatory evidence and the police investigator had falsely testified.
- Francis Choy, a seventeen-year-old Asian girl was convicted of murder for the arson deaths of her parents and sentenced to life in prison in 2003. She spent seventeen years in prison before being exonerated in 2016. The Massachusetts Superior Court judge cited the racial animus of the prosecutors and their use of known perjured testimony as to the reasons for her exoneration.
- In 2013, Kash Register, a black male, was exonerated and released from prison, where he was serving life without parole for a 1979 murder conviction in Los Angeles, California. The prosecutor in his case had deliberately concealed relevant information of his innocence and had concealed eyewitnesses. The city of Los Angeles paid Register $16.7 million, and California paid him $1.7 million.
- A thirty-year prosecutor for the New York Nassau County district attorney's office resigned after the judge criticized him from the bench for withholding exculpatory evidence from three men convicted of murdering an off-duty police officers twenty years ago (Rayman, March 11, 2021). The three men had been in prison for over two decades. The judge said that the prosecutor had "deliberately withheld" evidence of their innocence.

Forensic Analysts' Misconduct

Forensic analyst misconduct occurred in 3 percent of the Registry cases. Even at this low level, this is unacceptable; justice depends on the trustworthiness of the evidence presented for or against a defendant. The courts rely on forensic analysts to interpret trace and digital evidence, reconstruct crime scenes, and give valid and unbiased opinions on their findings. However, some police forensic analysts' false results supported cases against defendants. Some of this information was deliberately falsified, and some was not. Forensic analyst misconduct occurs in the United States and the United Kingdom (England and Wales).

United Kingdom

A 2015 US National Research Council report and the 2019 UK House of Lords report found that many of the methods used by forensic analysts did not meet scientific standards for validity (National Research Council 2015 and House of Lords, May 1, 2019). The UK report found that the lack of oversight, responsibility, and accountability of forensic-science providers was a major problem in England and Wales. The House of Lords reported that the England and Wales police-agency fragmentation created a situation where small forensic labs gave biased findings to secure contracts. This occurred because the chiefs and police crime commissioners of forty-three police agencies run the procurement of forensic services from private providers. The chiefs and commissioners could award contracts to those labs that supported the police. However, the most disturbing findings came in the Registry report, to wit, examples of American forensic analysts responsible for multiple wrongful convictions. Consequently, use of forensic analysts is a solution to and also part of the wrongful-conviction problem.

American Forensic-Science Misconduct

Garrett and Newfeld (2009) (Garrett is a law professor and Newfeld is cofounder and codirector of the Innocence Project) made it clear that the reliability and trustworthiness of the analyst depends on the interpretation of a valid scientific technique and the truthfulness of the testimony in court. However, there is no systematic collection and examination of forensic analysts' testimony in criminal cases. These noted jurists examined the trial transcripts from the cases of 137 of 156 exonerees who had been convicted of rape and murder in the 1980s and found that, in 82 cases—60 percent—the analysts provided invalid testimony. The invalid testimony came from seventy-two forensic analysts in fifty-two laboratories or medical practices in twenty-five states. Aronson and Simon (2009) report that the Houston Police Department's crime laboratory shut down in

2002 after it was discovered that forensic analysts regularly fabricated DNA evidence and lied in court.

The 2020 Registry presented examples of rogue forensic analysts who committed fraud or gave false or deceptive trial testimony in multiple cases.

- The most egregious example was a Texas pathologist in the 1980s and early 1990s, Dr. Ralph Erdmann, known as the pathologist from hell. However, local law enforcement officers liked Dr. Erdman; he would say whatever they needed to convict a suspect. At least twenty persons wrongfully convicted of murder successfully appealed cases he was involved in. He lost his license after it was revealed that he had filed reports on hundreds of autopsies he had not performed.
- Fred Zain was a forensic chemist for the West Virginia State Police Forensic Laboratory and the Bexar County, Texas, crime lab. A 1993 investigation of his work revealed that Zain had overstated the results of his work, misrepresented the frequency of genetic matches, reported inconclusive tests as conclusive, failed to report conflicting tests, and reported scientifically impossible or improbable results. The number of wrongful convictions he was responsible for is unknown, but some estimates are as high as 182.
- Joyce Gilchrist, a black woman, was a forensic chemist for the Oklahoma City Police Department for twenty-one years. She had a reputation for supporting the police and prosecution in criminal cases. She testified in twenty-three death-penalty cases, and twelve of those resulted in executions. Whether or not any of those executed were wrongly convicted is unknown; however, three of her cases resulted in exonerations. She was fired and moved to Texas, where she died in 2015.
- Pamela Fish, a Chicago forensic analyst from 1979 to 2004, was well known for her sloppy work and poor performance. She was responsible for ten exonerations.

There are other rogue forensic analysts listed in the Registry; however, a complete explication of the serious problems with forensic analysis in criminal cases is beyond the scope of the discussion of deviant police officers.

The Registry: A Valuable Source of New Information

Those persons listed in the Registry are described according to pertinent demographic variables and contributing factors. Therefore, this valuable source goes beyond the usual quantitative presentation of official and scholarly statistics in describing qualitative information. For example, Anthony Hinton was a twenty-nine-year-old black man convicted of murder in 1985 and exonerated in 2015. He spent thirty years experiencing the horror and pain of an innocent man wrongly convicted. From these bland statistics and facts, we cannot determine the answers to key questions, such as the following: Who was Anthony Hinton? What was his crime? What led to his wrongful conviction? What led to his release? The setting and circumstance of this miscarriage of justice never appear in scholarly research studies or official statistics. Now, any interested person can go to the Registry's open-source website and see the picture—not a mug shot—of a smiling Anthony Hinton on the day he was released from death row in the hell hole known as Alabama's Holman prison. I was interested in Mr. Hinton's information. Men I had arrested were in Holman prison when Mr. Hinton arrived. I remembered his conviction and release.

I read his best-selling book about how he existed during that isolation. I followed "his march till victory was won." If unfortunate prisoners were on death row, their normal human habits changed drastically, according to Anthony Hinton. Little things like times to eat changed. Condemned men in prison eat first—breakfast at 2 a.m., lunch at 10 a.m., and dinner at 2 p.m. They shower at midnight every other day—sometimes. Who keeps the schedule? No one. If their mother, brother, sister, or child died, did they attend the funeral? No. Even though they are innocent, they "live" with the thought that the state will kill them. They do not have a name. They are a number. Anthony Ray Hinton was Z468. The facts of his arrest, conviction, and exoneration are instructive for all those interested in American social justice and wrongful convictions.

Anthony Ray Hinton: Case Study. Hinton, a poor black man, was sentenced to death for the robbery and murders of two fast-food restaurant managers in Birmingham in 1985. He spent thirty years on Alabama's death row, waiting to "ride the lightning" in Yellow Mama's Lap—the popular name for Alabama's electric chair. The innocent man spent at least 10,220 nights sleeping with the rats and roaches crawling about, listening to the cries and moans of the soon-to-be dead waiting for their execution. Hinton complained about the horrid smell of burnt flesh and fried organs after executions on Alabama's death row. Hinton was told by a laughing guard, "You'll get used to it. Next year or one of these days, somebody's going to be smelling you just the same. What do you think you gonna smell like to everyone? Not too good" (Hinton, 2019, pp. 122–23).

How did Hinton end up on death row? The strange odyssey began when the investigating detective of two murders lasered in on Hinton in the available pool of usual suspects—poor black men with credibility problems. Hinton was a paroled ex-con who fit the suspect's general description. It appears from the published information and court documents, including a best-selling memoir, *The Sun Does Shine*, a 2018 Oprah's Book Club selection, that the investigator was convinced that Hinton was guilty and set out to prove it. From the beginning of the investigation, the likelihood of his eventual conviction increased. Hinton was unable to afford his attorney and was assigned an incompetent defense attorney who bungled the defense's investigation—or lack thereof—and courtroom defense. The US Supreme Court would vacate the conviction and remand it back to trial because of the constitutional deficiency of the defense counsel. However, in the end, a variety of factors contributed to Hinton's wrongful conviction: mistaken witness identification, misleading forensic evidence, inadequate legal defense, and police misconduct, including an attempt by the investigator to coerce a false confession. Hinton was convicted and sentenced to death after only one hour of jury deliberation in 1986. In 1998, Alabama's Equal Justice Initiative, a nonprofit group that provides legal assistance to indigent defendants and prisoners got involved. In 2014, the US Supreme Court vacated Hinton's conviction and death sentence and ordered a new trial. In 2015, the charges were dropped.

Hinton's race cannot be ruled out as a contributing factor in Hinton's case and in other cases in the Registry report. The colors of wrongful convictions and false confessions are black and brown with a sprinkle of white. Although black people are about 13 percent of the population, they account for 48 percent of all known exonerations (1,158/2,400), 52 percent of murder exonerations (468/908), and 63 percent of drug exonerations (200/317) (Gross et al., September 1, 2020). At the time of Hinton's trial and conviction, the victim's race, combined with socioeconomic status, was a factor in Alabama's criminal-justice system. The trial and conviction of the Choctaw Three in Alabama made that clear.

Choctaw Three: Manifest Injustice. In 2002, a bizarre Alabama case revealed that the effects of police psychological coercion on vulnerable suspects, combined with their race and socioeconomic status, produce false confessions and wrongful convictions. Three black suspects—two women and one man—known as the Choctaw Three because of the county in which the crime occurred were sentenced to fifteen years in prison for the murder of a child that was never born (www.wcjjn.org/Choctaw_3). All three black victims were poor and mentally retarded, with low IQs—40 to 57. They were members of the pool of people who are vulnerable to police misconduct. The tragic events leading to their false convictions were as follows:

In 1999, one of the convicted black women feigned pregnancy to get released from jail; the sheriff had two doctors examine her. One doctor found no evidence of pregnancy, and the other detected a fetal heartbeat. The woman was released on bond due to her pregnancy. Months later, the sheriff saw her and asked where the baby was. She told him she had had a miscarriage. The skeptical sheriff had her arrested and began an investigation into the "missing" baby. Her estranged husband and sister were also arrested for possible ties to the baby's disappearance. After three days of intense interrogation, without a lawyer, the mentally retarded husband "confessed" to murdering the missing baby. The sister also confessed to helping to dispose of the body. She later pleaded guilty to manslaughter and agreed to testify against the others who were found guilty.

Complicating the guilty verdict was that there was no evidence that a baby had been born. No one had ever seen a baby, there were no hospital records, and it was revealed that the supposed mother had a tubal ligation in 1995. How could this happen? The inadequate legal defense was a prominent factor in this miscarriage of justice. The innocent victims were represented by a "prison deliverer"——a public defender. The prosecutor ignored or withheld information. When the prosecutor was asked later what physical evidence he had that there was a baby, he replied, "Well, they all told us that." The police coerced false confessions. The Alabama Court of Appeals reversed the convictions and said that a manifest injustice had occurred in the case (Sherrer, October 12, 2020).

In Prison but No Crime Committed. This case points to a curious finding from the National Registry of Exonerations. Forty percent of the exonerations occurred because no crime had been committed (National Registry of Exonerations, 2022, p. 7). These cases include child-abuse incidents where the alleged victim recants his or her accusation, murder convictions that turn out to be accidents or the results of self-defense, and drug-possession cases where the substances turned out not to be drugs. The top five rank order of no-crime exonerations are murder (1,226); drug possession (585); sexual assault (357); child sex abuse (312); and robbery (158) (National Registry of Exonerations, 2022, p. 8). The registry gives the example of a Virginia man who was accused and convicted of sexually abusing the ten-year-old son of a former girlfriend. Thirteen years later, the alleged victim, now twenty-three years old, confessed that he made the story up because of the man's strict disciplinary practices (National Registry of Exonerations, 2022, p. 8). The State of Virginia provided him with a writ of innocence in June 2022. He received $59,000 in state compensation in 2023. In 48 percent of the no-crime wrongful convictions, the subject pleaded guilty. The registry report also points out that, in some cases, the officers planted drugs or falsely testified.

Cook County, Illinois, reported 198 exonerations of persons convicted of drug possession. Chicago police sergeant Ronald Watts and his anticrime crew planted drugs and gave perjured testimony in 189 of these cases (National Registry of Exonerations, 2022, p. 10). One victim from the pool of vulnerable defendants with credibility problems—here, a person with prior convictions—pled guilty to a false charge and agreed to a five-year prison sentence, because, if convicted, he was facing life in prison. At his hearing, he told the judge, "This is wrong. I am pleading guilty because I'm scared. That's the honest to God truth, your honor (National Registry of Exonerations, 2022, p. 11)." He wasn't, and isn't, the only person to plead guilty to a crime that he didn't commit or that never occurred. The top three reasons for no-crime exonerations are perjury or false accusations (882); official misconduct (685); and false or misleading forensic evidence (326).

Conclusion

The presumption of guilt colors the current American accusatory method of police interrogations with the goal of eliciting a confession. The method does produce confessions, both true and false. The American criminal-justice process produces true and false confessions. False confessions are a major factor in wrongful convictions, with innocent people spending years in prison. Misclassifying an innocent suspect as guilty is common in the accusatory method of interrogation and begins the journey to an erroneous conviction and false confession. The goal of police interrogations should be eliciting confession or discovering information from guilty suspects. We need to rethink the necessity of confessions as a gold standard of guilt. Lazy detectives should not end the investigative process when a suspect confesses. That assumes a realistic workload or caseload. In the interim, there is an obvious road to take.

To minimize miscarriages of justice, police interrogations, especially those of juveniles, should be recorded. The evidence clearly indicates that certain groups— mentally impaired persons and young persons—are especially vulnerable to the psychologically coercive Reid techniques. A video recording of the entire interrogation could add to or distract from the reliability of any elicited confession. At present, the FBI, DEA, and the ATF record interrogations. Twenty-six states also require that interrogations be recorded; these include Alaska, Colorado, Connecticut, Illinois, Indiana, Kansas, Maine, Maryland, Massachusetts, Michigan, Minnesota, Missouri, Montana, Nebraska, Nevada, New Jersey, New Mexico, New York, North Carolina, Ohio, Oklahoma, Oregon, Texas, Utah, Vermont, and Wisconsin. This ensures that Miranda warnings are given and explained. Legal consequences should result from the failure to record interrogations. Police officers that use illegal or physical techniques to obtain confessions must be identified and punished. Taping these interrogations protects all those involved, including the law-enforcement officers. All detectives and investigative officers should receive the latest up-to-date training. The book will return to reform issues in later chapters.

Discussion Questions

1. Why would an innocent person admit to a crime he or she didn't commit? Would you? This is not a yes or no question. Defend your answer.
2. Why was Anthony Ray Hinton convicted of a crime he didn't commit? Why is this case not just a Southern case?
3. Could the United Kingdom's appropriate adult program be implemented at the local or national level in the United States? Defend your answer.
4. What are the benefits of and problems with the Reid techniques used in the causational method of interrogation? Be specific in your answer.

CHAPTER 6

Expanding Police Misconduct

MISUSE OF CONFIDENTIAL INFORMATION, IDENTITY THEFT, AND STEALING TIME

Key Terms:

Confidential information
Identity crime
Identity theft
Police databases
National Crime Information Center (NCIC)
California Law Enforcement Telecommunications System (CLETS)
Gaming the system
Stealing time

Chapter Objectives:

After reading this chapter, the reader should be able to do the following:

1. Describe police databases and their misuse
2. Describe identity theft and how it is a police misconduct problem
3. Describe stealing time and how it is a police misconduct problem

The traditional police occupational/workplace misconduct patterns of abuse of authority, sexual misconduct, and lying have long histories in the police occupation. However, global events and technological changes since the beginning of the twenty-first century have changed the American policing landscape and have presented new opportunities and challenges. For example, the events of September 11, 2011 (9/11), led to the creation of an alphabet soup of new and reconfigured federal agencies, such as the Drug Enforcement Agency (DEA), Immigration and Customs Enforcement (ICE), and the US Customs and Border Patrol (CBP), which is now the most corrupt law-enforcement agency in the United States. New issues of police misconduct have come into being with the new agencies. Previous chapters have discussed the misconduct and crime of the CBP and have given examples of the deviant behavior of the Homeland Security Investigations (HIS).

The Transportation Security Administration (TSA) may be the most deviant American "non or quasi police" organization created since Prohibition and the creation of Prohibition agents. The TSA, created after 9/11, fired five hundred agents from 2001 to 2012 for stealing airline passengers' possessions. The agents stole items including cash, debit cards, laptop computers, iPads, and painkillers. But, technically, the TSA is not a police organization. That issue needs attention and research, but not here.

The creation of each of the new federal agencies mentioned above brought with it challenges to local police agencies, such as new crimes and new collusions between federal and local agencies. However, technology changes appear to have had the greatest impact on local police agencies in how they operate and respond to new and expanding opportunities. Three of those technological changes that have led to new patterns of police misconduct are the misuse of confidential information, identity theft, and stealing time.

Misuse of Confidential Information

The misuse of confidential information has been a thorny police problem since the founding of the police occupation and has steadily gotten worse with time and technological change and threatens to increase exponentially in the future. The possible disastrous consequences of the disclosure and/or misuse of confidential information by employees and staff of criminal-justice organizations are recognized as a possibility in codes of conduct, policies, rules, and regulations of law-enforcement agencies at all levels of government. State laws forbid the disclosure of confidential information by any official employee or staff member for his or her or others' personal gain. Why? The answer is obvious. Every official actor in the American justice system, or for that matter any country's criminal-justice system, has by their work duties access to personal information that can be used for nefarious purposes. The list of persons with the opportunity to misuse a citizen's personal data is voluminous and includes any police officer that a citizen has contact with. Consider the consequences of this short vignette, which is based on a police–citizen encounter that a neighbor told me about.

The first request usually made in any police–citizen contact in Texas is "Let me see some identification." In many states you don't have to show any. In Texas, unless you have a gun or are in a vehicle, you don't have to show an ID unless the officer arrests you. So, you refuse to show any ID, which is your right in Texas. But that may not be the end of the contact. Your legally challenged officer has just turned off his body camera and looks around. No one is watching or videotaping. That may be why you were stopped.

The smiling officer asks another question, "What hospital do you prefer?"

"I don't need to go to the hospital," you reply.

"Well, Mister Smart Ass, if you don't show me some ID, you're going to jail or the hospital. You don't need to show an ID to get in either one. But you will need to show an ID to get out."

You come to your senses and show "Officer Friendly" your driver's license, your bank debit card, two credit cards, your laminated social security card, and your college ID card. But suppose you persist in voicing your civil rights, then the ambulance drivers, the hospital in-take staff, the jail trustees, and the detention officers may go through your wallet, write down the information, and keep it or make copies of it. This happens every day to someone in the United States. In the twenty-first century in the United States, information technology records, manages, and stores confidential data. Such data are often in the hands of someone who wants to use the data for personal reasons. Law-enforcement officers are included in that large category of persons who may want to do you harm. Knowing this, you object.

He can't do that, you may protest. Yes, he can. It violates police ethical standards—agency policy and rules and the law—but he can do it. It is your word against his. It happens every day to someone in the United States. The misuse of confidential information by law-enforcement officials is a worldwide example of occupational/workplace deviance. Misuse of confidential information is police deviant behavior that occurs when the police actor believes the act is safe to perform and the benefits outweigh the possible punishment. We will see that many police malefactors are repeat offenders. They feel safe in this behavior. To deter this behavior, we must improve the methods to detect it and increase the certainty of meaningful punishment.

Technological change and the identification cards that you are carrying have produced new forms of police misconduct and crimes that could not be foreseen in the early development of the police occupation. Misuse of confidential information and police identity theft are two new police misconduct patterns that have become persistent police problems in the twenty-first century. How much of a problem these are is unknown because only a minority of incidents become known (Rajakruna, Henry, and Scott, May 7, 2019). Stealing time, policing for profit, and abusing facial recognition technology are also new means of police misconduct and will be addressed in the next chapter. How the police use these new technological tools raises privacy, personal freedom, and abuse issues. These tools should be controlled and monitored by someone. Who is that someone in America? The police? How did this situation become a problem?

POLICE DATABASES

Fifty-six years ago, an idea attributed to J. Edgar Hoover, the often-maligned FBI director, and an American law-enforcement pioneer, came into being (Anon, October 5, 2020). Hoover had often thought of a national database for crime control that would revolutionize policing. The new technology was the National Crime Information Center (NCIC), and it impacted the nature of policing worldwide, for the good and the bad. Today, NCIC is a computer located at the FBI headquarters in Washington, DC. It provides rapid responses to police officers through their regional or state systems or with a direct tie-in to the NCIC computer. Today, American police officers have easy access to the NCIC or other databases via the laptops in their police cars, on their smart phones, or using any other device to do a Google search.

The National Crime Information Center The NCIC computer has twelve files containing data on articles, boats, Canadian warrants, guns, interstate identification, license plates, missing persons, securities, US Secret Service information, unidentified persons, vehicles, and wanted persons. In addition to the NCIC, state and local police agencies, depending on size and funds, have databases on persons and other relevant information, such as arrests, warrants, and driver licenses, too numerous to list. Today's world is truly a "surveillance" world. Everyone is in some official database somewhere. It is curious that the United States has at least one national database on crime issues (the NCIC), and most states have one or more databases on criminals and other issues, but there is not a national database on American police misconduct. This access is crucial to modern police work; however, this power and easy access is subject to abuse. How much? We don't know. Most of what we know about the misuse of police confidential data comes from the media after a scandal. Violations or misuse of confidential information are not required to be reported to anyone.

Misuse: Impression Management Technique

The first misuse of the new crime data was the data's use as an impression-management technique. As soon as the politicians and the police realized that crime rates could fluctuate, crime went up or down with the pencil or erasure (personal observation). Manipulating the data to create a favorable impression of the department when it comes to crime control or integrity has a long history in the police occupation and only got worse with the creation of crime databases. Manipulating the data, called "good housekeeping" in the United States and "fiddling the figures" in the United Kingdom, is a standard impression-management technique (Patrick, 2011). Patrick refers to this practice as "gaming" and calls it a pattern of police misconduct. Such impression management is an example of organizations "gaming the system." The "gaming" of the system went on in American police agencies, with an added wrinkle. As soon as crime and crime-related databases became ubiquitous in the NYPD, selling confidential data became the most common form of misconduct in the department, according to one source (Lawson and Oldham, 2006). There were some hideous consequences to this new form of police misconduct. The misuse of a database search, which led to an innocent person being murdered, would be used in the prosecution of two retired NYPD detectives who acted as Mafia hitmen (Barker, 2020). The consequences are not usually this dire, but they often involve an individual's liberty. Nevertheless, the misuse of police databases receives little attention in scholarly literature. That trend is changing as this area of police misconduct has become a worldwide police problem.

WORLDWIDE POLICE DATABASE MISUSE

United Kingdom

A UK think tank, Parliament Street, examined data it received in an FOI request sent to twenty-three police agencies in England and Wales from 2017 through 2018. They found that 237 officers were disciplined for misuse of confidential information. Six resigned, and eleven were sacked. One police agency had fifty officers disciplined and the London Metropolitan Police Service, the largest UK agency, had eighteen sacked for misusing the Crime Reporting Information System (CRIS) (Muncaster, November 8, 2019). Similar studies, done in 2017 by other public groups, found similar results. In 2017, a security company revealed that UK police had investigated eight hundred cases of data misuse in 2016. A community-action organization, Big Brother Watch, reported in 2016 that it had found 2,315 cases of data misuse from 2011 to 2015.

In the United Kingdom, the Law Enforcement Assistance Program (LEAP) is an online database that reports and catalogs alleged crimes, including family violence, and missing persons. In 2019, the Victorian police investigated serious police misconduct cases where officers had used the information for sexual purposes with juveniles (Marozzi and Taylor, December 14, 2022). Three women reported that they had been stalked and harassed. The same report said that, in the last five years, 178 police had been complained about for misusing LEAP.

Australia

Australia has had numerous problems with police abuse of power, misconduct, and corruption throughout its history. Since 2016, the state of Queensland's Crime and Corruption Commission (CCC) has been investigating the unauthorized use of sensitive databases by the state's police service. According to this report, from July 2015 to May 2016, there were fifteen investigations into this misuse, resulting in eighty-one criminal charges and eleven recommendations for discipline, including suspension (Nedim, May 2016). Officers named in misconduct complaints included a police officer who hacked into the crime database fifty times to check on women he met on online dating services and another male officer who obtained the phone numbers of men for sex purposes. Another officer received a six-month suspended sentence for leaking information to a private investigator. A 2017 article stated that five Queensland police officers, including three sergeants and two constables, were given notice to appear in court for unauthorized use of a Queensland Police Service database (Barbaschow, June 12, 2017). Three of the officers were alleged to have made ten or more unauthorized uses. The article reported that, from July 1, 2015, to June 30, 2016, there were 4,308 allegations of police misconduct made to the CCC, and 11 percent were for computer hacking and misuse of information. In 2019, the commissioner of the Queensland Police Service issued a statement before the opening of a CCC investigation into police public safety data. She said the police misuse has "brought our organization into disrepute" (Smee, November 6, 2019).

New Zealand

Two recent cases were reported in New Zealand (Leask, January 4, 2023). New Zealand has a National Intelligence Application and record of stolen property database. A female Christchurch constable was accused of using this database for personal gain. A second New Zealand constable was accused of using a national police database to sexually prey on female victims and witnesses. A New Zealand article reports that, from 2015 to 2022, five New Zealand police officers were charged with murder, manslaughter, and attempted murder and 157 officers were discharged, dismissed, and acquitted for crimes ranging from theft to sexual assault and for other police occupational/workplace deviance.

American Crime-Sharing Database Misuse

ASSOCIATED PRESS STUDY, 2016

The latest report on US police officers abusing confidential databases for personal reasons was written by two Associated Press journalists and published in September 2016. The excellent report was long on talk and short on specifics. That was no surprise because their data came from record requests to state agencies and big-city police departments, agencies not known for cooperation on police misconduct or police crime. Impression management is the name of the

game that police senior executives play 24/7 (personal observation). The journalists contacted all fifty state agencies and three dozen of the nation's largest
police agencies and requested the abuse information. They also examined the
NCIC database. As expected, many agencies did not respond or said they didn't
collect such data. The lack of cooperation was not surprising or unexpected.
As stated, there is no national database on police misconduct, police crime, or
police corruption. The Uniform Crime Statistics touted by police executives,
politicians—left and right—and the media are not really accurate. It says so on
the first pages. Not every police agency reports the data. It is strictly voluntary.
Therefore, what the Associated Press found is an undercount of American police
abuse of confidential databases. However, what they found was damning and
cause for alarm.

Overall, they found that, between 2013 and 2015, 325 law-enforcement
officers were fired or suspended—or they resigned—because of allegations of
or administrative convictions for misusing official databases. Another 250 officers received reprimands, counseling, or lessor discipline. There were another
ninety incidents where unspecified or no discipline was applied. Police mining
of police databases was for officers' personal use and for others' personal use,
such as getting information for a friend or relative. According to the Associated
Press study and the interest it elicited, the opportunities for and the misuse of
police database information were mind-boggling and ranged from the curious to
the criminal. The misuse amounted to, in many cases, the unchecked power to
collect, use, and share confidential information, most of which went unreported
and unpunished. Sometimes the searches are ridiculous, but, still, they happen
because they can. One reported search involved a law-enforcement officer want-
ing a search run on every white truck because his girlfriend was cheating on him
with a man driving such a truck (Storm, September 28, 2016). Obviously, that
was not in Texas.

STATE DATABASES

Officers gathered personal information on celebrities, cop haters, and cop supporters. An audit of the Boston Police Department's record system revealed 968
personal searches on then–New England Patriot quarterback Tom Brady (Anon,
July 2009). The police searchers were looking for information on his driver's
license and his home address and phone number. Some wanted to know if he
had ever purchased a gun. Other searches were for information on Matt Damon,
James Taylor, Boston Celtics players, and the owner of the Boston Red Socks.
This information could lead to more than fan interest.

Many states and the federal government have massive "intelligence sharing"
databases of criminal records, driving histories, car ownership records, probation

histories, FBI crime information (NCIC), social security information, firearms purchase records, and other information that can, and is, misused by American police officers. There is controlled access to all these databases, and security, in theory, is supposed to work by identifying in policy and rules what is confidential and who has and doesn't have access. Those with access are supposedly trained in these factors. Finally, misuse is prevented by regular audits and by punishing the violators. Unfortunately, the security theory is not put in practice by many American police agencies. At a minimum, there should be a record of who accessed the database, for what purpose, and what was the final disposition. The records should be audited on a regular basis.

California's statewide police database, California Law Enforcement Telecommunications System (CLETS) is notoriously abused, and discipline for offenders is lax. A 2019 article reported that over one thousand officers, including California Highway Patrol (CHP) officers had accessed the CLETS database for no legitimate reason in the previous decade (Staten, Smith, and Walloo, November 2019). Examples cited included a San Francisco police sergeant who ran searches on tenants renting apartments from his girlfriend. The sergeant retired and pleaded guilty to a misdemeanor and was fined $150. A female CHP officer looked up information on a romantic rival and allegedly drove to her residence and keyed her car. A West Sacramento police officer wrote phony traffic tickets to two men involved in a lawsuit with him five years earlier. During the time investigated, 82 law-enforcement officers resigned, 86 were fired, and 125 were suspended, but none were criminally charged. According to a 2017 article, CLETS was established in 1970 as a statewide system to allow public law-enforcement agencies to look up criminal data, and the California Department of Justice is directed to make reports of misuse available to the public. That is in keeping with the civilian oversight responsibility function of the people in democratic societies.

Many of these abuse examples, in the United States and worldwide, involve what one police chief told a sexual predator he fired. The officer was using the state police databases as "your personal Google" (Parnass, August 2, 2021). The Lanesborough, Minnesota, officer violated department policy and the law by looking up women on a state criminal-justice database without a valid police purpose. His targets included women he was dating, had dated, or wanted to date. Other searches for information about women mentioned in the Associated Press report involved stalking ex-girlfriends or ex-spouses. Many searches looked for information or phone numbers of attractive women. One Denver police officer, who became acquainted with a hospital worker during a sexual-assault investigation, looked her up on a police database, found her phone number, and called her—a clearly forbidden act. Police databases are not personal Google search engines for police dating services and curious cops.

A main reason to maintain security and audit use of police databases is that, even though some of the abuse, probably the majority, is curious and ridiculous behavior, an unknown portion of this misconduct is criminal, with the unauthorized searches being used in corrupt acts or as a technique to engage in identity thefts.

SELECTED EXAMPLES OF POLICE CRIMINAL MISUSE OF POLICE CONFIDENTIAL INFORMATION

- A Harris County, Texas, deputy sheriff was indicted for swapping police restricted information from the NCIC to nonpolice persons for cash (DOJ, February 24, 2010).
- An Arlington, Texas, police officer with access to the Texas Crime Information Center and the NCIC, with extensive training on the authorized use of this information, was charged with providing information to known drug dealers (DOJ, June 12, 2013).
- A detective with the Dunwoody, Georgia, police department, who also served as a member of a DHS federal task force, swapped information from searches of the Georgia crime information database for airline tickets and other property and money. His corrupt actions allowed criminals to be notified of pending arrest warrants, allowing them to flee before arrest (DOJ, March 23, 2015).
- A Cumming, Georgia, police officer was arraigned and charged with accepting a bribe to access a police database. The officer and the victim met when the officer answered a 911 call that resulted in the citizen's arrest. Following the arrest, the officer had other contacts leading to the officer asking the man for a loan. The citizen suggested that he would exchange $1,000 for a search of police databases to see if an individual was an undercover police officer. The officer agreed, and the citizen cooperated with police authorities. The officer was arrested and resigned before his indictment (US Attorney's Office, July 7, 2016).
- An officer in the Metropolitan Police Department (MPD) in Washington, DC, pleaded guilty to accepting $40,000 in bribes in exchange for providing traffic accident data to two "runners" who provided the information to lawyers. One runner paid her $400 to $500 a week, and the second paid her $250 a week. The MPD officer was assigned to the patrol division and the school safety bureau. Her police assignment provided access to the traffic crash reports. Her sentence was seventy-eight days in jail, to be served on weekends. An MPD audit after her conviction revealed that she had accessed 3,376 traffic crash reports from June 1, 2017, to October 6, 2017 (DOJ, October 6, 2021).

Identity Theft by Law-Enforcement Officers

Identity Crime is a category of crimes committed worldwide that involve the theft of identity information for personal gain; creating false identities for criminal purposes, such as using another's name when arrested or convicted of a crime; or identity fraud that would include using another's identity to obtain medical treatment or benefits. Local police are most involved in what the National Council on Identity Theft and the US Department of Justice defines as financial identity theft—someone stealing the personal information, such as the social security number, credit-card information, or other information, such as that contained in a police database, of another to obtain cash, credit, loans, or other financial benefits (National Council on Identity Protection, US Department of Justice, April 2021). For example, a sixteen-year veteran LAPD officer was recently arrested on suspicion of theft and fraud for using a woman's stolen debit card at a home improvement store. The woman had recently gone to the police station—no reason given—and noticed unusual transactions on her statement. She, on her own, visited the store and watched the officer making the purchases and notified the police (Winton, August 9, 2023).

Identity theft is a worldwide problem. In 2018–2019, the estimated cost of identity crime in Australia was $3.1 billion in Australian dollars (McAlister and Franks, 2021). The report said that identity crime included credit-card fraud against individuals and other financial frauds against individuals; frauds against government agencies; and money laundering by organized crime groups. Reports from Canada indicated that identity theft included stolen credit cards and sophisticated scams (Office of the Privacy Commissioner of Canada, October 2020). Canadian identity theft increased 218 percent after the COVID-19 pandemic. The same report stated that 6 percent of European Union residents experienced identity theft between 2016 and 2019. In 2018, an estimated twenty-three million US residents sixteen and older were victims of identity theft (Harrell, 2021).

Identity theft is not a "new" crime; however, it became a major criminal-justice problem with the technological advances in computing and communication of the 1990s (Newman, 2004). The improved technology and a global economy have increased the losses and opportunities for certain occupations to take advantage of vulnerable persons and groups. This is especially true for criminal-justice personnel involved in arrest and detention duties. However, this is seldom mentioned in the listing of ways that information can be obtained for use in identity thefts. For example, a 2013 UK article listed various ways such theft occurs: dumpster diving is the most conventional method, followed by phishing or indiscriminately sending emails to trick a person into providing personal information; pharming is a technique that allows the sender to invade a computer when an email is opened; and introducing malware or other viruses is another common method. These are methods and techniques commonly used. However, the article fails to recognize the occupations, such as first responders like the police, that have easy access to personal information that is fertile territory for identity theft.

POLICE OCCUPATIONAL OR WORKPLACE DEVIANCE: IDENTITY THEFT

Identity theft is a unique crime because most acts occur electronically, either on the Internet or through credit-card transactions. The police cannot prevent or easily identify the victims or the perpetrators. Corrupt police officers use these factors to their advantage. The police identity thief uses information obtained from sources such as social security cards, drivers' licenses, credit cards, bank accounts, tax returns, passports, and citizenship paperwork. Law-enforcement and detention officers routinely possess or have access to these data sources in their daily activities, making this crime a relatively "safe" theft. Identity theft by a law-enforcement officer or another criminal-justice worker fits into the rational choice paradigm: inclination + opportunity in a real or perceived low-risk setting = occupational/workplace deviance.

Although there are few scholarly studies of law-enforcement officers and identity theft at this time, following are illustrative, not exhaustive, examples from Barker's files.

- Identity Theft to Murder. In 2007, a Jefferson Parish, Louisiana, deputy sheriff investigated a traffic accident and stole the driver's bank debit card and checkbook. The deputy then made purchases using the debit card and withdrew funds from the victim's accounts from ATMs. When the victim got a replacement card, the deputy tried to cash forged checks. The thefts were discovered, and the deputy was arrested. The victim disappeared and was never seen again. In July 2014, following an evidentiary hearing, the judge found clear and convincing evidence that the deputy was responsible for the death and disappearance of the victim. The former deputy was sentenced to ninety-two years in prison and ordered to pay $13,215.22, split between the bank and the estate of the victim (Office of Public Affairs, Department of Justice, November 10, 2014).
- A Hialeah, Florida, police officer pleaded guilty to identity fraud charges and was sentenced to five years in prison (DOJ, July 18, 2017). The officer accessed restricted database information on twenty-five persons and gave their personal information to a civilian accomplice who fraudulently obtained

merchandise from retail stores throughout Florida. The accomplice received eighty-one months in prison after his guilty plea.

- A Mississippi County, Missouri, sheriff was indicted for eleven identify-theft charges (DOJ, March 20, 2018).
- A female St. Cloud, Florida, police officer was fired and is facing fraud and identity-theft charges. She responded to a man's 911 call. The man died, and the officer took pictures of his credit cards and charged personal purchases to his credit cards. The man's wife noticed suspicious charges and reported them to the police (Boey, May 10, 2023).

Police Misconduct: Stealing Time

WHAT IS STEALING TIME?

Time stealing or getting paid for not working while on the job is one of the oldest forms of police occupation/workplace deviance. For example, sleeping on duty in designated "holes" began with the first nighttime walking assignments in London and the practice continued in the colonies. American police officers on patrol played "hide and seek," hiding with supervisors as they "goofed off" in saloons. Police officers were supposed to be constantly on the move; that was the idea behind a preventive police occupation in 1829. But it was hard then and harder now to determine where the beat cops were and what they were doing. In the earliest days of American policemen "shooflys were constantly looking for meat" (Lardner and Reppetto, 2000). "Shoofly" was the police term for the precinct roundsman whose primary duty was checking on the walking beat officer to deter him from taking a smoke break, grabbing a beer in a saloon, sleeping in the back room of a store to get warm, or, as frequently happened, going to a "coop" or "hole" to sleep. Quotas or "performance" indicators were the crude attempts to ensure that officers were working.

Today's police officer, in addition to using work avoidance techniques, can "goof off" on the Internet or on a mobile phone. A common workplace time theft occurs when workers, including police officers, chat, play games, and shop while "working." It is not unusual for a police officer going to college or law school to park in a "hole" and study or prepare for a test. Other workers in other jobs steal company time in the same manner. Such acts of time stealing may get the officer fired or disciplined because of policy infractions. However, the infractions are not considered corrupt acts. There is no monetary gain or a quid pro quo relationship between a cop and a corruptor. However, there is a problem with time stealing in today's world. Some police time thefts are considered crimes and are prosecuted as such.

OVERTIME FRAUD

"There is a general sense both inside and outside the law enforcement that overtime is overused, and only halfheartedly controlled" (Bayley and Worden, 1998). The key issues that these two police experts arrived at were 1) police overtime was overused, misused, and inadequately regulated from 1985 to 2000; 2) federal monies to support police overtime at the state and local level have grown (in the late 1990s, 60 percent of the federal monies going to state and local police agencies for overtime came from the Department of Justice [Bayley and Worden, 1998]); 3) concern over the misuse of overtime has increased; and 4) there are few if any studies of the misuse of police overtime. To determine if there is misuse of police overtime, there is a need to know if work is being done, what sort of work is being done, and under what circumstances. The issues and questions remain today as the costs of police overtime rise to astronomical numbers as individual and groups of American law-enforcement officers systematically take advantage of new opportunities to engage in this burgeoning pattern of police misconduct.

From June 2021 to June 2022, the NYPD had its second-highest overtime costs for uniformed officers: $782 million. That figure passed the allotted budget by $100 million (Gilardi, November 16, 2022). One K-9 handler worked 2,002 overtime hours. That is akin to seventy-nine-hour work weeks for the year. The officer and eight other members of the Transit Bureau K-9 unit averaged 1,700 overtime hours for the 2022 year. Altogether, the forty-five-member K-9 unit cost the city $2.3 million in overtime. How much of that cost is the result of time theft is unknown. It is known that overtime fraud was occurring in the NYPD at the time. An NYPD police captain was allowed to retire after admitting that he received $60,000 for 400 overtime hours he didn't work from 2019 through late 2020 (Ke, January 17, 2022). In 2021, a whistleblower—a detective—alleged that an NYPD internal affairs lieutenant was "manipulating" sting operations against fellow officers to collect overtime pay (McCarthy, March 17, 2021). He reported this to a deputy commissioner and was promptly demoted and transferred. He filed a lawsuit. The detective has been reinstated and is asking for the newly elected New York mayor to investigate his allegations of overtime misuse (McCarthy and Reilly, February 5, 2022).

The opportunity for police misconduct has expanded with the increased rise of police overtime—an occupational hazard; however, not all police overtime costs are the result of overtime misuse. The Dallas city auditor reported that, from October 1, 2018, to December 31, 2020, the Dallas Police Department received $78,695,699 for 1,305,750 overtime hours for both uniformed and civilian members. The auditor concluded that, although there were isolated cases of overtime misuse, the overall control and written procedures were working (Swann, August 9, 2022). Stealing time as a pattern of police misconduct cannot be eliminated but it can be controlled. The key to control is recognizing the occupational opportunity as a police misconduct hazard.

STEALING TIME IS POLICE MISCONDUCT

Police misuse of overtime is not often considered an example of police corruption. When Barker presented the typology of corruption in the 1970s, stealing time from the job was not recognized as a police corruption problem because there was no material reward or gain, and it was primarily an agency rule violation. Today, when it is common to use federal monies to pay for stealing time, it is often treated as a fraud felony matter. For example, a Dallas, Texas, police officer was charged with submitting a false report to receive federal monies from a federal grant awarded to the Dallas Police Department (Office of Inspector General, September 16, 2019). The grant covered overtime pay to increase traffic enforcement and reduce fatal and serious accidents.

His elaborate scheme involved submitting false traffic tickets to people who did not exist in connection with events that did not happen. He would unlawfully access law-enforcement databases to get driver and automobile information and then, using phony dates of birth and forged signatures, he would create a traffic citation and submit it as proof of his overtime work. He also issued citations to people after they left traffic stops. He was paid for 160 overtime hours before his scheme was discovered. The former Dallas police officer pleaded guilty to submitting a false report to the Dallas Police Department. He was sentenced to three years' probation, 120 hours of community service, and $10,691 in restitution.

The workplace problem occurs with profit-motivated time thefts when the officer claims to have worked and is paid for it but does not perform the work. This pattern of overtime fraud has increased in recent years and has been attributed to police overtime escalation due to the pandemic, riots and demonstrations, and staffing issues. There has been a critical shortage of police officers in many American cities after the 2020 killing of George Floyd and the social unrest that resulted. Nowhere is this more evident than in the murder site—Minneapolis. There are about 780 police officers in the Minneapolis Police Department (MPD) and 70 percent of the officers make six-figure salaries because officers are leaving in droves and those remaining are working unbelievable and unhealthy amounts of overtime (Winter, June 19, 2023). Thirty-nine officers make over $200,000, and one sergeant makes $390,000 with overtime pay. The chief makes $271,721 annually. The chief is aware that too much overtime without adequate rest leads to fatigue, increased citizen complaints, elevated use-of-force incidents, impaired driving skills, and a host of medical issues, but what is he to do? No one wants the police job in Minneapolis. Other American cities are having the same problems. The staff-shortage problem exacerbated the overtime problem. The MPD overtime budget went from $6.4 million in 2019 to $10.3 million after Floyd's death. Some of the officers took advantage of the new financial situation and engaged in time stealing.

Nevertheless, police workplace time stealing is present in police agencies worldwide at all levels, from the top down, although it is most prevalent in the lower ranks. Police time stealing has two categories: 1) not working while on the job, which has a long history in the police-work occupation; and 2) overtime fraud, which is a recent phenomenon and a pattern of possible police misconduct with the police officer gaming the system without a corruptor or a quid pro quo relationship.

POLICE TIME-STEALING OPPORTUNITY STRUCTURE: OVERTIME FRAUD IN THE UNITED STATES AND OTHER COUNTRIES

Police stealing of time, consisting of not working while "on the job" or claiming to work when one has not and being paid, occurs whenever the *inclination and opportunity intersect in a low-risk work setting*—the necessary conditions for occupational/workplace deviance. The opportunity for these police deviant behaviors has increased exponentially worldwide. Police in the United Kingdom registered some disturbing overtime findings in a 2009 online newspaper report (Hughes, August 17, 2009). Twelve thousand police constables—the lowest rank—increased their salary by 20 percent in overtime pay. One London Metropolitan police constable earned almost €15,000 more than a chief superintendent six ranks above him. Some police constables doubled their salary. To do that, the officers would have to work at least sixty to seventy hours in overtime per week. This raised a red flag and a call for an investigation. However, the increase-in-overtime trend continued in the United Kingdom. Nine years later, a BBC article reported that UK police forces spent €1.7 billion on overtime from 2013 to 2018 (Mackintosh, August 11, 2018). The BBC reported that the officers in their study averaged ninety-seven hours of overtime in one year. The money spent on overtime could have funded the hiring of ten thousand new police officers. The police said that football matches and the high terror threat along with staffing problems led to the high overtime expenditures. In 2015, the German police overtime hours increased by half a million hours during an invasion of migrants seeking asylum. In 2017, the German border guards' overtime rose to 2.7 million hours (Hall, March 23, 2016). There is no available information on how much of that increase was the result of fraud; however, there is evidence of overtime fraud in the United States and in some European countries.

OVERTIME FRAUD EVIDENCE: UNITED STATES

Individual and Group Overtime Fraud, 2022 and 2023

(The following examples are illustrative, not exhaustive.)

January 26, 2023. A Columbus, Mississippi, police officer (population, 23,319) was fired for "fudging" his time sheets for extra pay. According to the city officials, the officer was saying he was at work when he wasn't. He was stealing time. The year before, a police officer was suspended for thirty days for claiming overtime not worked (Jones, January 26, 2023).

January 26, 2023. A Scranton, Pennsylvania, police sergeant (population, 78,874) pleaded guilty to theft of federal monies for time-stealing offenses. He received $11,243 for extra-duty shifts at Scranton area lower-income housing complexes he did not perform (DOJ, January 26, 2023).

January 24, 2023. A bizarre case of law-enforcement occupational/workplace crime involved an HIS agent. The HIS agent, while supposedly on duty, used his government-issued vehicle while working for Amazon, Uber, and Lyft. He was sentenced to two years' probation and ordered to pay $133,999 in restitution to the DHS.

December 1, 2022. A Fairfax Borough, Pennsylvania, police officer was arrested for allegedly submitting fraudulent time sheets that lead to the theft of $98,754 dollars. He was also charged with stealing three firearms from the evidence locker (Wesser and Stockburger, December 1, 2022).

August 24, 2022. The city of Shreveport, Louisiana, received a Community-Based Crime Reduction grant in 2020 from the US Department of Justice to pay for police overtime in high-crime neighborhoods. The officers would receive 1.5 times their regular rate of pay for this overtime. A Shreveport police officer was arrested and indicted for allegedly submitting at least six false claims for working overtime. The records show that he was working at another job at the same time as he purported to be working overtime (DOJ, August 24, 2022).

January 26, 2022. An officer with the small town of Alarton, Illinois (population, 262) was sentenced to ten months of confinement—five months in prison and five months at home—for falsifying thousands of hours on his time sheets. He usually stayed home, with his patrol car parked outside his house, which was out of the city. He sometimes ignored calls from the dispatcher, even though he was the only officer "on" patrol (DOJ, January 26, 2022).

Recent American Police Department Systematic Overtime Problems

New Orleans Police Department (NOPD). The NOPD is no stranger to systematic police corruption, from the top down; therefore, it is not surprising that time stealing would occur at all ranks. A female captain was demoted to lieutenant when she was caught logging herself as on-duty while she was being paid as a private security guard—double-dipping and time stealing (J. Gordon, October 7, 2022). She was caught twenty-six times being paid for off-duty and on-duty work. Prior to her present assignment, she had worked in the NOPD Public Integrity Bureau, which is responsible for investigating NOPD misconduct. NOPD policy allows officers to work off-duty details but not at the same time as they are on duty. However, journalists at a local TV station found numerous examples of NOPD officers being paid twice, for on-duty and off-duty work done at the same time (Zurik and Lillich, November 17, 2021). As a result of the TV exposé, twenty-six officers were suspended from working off-duty details.

California Highway Patrol (CHP), February 18, 2022. According to Bloomberg.com, fifty-four CHP officers—current and former—were accused by the California attorney general of engaging in a systematic scheme to collect over $200,000 in fake overtime expenses from 2016 to 2018. The officers would claim eight hours of overtime when they worked only two or three hours (Schneider, February 18, 2022). The CHP overtime fraud case came to an ignoble end on December 4, 2022. A Los Angeles county judge reduced the felony charges to misdemeanor offenses and then dismissed them if the officers would pay back the money that they were accused of improperly receiving. They would not be required to admit guilt (Associated Press, December 4, 2022).

Massachusetts State Police. Forty-six Massachusetts state troopers were discovered in 2018 submitting claims for overtime they did not work. Their unit patrolled the Massachusetts Pike. It was disbanded after the overtime scheme was discovered. Twenty-four troopers retired during the investigation or were fired after they were criminally charged. The remaining troopers kept their jobs and received unpaid suspensions, ranging from 60 to 841 days, paid restitution for the money stolen, received a reduction in seniority, and waived their rights to appeal (WBUR Newsroom, July 10, 2020).

Boston Police Overtime Fraud. In September 2020, nine Boston Police Department (BPD) members who worked in the department's evidence warehouse were charged with conspiracy to commit theft from programs receiving federal funds and embezzlement from an agency collecting federal funds. Since then, five have pleaded and are awaiting sentencing (DOJ, February 2, 2023). Four, including a lieutenant, a sergeant and a female officer, face additional charges and are awaiting trial. According to court documents, the defendants were responsible for storing, cataloging, and receiving evidence at the warehouse. They falsely claimed overtime amounting to over $200,000, which was paid for by federal grants from the US Department of Transportation and the US Department of Justice.

OVERTIME FRAUD OUTSIDE OF THE UNITED STATES (SELECTED EXAMPLES)

The Police Service of Northern Ireland spends €100,000 a day on police overtime, with some officers receiving €40,000 a year (Hewit, 2019). One officer was investigated because he worked 1,758 hours of overtime in a single year. Malta, the smallest republic in the European Union, was part of the United Kingdom until 1964. In 2020, Malta had 2,400 police officers and 40 of them had been arrested for systematic overtime abuse and police corruption (Anon, February 13, 2020). A police whistleblower said that traffic officers, particularly motorcycle officers, had submitted overtime sheets for hundreds of hours they had not worked for the past three years. The corrupt officers were also accused of misappropriating fuel for their own vehicles, another example of police occupational/workplace crime. In Canada, during the 2022 truck-driver demonstrations, Winnipeg police overtime expenditures rose 29 percent, sparking concern about police overtime abuse. As noted above, police time theft also appears to be an American police corruption problem.

Opportunities for American time theft increased as police unions and collective bargaining contracts required extra pay for work outside the forty-hour work week, usually at time and a half. This made "fudging" time sheets more profitable as the opportunity for workplace misconduct and crime exponentially expanded. There have been several notable time-stealing scandals in recent years.

Conclusion

Police occupational/workplace deviance, including misconduct and crime, has always varied in any individual police agency according to the opportunities present in the workplace. This is made clear by the technological changes affecting the exponential growth of the storage of and access to data on American citizens—both criminal and law-abiding citizens. Therefore, it is hard to make general statements about police use or misuse of new techniques and practices, which vary with the size and complexity of the police agencies. We can say, depending on the workplace setting, American police officers can access local, state, federal, and national databases from the laptop computer in their cars, their smart phones, and their home computers. The potential misuse of these databases includes converting confidential information to their own use and profit, identity theft, and stealing; these are some of the fastest growing crimes in the twenty-first century. This misuse is affecting the trust that Americans have in their police. That may be the real consequence of new police misconduct forms and practice.

The public expects the police to use confidential data responsibly for prevention of crime, detection of offenders, and their apprehension, not for frivolous personal interests or gain. The publicly paid police occupation in democratic societies is based on having the consent of the public and the public's trust that police officers will do the right and fair thing. As this chapter has shown, new police technologies lead to police abuse of authority. Several chapters have argued that a law-and-order objective of making the police more efficient and effective should not be made at the expense of our liberties. What the American police do and how they do it should always be legal, transparent, and in keeping with procedural justice.

American policing is a diverse institution serving diverse communities. Our fragmented system works against police reform. However, the documented misuse of confidential information by some American police officers and agencies and the cavalier attitude shown toward citizens' personal information by these officers and agencies are disturbing. This calls for tightened control and increased sanctions on offending police officers and law-enforcement agencies by some central authority. Open and spirited debate should occur before new technologies are introduced. The worst possible examples of police misconduct, in which police did not act legally, with transparency, or according to procedural justice, are revealed in Part 3, which examines police malfeasance.

Discussion Questions

1. How does technological innovation affect police occupational/workplace deviance?
2. Describe the benefits of and problems with easy access to police databases.
3. What would you suggest are the precautions a police agency can take to prevent police identity theft?
4. Put on your thinking cap. What do you believe will be the next technological innovation to be misused by the police? Hint—what about facial recognition techniques?

Discussion Questions

PART III

POLICE CORRUPTION AND CRIMINAL LAW-ENFORCEMENT OFFICERS

MALFEASANCE

Law-enforcement occupational/workplace deviant behavior violates accepted ethical standards, agency rules and regulations, and the law. Part 2 examined the police-misconduct violations of ethical conduct or rules violations, or at least the patterns of police deviance that are treated that way when exposed. Police misconduct may or may not be viewed or acted upon as criminal, depending on the presence or absence of a material reward, the presence or absence of a victim, and the reaction to it. On the other hand, Part 3's chapters examine proscribed behaviors that are always criminal. These acts are typically known as "police malfeasance" because they are official misconduct for personal gain. Recall that this book previously defined police malfeasance as illegal actions by a public official for personal gain. This definition included individual, group, and systematic behavior, ranging from profit-motivated crimes to payoffs and shakedowns. Unfortunately, police malfeasance has always been a part of American police history.

The data from the 1931 Wickersham National Commission on Law Observance and Enforcement and its bombshell report, *Our Lawless Police: A Study of the Unlawful Enforcement of the Law*, documented for the first time the "not so secret, secret" that American police were committing serious crimes and using violent "third-degree" methods to extract false confessions to conceal their deviant behavior (Hopkins, 1931). This was the first, but not the last, revelation of widespread American police malfeasance in the forms of criminal behavior and the accompanying extreme violence. Other American police scandals, which revealed other crimes and violent actions by American police officers, followed. The 1960s American police crisis—from 1964 to 1968—resulted from media reactions to incidents of violent criminal acts of primarily local or municipal police officers (Barker, 2011). The reports and, for the first time, the scientific research that followed led to the conclusion that there was a substantial number of American criminal cops. These criminal cops were erroneously described in professional literature and the media as "rotten apples" or rogue police officers, and some criminal cops were considered bad by even corrupt cops. A small cadre of former police officers going to college on federal funds and the GI Bill and developing a new field of study—criminal justice—knew these criminal cops had always been there and it wasn't a few "rotten apples" that was the problem (Barker, 2011).

Criminals joining police agencies and exploiting the police-work setting became routine in many US police agencies during the 1970s "war on crime" and what became known as hot-rod statistical policing. Some of these criminal cops were gangsters, members or associates of organized crime enterprises, who seized on the police occupation's opportunity structure. As one criminal Chicago cop, Richard Cain, reportedly said about police work, "it's the best job, there is. It's a fucking license to steal" (Cain, 2007). Richard Cain became a "made" member of the organized crime group, the Chicago Outfit—the Mafia. Cain bragged that after an Outfit boss gave him his police position, he went to the police uniform store with a booster—professional shoplifter—and got all his gear without paying for it. Chicago was not unique. There were criminals who became cops or cops who became criminals in many American cities of all sizes. However, a caveat is necessary at this time: criminal cops are a minority in American police work as an occupation, but that gives little solace to their victims. However, we do not intend to paint the entire police-work occupation with the sordid brush of corruption and crime of some police officers. Nor should we accept the lofty accolades from the "police apologists." Police officers are not all brutal crooks or saints. The evidence indicates that the traditional uniformed "on the job" local American police officers can be placed on a continuum of their involvement in prohibited behaviors (Barker, 2011).

"White knights," who engage in no prohibited behaviors, or those who say they don't, are in police agencies (figure 7.1). How many? No one knows. Police officers of this ilk often leave the job because they can no longer tolerate the temptations or the behavior of their peers. The next category, "straight shooters," are in the majority in most local police agencies. They rarely engage in prohibited behaviors involving corrupt acts for personal gain, except when accepting a free meal or another small gratuity. They sometimes yield to temptation and engage in consensual on-duty sex; however, they do not actively search for sexual opportunities. Sometimes, out of anger or frustration, a straight shooter will "thump" or "tune-up" a belligerent drunk, suspect, resistor, or another dirtbag—thugs, rats, and assholes. Cops will tell you that the most frequent offense that gets a citizen arrested or beaten is "C.O.P."—"contempt of cop." However, this is risky behavior. Stepping in quicksand can be dangerous. A known straight shooter who lets his emotions dictate his behavior told me about the following incident.

| White Nights | Straight Shooters | Grass Eaters | Criminal Cops (aka Meat Eaters/Rogues) |

◄──►

| Break no Rules | On Occasion | Depends on Opportunity & Risk | Criminals With Badges |

Figure 7.1.   Continuum of Rule-Breaking Cops. *Source:* Created by author.

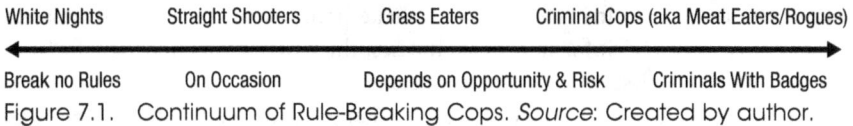

A veteran police officer who answered a domestic disturbance call on Christmas Day told me the drunken husband had broken all the kids' toys and had thrown them in the yard. The enraged officer spread the drunk across the bed, pulled down the man's pants, and whipped him with a belt. That set in motion a series of lies the officer had to tell to keep his job. He had to lie to a police investigator after a complaint was filed. He then gave perjured testimony in court to save his job. He became a member of a large group of straight shooters who wished they had been honest and truthful. His not-so-straight peers reminded him of the incident on occasion. Any cop who engages in excessive force will sooner or later have to lie. Lying, including perjury, may then become routine. They, the straight shooters, have, in most circumstances, occasionally engaged in the common use of excessive force after pursuits or resistance of arrests. Most injuries to drivers that flee, resulting in high-speed chases, occur after the chase is over. The adrenaline-charged officer exacts their revenge. This bad decision leads to civil or criminal liability and the necessity to lie and commit perjury.

Straight Shooters sometimes feel it is necessary to "fluff up" the evidence of guilt to convict a known dirtbag. Everybody does it, they rationalize. However, these "honest" cops are a major police problem because their lies cover up and give tacit support to brutal and criminal police officers. It compromises the straight shooter's ability to intervene or report police misconduct and crime. Even in the recent most corrupt group in Baltimore Police Department history, the Gun Trace Task Force, there were two officers who took no money. However, they overlooked the egregious crimes of their fellow squad members because of their tainted history of engaging in small acts of corruption and crime and the supposed feelings of brotherhood (Woods and Soderberg, 2020). Why would an "honest" police officer lie? A frequent comment in police work is "I'm not going to be a rat. We have to protect each other. Cops don't rat out other cops." This results in straight shooters suffering in silence or finding assignments in corruption-free environments because they are compromised.

Next along the continuum are law-enforcement officers who respond to the inherent temptations sporadically—just enough to be part of the group. But they have been sucked into the dark abyss of police malfeasance, including corruption and other crimes. In most police agencies experiencing corruption and crime scandals, every officer has secrets. Ever wonder why most cops who testify against other cops are granted immunity? This prevents them from facing charges themselves when the defense brings up their prior criminal behavior.

However, sometimes it is necessary to "shake hands with the devil" to make a case and use a "dirty" informer. In such cases, the worst actors may benefit from the rule that "the first rat gets the best deal."

The next category of police officers who engage in rule breaking appears to be the more numerous deviant cops in American police agencies—"grass eaters." They engage in sporadic individual corrupt or minor criminal behaviors. Grass eaters are officers with weak social control systems who engage in corruption, sexual misconduct, lying, and brutality on occasion, as the opportunity presents itself and the real or perceived risk of exposure is low. The 1970s Knapp commission, which examined the systematic networks of NYPD corruption, was the first to give a name to these officers. Grass eaters, according to the commission, take advantage of the opportunity when the risk is low. They engage in quick shakedowns of traffic violators or legitimate businesspersons, bars owners, contractors, and towing companies who commit technical violations, but grass eaters do not set up or participate in networks of protection payments. They are typical secret deviants that can be found in most occupations or workplace settings. The mask of respectability hides their deviant behavior. Often, grass eaters' violations are an effort to show they can be trusted—*see, I ain't no snitch—but I have my limits.* The Knapp commission pointed out that, "Accepting payoff money is one way for an officer to prove that he is one of the boys and that he can be trusted (Knapp Commission Report, 1972, p. 65). But this rationalization has consequences. In the words of one officer caught up in a 1970s NYPD corruption scandal, "From an inexperienced rookie, it hasn't taken long to evolve into a hardened thief and, ever so slowly, I began to realize it" (Droge, 1973). The discovery of corrupt and criminal cops in New York was not an anomaly. The social scientists and academic researchers found what working American police officers had known for decades.

American police agencies prior to the 1960s were off limits to social-science researchers. There weren't many former cops with college degrees, let alone PhDs. When I became a police officer in the 1960s, there was only one officer among the more than six hundred white men in the department who had a college degree. That changed dramatically in the late 1960s and 1970s.

The early 1970s police research studies conducted by the noted criminologist Albert Reiss through observations, police self-reports, and other data in three urban cities found that one in five—20 percent—of American police officers engaged in serious criminal forms of police corruption for personal gain (Reiss, 1992). Police protection networks of police officers, vice operators, and gangsters found by the 1972 Knapp commission also existed in Baltimore, Birmingham (Alabama), Chicago, Houston (Texas), Los Angeles, Miami, New Orleans, Newport (Kentucky), Philadelphia, and other US cities, large and small (Barker, 2011). The Knapp commission and other inquires of that time exposed the worst features of police offenders, namely, badge-packing criminals. We will discuss this fully in the next chapter. However, that brings us to the last category on the continuum—criminals with badges. New York City's former police commissioner William Bratton, commenting on the Mollen commission's report on NYPD corruption in the 1980s, said "we have criminals in blue uniforms who are more vicious than some of the criminals they are supposed to be policing" (Bratton, 1995, p. 3).

The final category of "bad" cops are "meat eaters" or, as the media and popular culture called them, "rogue" police officers. They are, then and now, criminals with badges. These cops are constantly on the lookout for some material gain. Everything they do has a dollar sign attached to it. They commit any crime when they believe they can get away with it. Every arrest has a price tag. For example, in 1980, five men, including three police officers, burglarized a Medford, Massachusetts, bank for $10 million in cash and valuables from the safety boxes. Criminal cops became a national problem in the late 1970s and early 1980s. This book will discuss them later.

CHAPTER 7

Rule-Breaking Cops

MALFEASANCE

Key Terms:
   Police corruption
   Quid pro quo
   Criminal cops
   Mafia cops

Chapter Objectives:
   After reading this chapter, the reader should be able to do the following:

1. Identity and discuss each pattern of police corruption
2. Identify and discuss corrupt cops and their categories
3. Place corrupt cops in a historical context as an occupational/workplace police problem.

Patterns of Police Corruption

The morally dangerous police-work occupation presents so-inclined workers with numerous opportunities to commit work-related misconduct and criminal behavior. Some, but not all, of these behaviors result in a monetary reward or the equivalent going to the law-enforcement officer—police corruption. Police corruption is any *forbidden* act that involves the *misuse* of a law-enforcement officer's official position for *money or material gain* (Barker, 2011). The public agrees that police corruption is abusing one's power for personal gain (IPCC, 2011). Money-related corruption is the classic definition of public-official malfeasance. There are three necessary conditions for police corruption to occur. First, the act must violate a law, an agency rule or regulation, or a prescribed ethical standard. The officer does something he or she should not do (a commission) or fails to do something he or she should do (an omission). Second, the act must involve the misuse of the officer's official position. These acts can involve off-duty acts, if there is a link between the off-duty act and the officer's official position. For example, access to police databases has made it possible for police officers to sell or destroy this information while on or off duty. Corrupt officers can take confidential information routinely learned while on-duty and engage in corrupt off-duty acts, such as identity theft. Lastly, a necessary third element for police corruption to occur is a personal material gain. Barker and Roebuck (1973), in the first empirical study of police corruption by behavioral scientists, identified eight patterns that varied in seriousness, support from the peer group, and organization. The identified patterns ranged from the quid pro quo exchange of money or the equivalent to influence the officer's decision-making to direct criminal actions.

TRADITIONAL PATTERNS OF QUID PRO QUO POLICE CORRUPTION

The traditional patterns of police corruption are found to some extent in the history of all local American uniformed police departments. Local uniformed police officers have the largest number of opportunities for corruption due to the close nature of police–citizen contacts under largely secret and unsupervised settings. Some of the patterns are present in federal and special district police agencies with less of an opportunity structure. Many of these federal agencies, such as the FBI, DEA, and ATF, are ununiformed special agents primarily engaged in investigations with less direct contact with citizens. However, these special agents have their opportunities for corruption. The "traditional" patterns of police corruption engaged in by local police officers are discussed below (Barker and Roebuck, 1973; Barker, 2011).

Pattern: Corruption of Authority

Acts. A police officer's discretionary decision-making is corrupted or compromised whenever he or she enters into a quid pro quo arrangement for implicit or explicit material gain. The reward for elected law-enforcement officers, such as sheriffs, can be in the form of a campaign contribution. The value of the material gain depends on the officer's assignment, rank, or influence. The material "reward" can include, but is not limited to, cash, meals, liquor, services, merchandise, and admission to theaters, concerts, and sporting events. Even though the claim is often raised that there were no conditions attached to the "gift" or "gratuity," the reward obligates the officer to some extent to the gift giver.

It also gives the appearance of evil. The practice of accepting free meals by police officers is called "mumping"—to cheat or beg—in London (Rubinstein, 1996).

There are two common views about the police acceptance of minor gifts and gratuities. One view would allow minor gifts and gratuities by the public for their police–community relations benefit, especially in the era of community policing (Kania, 1988; Prenzler, Beckley, and Bronitt, 2013). On the other hand, as we saw in Chapter 1, the codes of ethics from the College of Police in the United Kingdom and the IACP both forbid the acceptance of gratuities. The gift or gratuity creates the expectation that a favor or service will be returned, and it makes the officer look corruptible to observing citizens. There have been police scandals involving gratuities in Australia, England, and New York City (Barker, 2011; Prenzler, Beckley, and Bronitt, 2013).

One of the most widely publicized quid pro quo exchanges in American police-corruption history occurred in New York City with the convictions of the former New York City police commissioner Bernard Kerik in 2006 and 2009 for state and federal crimes committed while in public office. Kerik pleaded guilty to accepting $250,000 from a New Jersey construction firm to renovate his home in consideration for helping the firm obtain a city license. He was sentenced to four years in federal prison and was released in 2013. This former NYPD commissioner, who confessed to corruption-related crimes and lying, is now a frequent TV guest as a crime expert. His corrupt acts are viewed as business as usual in New York City and other large cities.

The Strange Odyssey of NYPD Commissioner Bernard Kerik—Bent or Criminal Cop. Bernard B. Kerik was the fortieth NYPD police commissioner, serving from August 21, 2000 to December 31, 2001. Prior to being appointed to that position by New York City mayor Rudy Giuliani, Giuliani appointed Kerik commissioner of the New York City Department of Corrections, where he served from 1998 to 2000. Kerik is the only NYPD police commissioner to be charged with a crime committed while in office. He is a convicted felon (tax fraud, ethics violation, and false statements), an ex-con (four years in federal prison), a police-issues consultant, a white-collar criminal, and a media celebrity. At the time of his appointment as commissioner of the NYPD, Kerik was a high-school dropout with a GED with no police experience above the rank of detective, leading many to question his qualifications for this position, other than being the mayor's bodyguard and driver during the mayor's 1993 election campaign. At the time, a college degree was a requirement to promotion to the rank of captain and above. The new mayor, Giuliani, made this appointment after rejecting the advice of the former police commissioner, Howard Safir, and ranking members of the police department (Lipton, August 21, 2000). Mayor Giuliani passed over the recommendation of the chief of the department, a thirty-one-year NYPD veteran who had the support of the rank-and-file and the top brass. Future events proved that the mayor should have listened. Kerik's brief sixteen-month tenure was marked by allegations of abuse of power, sexual misconduct, and criminal conduct. The evidence suggests that Kerik, who was the NYPD police commissioner during the 9/11 terrorist attack, used an apartment set aside for weary rescue workers as a love nest for extramarital affairs (Powell, November 3, 2007). Reports of sexual misconduct by Kerik go back to his time as corrections commissioner (Hosenball, April 16, 2007). After Giuliani left the mayor's office, Kerik resigned as police commissioner and joined the Giuliani consulting firm. The proverbial sh—t hit the fan.

In 2004, Rudy Giuliani pressured then-president George W. Bush to nominate Kerik to become the DHS secretary, and the house of cards built by Kerik collapsed. The subsequent federal investigations for the vetting process revealed Kerik's secret past. Seven days after the nomination, Kerik abruptly withdrew his nomination, with the statement that it had been brought to his attention that he had not paid the required tax payments on his immigrant housekeeper. He added that would serve as a distraction if he became the DHS secretary (Veith and Chen, December 11, 2004). It also came to light that he had business dealings with a stun-gun manufacturer while he was the NYPD police commissioner. That dealer had sold the weapons to the DHS. Additional questionable and possibly quid pro quo dealings kept coming to light. The best man at Kerik's wedding, an executive with a construction company with suspected ties to organized crime, revealed that he had given Kerik $7,000 in gifts while Kerik was corrections commissioner and police commissioner (Rashbaum and Flynn, December 13, 2004). It was later revealed that, a month after 9/11, Kerik persuaded a property developer to pay two years of rent—$236,000—on his apartment (Leonard, November 10, 2007).

In 2006, the disgraced former police commissioner pleaded guilty to two state misdemeanor ethics violations and was fined $221,000. In 2009, Kerik pleaded guilty to eight felony charges of tax fraud and obstruction and was sentenced to four years in federal prison. The judge admonished Kerick for engaging in a ten-year pattern of abuse of power while serving as corrections and police commissioners and said that he had used the 9/11 events for personal gain—writing books and speaking arrangements (Esposito, November 10, 2009). The final twist to this bizarre odyssey occurred in 2020. On February 18, 2020, President Donald Trump granted Kerik a full pardon for the federal convictions. Today, Kerik is a frequent spokesman on police issues in print and nonprint media, including numerous TV appearances. Is Bernard B. Kerik a bent cop who succumbed to the corruption opportunities of the job or a criminal cop who was finally exposed?

Although former NYPD commissioner Kerik was sentenced to prison for "favors" extended to him, the practice of businessmen lavishing money and services on high-ranking police officers to have "a private police force" for themselves and their friends is often considered an NYPD tradition. Levitt (2010), writing in the popular *NYPD Confidential—One Police Plaza*, documents corruption-of-authority activities, beginning with the revelations from the 1970s Knapp commission. According to Levitt, New York businesspeople have always enticed senior police officials with fancy dinners and expensive trips to perform personal favors. The latest quid pro quo scandal of this nature occurred in 2016 when four senior NYPD officials were charged with federal corruption offenses. The specific charges were conspiracy to commit "honest services" wire fraud during a bribery scheme. The officers received tens of thousands of dollars in meals, trips, home renovations, and other benefits. In return, the businessmen received private police escorts, ticket fixing, and pistol licenses (see Textbox 7.1). According to one source, corruption of authority is so rampant in the NYPD that officers are prohibited from accepting any gratuities, even a cup of coffee. The only exceptions are the pen and pencil sets, plaques, and other common tokens of appreciation (Kashbaum and Goldstein, June 20, 2016). This policy appears to not be working.

An NYPD officer has filed a lawsuit against the police department alleging that he was unfairly disciplined for violating the unwritten police policy of not ticketing "courtesy card" holders (Anon, May 31, 2023). According to the lawsuit, NYPD police unions and police executives pass out laminated cards to friends, relatives, politicians, and businesspersons to be shown if they are stopped for traffic offenses. This is a common practice among American police agencies and a ubiquitous example of corruption of authority (personal experience). The author has shoeboxes full of these cards that he used in classroom and training sessions.

Their Own Private Police Force. Two New York businessmen who were major contributors to and fund raisers for Mayor Bill de Blasio's campaign fund used their political influence to create their own "cops on call," according to the US Attorney for the Southern District of New York (Kashbaum and Goldstein, June 20, 2016; Vasilogambros, June 21, 2016). Three senior NYPD officers and a patrol captain were arrested—a deputy chief, a deputy inspector, a sergeant, and an officer. All those arrested were accused of taking at least $100,000 of gifts in exchange for acting as a "private police force for themselves and their friends"—bodyguards, chauffeurs, and concierges. The deputy chief and the deputy inspector allegedly received expensive meals and free overseas and domestic flights. The deputy inspector received a trip on a private jet to Las Vegas for the Super Bowl weekend in 2013. A prostitute accompanied him on the trip. One of the businessmen "ratted out" the police in exchange for a lesser sentence. Once the scandal became public, nearly a dozen senior officers were disciplined, and several retired.

Other select examples include the following:

- The longest-serving sheriff of Philadelphia was sentenced to five years in prison and the forfeiture of $78,581 dollars for exchanging sales of homes at sheriff's sales for city work. The sheriff had served for twenty-five years as a police officer and was the elected sheriff from 1988 to 2010 (Dale, August 1, 2019). The US district judge at sentencing reportedly said, "This is the city that time and time again has been roiled by this kind of corruption. You were supposed to be one of the good ones. The shame—your shame and the shame of the city—is that you were not (Dale, August 1, 2019). A local businessman made $33 million in sales as a result of the quid pro quo arrangement, even though he claimed there was not an exchange relationship for his "gifts" to the sheriff. The jury found otherwise. The sheriff received over $675,000 in money and material gains, including a rent-free home and then the purchase of the home at a discount; $65,000 in hidden campaign funds; and $320,000 to buy a retirement house in Florida.

- In 2019, a sheriff of the city of Norfolk, Virginia, was indicted for engaging in a suspicious quid pro quo arrangement with the chief executive officer of a company that provided medical services to the inmates at the Norfolk City Jail. The eventual court case showed that from 1994 to 2016 the sheriff received cash, travel, entertainment, gift cards, catering, personal gifts, and campaign contributions from a number of vendors who had contracts with the Norfolk City Jail (US Attorney's Office, Eastern District of Virginia, Department of Justice, May 20, 2022). In addition, a food services company provided free catering at the sheriff's home, his annual golf tournament, and other political events. Although this example is classified as corruption of authority, it, like many other such cases, can shade into "kickbacks."
- An interesting case just occurred in the United Kingdom where a nightclub boss was sentenced to four years in prison for lavishing a corrupt cop with free holidays, nights with call girls, fine dining, tailored suits, hotel stays, and house renovations (James, September 25, 2023). The police sergeant was convicted and sentenced to seven years in prison.

Pattern: Kickbacks

Acts. Law-enforcement officers receive money, goods, and services for referring business to towing companies, ambulances, garages, lawyers, medical professionals, bondsmen, funeral homes, taxi cabs, service stations, moving companies, and others who sell services or goods to those the police routinely encounter. These activities are not contained in the corruption-of-authority pattern because the link between the act and the reward is direct and outlined by the corruptors: "I will pay you for doing this."

The corruptors in these incidents have a lot to gain from quid pro quo relationships with the police. The acceptance of kickbacks varies with the police agency and the "legitimacy" of the giver. Acceptance of money or other material rewards from a trustworthy giver with high social status and professional standing is rationalized as a "clean" benefit of the job. Corruptors are not engaged in criminal activity. Supposedly, this fact "whitewashes" the act. Ambulance-chasing lawyers provide free services or monetary rewards for referrals. It is not uncommon for police officers to have cards from lawyers, bondsmen, garages, and towing companies to pass out to accident victims. These corrupt acts are treated differently in the police agency and reacted to less severely than acts involving money and material gain from criminal shakedowns or protection money from criminals.

Within the police agency, certain assignments have increased opportunities for kickbacks. All patrol officers investigate traffic accidents; however, most police departments have specialized accident investigators for serious injuries and fatalities, which almost always result in civil litigation. The latter groups of accident investigators are prone to lawyer–police conspiracy arrangements. Complaint-desk assignments increase the likelihood of lawyer–police or bondsmen–police conspiracies.

National Lawyer Reference Service Kickbacks. Two veteran Chicago police officers were indicted and pleaded guilty to accepting kickbacks from a National Lawyer Reference Service owner. The service was based in Bloomingdale, Illinois. The lawyer service got paid for referring clients to lawyers. The officers received cash payments of $6,000 for one officer and $7,300 for his partner between 2015 and October 2017 (Caruso, September 10, 2018). The officers transmitted insider information about traffic crashes—the misuse of official information. The transmitted nonpublic information included personal information on the victims. In Chicago, traffic-accident information becomes public after a processing period lasting from twenty-four hours to several weeks, depending on the seriousness of the injuries or death and the required investigation needed. However, the reports are available to police officers with legitimate law-enforcement reasons. The two cops were accessing them, sometimes as many as three hundred a month, before the reports became public.

Bail Bondsmen. The bail system is notorious for its failures and problems, especially the disproportionate impact on the poor and the powerless. Nevertheless, the bail industry is highly profitable and competitive. The profit motive and the competitive nature of the business create the opportunity for quid pro quo arrangements between police/detention officers and bail bondsmen. In 2017, federal authorities busted up an elaborate long-running bribery/kickback conspiracy that involved licensed and unlicensed bail bondsmen, deputy clerks, and sheriff's deputies in the Orleans Parish Criminal District Court of New Orleans (US Attorney's Office, Eastern District of Louisiana, Department of Justice, August 25, 2017).

- A 2009 North Carolina case involved jail detention officers accepting case kickbacks of 1 percent of each client's bail for referring inmates to four bail bondsmen (Anon, August 13, 2009). Similar arrangements occur in numerous jails throughout the United States.

- A sergeant with the Portsmouth, Virginia, sheriff's department pleaded guilty to accepting $5,000 in kickbacks from a bondsman between 2008 and 2012 in return for referrals. He was sentenced to thirteen months in prison. His coconspirator, a female magistrate who set the bond's amount, was sentenced to a year in prison. The scheme worked like this. A suspect would call the sergeant, who was known as a "fixer," and then they would set up a time to appear before the magistrate. She would set the bond, and the cooperating bondsman would pay it. The bondsmen would pay the cop, and he would pay the magistrate.
- A 2007 New Haven, Connecticut, police–bail bondsmen kickback scheme involved a unique arrangement. A lieutenant with the New Haven Police Department's narcotics division was paid to act as a bounty hunter to track down bail jumpers who failed to show for their court dates. I have personal knowledge of bondsmen paying cops to arrest bail jumpers. On occasion, the cops would not take the bail jumpers to jail but would call the bondsmen to come pick them up. The cops were modern-day bounty hunters.

Majestic Towing Auto-Repair Scandal, Baltimore, 2011. Towing and auto-repair police kickback scandals are a recurring police-corruption problem. The 2011 Baltimore Majestic Auto Repair scandal is emblematic of this kickback scheme that appears episodically throughout the United States. According to one source, Baltimore has had police towing scandals in 1956, 1965, and 2011 (Hermann and Scharper, February 23, 2011). In 1956, a Baltimore cop got $5 for steering a towed vehicle to certain repair shops. Ten dollars a car was the rate in 1965, and in 2011 cops got as much as $300 a car. In 2011, car towing was a $12-million-dollar industry in Baltimore, with sixty thousand cars towed annually, some from private lots and others due to parking violations and traffic accidents. That is a lot of opportunities for police corruption. One tow-truck driver testified in 1964 that he had given one police officer $9,000 in one year and that other officers averaged about $4,500 annually. Cops testified in 1965 that everyone is doing it and no one is being charged. That attitude set the stage for the 2011 police towing scandal.

In 2011, two brothers, owners of the Majestic Auto Repair in Baltimore, Maryland, a non-city approved towing company pleaded guilty to paying kickbacks to over fifty Baltimore Police Department officers who steered automobile-accident victims to them. In 2008, the brothers "retained" two department officers to contact the brothers, instead of city-authorized towing and repair shops, from accident scenes. The officers were given the brothers' cell-phone numbers so they could call from accident scenes. The two corrupt cops recruited other officers into the scheme. The three-year scam involved the businessmen paying up to $1 million to the officers in kickbacks at $200 to $300 per referral. The car owners were told that the towing fee and their insurance deductible would be waived if Majestic repaired the vehicle. The officers were coached to tell the wreck victims to lie on insurance claims. Officers falsified or increased the damage to cover their corrupt fees. At least seventeen officers pleaded guilty to accepting bribes (DOJ, July 11, 2011).

Florida Highway State Trooper: Kickbacks from Tow Trucks and a Chiropractor. Florida law prohibits the release of vehicle crash information to third parties during a sixty-day processing period. The time frame makes it unlawful to solicit business from towing companies, auto repairs, and medical care. A Florida state trooper violated all the provisions of the law. The FBI opened up an investigation into the towing-company industry in the Miami area and snared the trooper along with three Miami Police Department officers and several police officers from adjacent communities. A confidential source told the FBI that he had paid the trooper between $100 and $1,000 per accident referral, depending on the damage.

The trooper was also accepting money from a chiropractor for business referrals. The FBI ran a "sting" on the trooper, using a fictitious corrupt chiropractor. The trooper supplied the personal information of one hundred accident victims to this imaginary chiropractor for $5,000. The Florida former state trooper pleaded guilty to federal extortion conspiracy charges in May 2015 and was sentenced to four years in prison (US Attorney's Office, Southern District of Florida, Department of Justice, August 20, 2015).

Detroit Police Department Deputy Chief, 2018. Law-enforcement officers that enforce licensing ordinances take kickbacks from legitimate business operators. A black female Detroit Police Department deputy chief with a law degree who oversaw the licensing and operation of private towing companies pleaded guilty to bribery and conspiracy in 2018. She took kickbacks from the owner of a large towing company and assisted him in getting towing permits and rotation placement. She pleaded guilty and was sentenced to one year and one day in prison (Meloni, April 18, 2018).

St. Louis, Montana, Police Kickbacks from Chiropractors, 2019. The policies and rules of the Metropolitan Police Department–City of St. Louis prescribe that unredacted reports of an accident will only be released to persons involved in the accident, the companies that insure them, or the lawyers that represent them. The policy exists because unredacted reports contain addresses, telephone numbers, birth dates, and insurance information. A department officer was sentenced to thirteen months in prison for accepting kickbacks from a chiropractor for providing her with the unredacted reports. The chiropractor identified victims from low-income areas and offered her services.

Massive New York and New Jersey Kickback Scheme Relating to No-Fault Insurance Policies, 2014–2019. A five-year investigation into a bribery, corruption, and kickbacks scheme related to New York and New Jersey no-fault insurance resulted in the arrests of twenty-seven persons, including NYPD officers. It is alleged that the Rose Call Center bribed 911 operators, medical personnel, and police officers for information from sixty thousand no-fault insurance motor-vehicle accident victims. New Jersey and New York requires insurance companies to automatically pay claims for certain types of motor-vehicle accidents if the claim is legitimate and below a particular injury or damage threshold. This practice is subject to insurance fraud. For example, the victims were directed to handpicked clinics and lawyers. The clinics and lawyers then paid kickbacks back to the Rose Call Center coconspirators. These kickbacks were then distributed to the medical personnel, 911 operators, and police officers who supplied the insurance information. It appears that each referral averaged about $3,000 a victim. Currently, the extent and gravity of the scheme are not known; however, it appears to be the most massive kickback scheme in US history (US Attorney's Office, Southern District of New York, Department of Justice, November 7, 2019).

Pattern: Shakedowns

Acts. Shakedowns are opportunistic forms of police corruption, and they involve quid pro quo acts. A law-enforcement officer observes a criminal violation or gains knowledge of the criminal act and accepts a bribe not to make an arrest or pursue prosecution. The most common shakedowns occur during traffic stops. However, since the "war on drugs" was declared, US police officers are often arrested for stopping drug dealers and shaking them down for money and drugs. We will discuss this in the next chapter on criminal cops. This corrupt behavior is safe because the victims are unlikely to complain because they are engaged in law-violating behavior. The shakedown practice is known in the police argot as "hitting a lick" (personal experience and numerous semi-structured interviews).

Hitting a Lick or Scores. Shakedowns are a typical pattern of police corruption in local, county, and state uniformed police agencies. However, shakedowns also occur in ununiformed federal agencies when investigators accept bribes to close, not open, or pursue a criminal case. The typical shakedown occurs when a uniformed officer observes a "respectable" citizen committing a traffic violation or "catches" a criminal in the act, and the officer "street settles" the violation with an on-the-spot fine. The officer operates a roadside fee scheme for traffic violators. He or she gives violators choices: contest the violation in court, pay the fine, and receive points on their driving record, or pay the roadside fee. Illegal immigrants are frequent victims of this scheme. They are safe targets. As stated, shakedowns are perceived as "safe" acts because the victims are commonly involved in criminal behavior or are a member of a marginalized class. The majority of all shakedown offenses involve money or money's worth gain; however, shakedowns include quid pro quo sexual acts.

Shakedowns, because they involve direct contact with persons who are not criminals and who may be offended by this police behavior, are risky. In police argot, there is a shakedown caution known as a "no come back rule":

> Remember one thing—don't ever go back for a note [money]. If it's there and you want it, take it, but don't ever go for no come backer! That's when they are going to set you up for something. The guy drops a dime [complaint] and you walk in and the ginks [the internal affairs unit] have given him marked money or they give him your picture. (Policeman quoted in Rubinstein, 1996)

Cardinal Rule Violation: No Come Backs. A San Antonio, Texas, police officer was sentenced in 2014 to eighteen months in prison for shaking down an individual involved in an assault. The suspect had a user amount of marijuana when the police questioned him. The officer said he would not file the possession charges in exchange for a $500 bribe. The officer then violated one of the cardinal rules of criminal cops—never arrange a come back. The man didn't have the money on him. The officer arranged for a time to receive the bribe. The suspect reported the shakedown to the FBI, who recorded multiple cell-phone conversations and filmed the officer coming in his marked police vehicle to pick up the envelope with the money in it (US Attorney's Office, Western District of Texas, Department of Justice, January 4, 2013).

Making Charges Go Away—Not. The following attempted shakedown case has an unexpected but commendable result. In 2015, a rookie Huntsville, Alabama, police officer working out of the North Precinct, made a traffic stop and recovered three ounces of cocaine. He turned the case over to a multijurisdictional drug task force, which in turn arrested the suspect and charged him with cocaine trafficking in state court. The suspect was already under released federal supervision from a previous drug conviction. Sometime later, the rookie officer was approached by a twenty-one-year highly decorated fellow officer who worked out of the same precinct. The fellow officer told the rookie that a friend of his knew the suspected drug courier and wanted the rookie to make the charges go away. The veteran officer said the drug suspect would give him $5,000 to "queer" the original search and get the evidence thrown out. The disturbed rookie reported this to his supervisors, who, in turn, reported it to the FBI. A covert combined operation of the city and federal agents recorded the conversations and arrested the rogue officer. He pleaded guilty and was sentenced to two years in prison (Staff, February 25, 2015).

As a part of a towing bribery scandal, a retired Detroit Police Department detective—with twenty-one years of service—went on trial on January 13, 2023. It is alleged that he received $7,724 dollars in things of value from shaking down a towing company and an undercover FBI agent. He also was accused of receiving $3,000 in cash from a used-car businessman (Snell, January 13, 2023).

Shakedowns Worldwide. As is true with most patterns of police deviance, they occur worldwide wherever the law-enforcement occupation is found, no matter what form of government exists.

- The Royal Thai Police is a national police of approximately 230,000 armed officers and is considered to be a military force if needed. Forty-two members of the highway police division were transferred to inactive posts for shaking down overloaded truck drivers (Anon, June 9, 2023). Truck drivers who paid into the bribery scheme were given a special sticker to put on their trucks so they wouldn't be stopped. The country's counter corruption department is investigating the scandal currently. Shakedowns of overloaded trucks occur in other countries, including the United States, but I am not aware of another scheme this organized.
- A former London Metropolitan Police sergeant was sentenced to seven and a half years for shaking down bars and nightclubs in the London's West End (Busby, July 18, 2023). He was responsible for premise licenses and inspecting the bars and nightclubs for compliance. He accepted luxury family vacations, tickets to Elton John events, and money along with other gifts.

Pattern: Protection of Illegal Activities

Acts. The corruptors in this pattern of police corruption are engaged in systematic illegal behavior and want to conduct their illicit operations without police harassment. So-called victimless crime activities—illegal gambling, drug sales, liquor violations, and prostitution—are common in this pattern. We are aware of police protection payoffs in drug conspiracies from the media attention these criminal activities receive. Nevertheless, the same sort of systematic payoff conspiracies occurs in gambling operations, large and small. Since the nineteenth century, US police officers have protected illegal gambling and prostitution operations (Fogelson, 1977). In New York, Lieutenant Charles Becker was the first known American police officer to be executed for on-duty murder. He killed a potential "rat" who was going to disturb his graft operation in Midtown Manhattan. He will appear again in the next chapter. The area was known as Satan's Circus (textbox 7.1) because it was New York's entertainment center and the heart of the vice trade (Dash, 2007).

Textbox 7.1. Satan's Circus

Satan's Circus was a square mile of Midtown Manhattan where vice ruled, sin flourished, and depravity danced in every doorway. At the turn of the twentieth century, it was a place where everyone from the chorus girls to the beat cops was on the take and where bad boys became wicked men. It was the place where a young policeman, Charles Becker, became the crookedest cop who ever stood behind a shield (Dash, 2007).

By the 1950s, systematic gambling payoff schemes were in operation throughout all the boroughs in the NYPD's jurisdiction. A description of the Harry Gross gambling syndicate provides a description (textbox 7.2). In the 1950s, gambling was the major source of systematic police corruption in most US cities. Liquor sales and drug dealing would outstrip gambling in later years in many cities.

Textbox 7.2. Harry Gross Gambling Syndicate

On the first and fifteenth of each month Gross paid the plainclothes squad in every division in which he had a gambling spot. In addition, he paid a set fee for each telephone [bookmaker] used in a given division. There were extra payments to precinct plainclothesman and precinct commanders. The borough plainclothesmen squads were paid for each location in their jurisdiction. The chief inspector's squad and the police commission's squad, having citywide jurisdiction, were paid off for all locations. Inspectors in charge of divisions received regular payments as did lieutenants in charge of plainclothes squads.

Systematic networks of payoff schemes, such as what happened in New York City, were used in southern states for liquor shot houses in black areas where blacks could not get legal licenses to operate or buy liquor in quantity (personal experience). An example includes the following.

The bloodiest riot—forty-three dead—in American history occurred on July 21, 1967, in Detroit. After four days of rioting, the disturbance was brought under control when President Lyndon Johnson sent in the US Army. Tradition has it that the rioting began when the Detroit police used excessive force in the raid on a "blind pig"—an illegal liquor house and after-hours club in a black neighborhood. The "blind pig" had stopped paying the police, and they retaliated with the forceful raid. Eighty-two black persons were arrested. Raiding illegal liquor houses that didn't pay or stopped payments and destroying the property and arresting everyone in them in a rough manner was common practice among police departments with systematic protection schemes (personal knowledge). Today, the most numerous egregious protection payoff conspiracies occur during drug-trafficking operations as cops rent their badge to dope dealers.

Police drug-related corruption differs from the other forms of police corruption subsumed under the pattern of protection of illegal activities, such as the vice crimes of gambling, prostitution, and others. Police drug-related corruption includes individual armed criminal police officers committing direct criminal activities—committing robberies, dealing drugs, escorting drug dealers in marked cars, and engaging in elaborate payoff conspiracies protected by groups of police officers or drug units.

Prostitution Payoffs. A retired former NYPD vice detective and his wife, a former prostitute, were the ringleaders for a complex system of brothels in Brooklyn from 2015 to 2018 (Anon, July 24, 2019). They recruited on-duty NYPD officers to help them in their protection conspiracy. The profitable illegal operation took in $2 million in the thirteen months before it was busted. One corrupt detective was paid regular weekly installments of $500. The three-year-long investigation began after an anonymous tip from an officer. During the investigation, two brothers who were also NYPD officers were caught on videotape, acting as doormen for brothels. They were also taped accepting large amounts of cash. One of the brothers set the price for sex at the brothel. Seven NYPD employees were arrested and charged—three sergeants, two detectives, and two officers. The majority of the women detained were immigrants from Central America.

Sex Trafficking Payoffs, 2022. A former Kansas City, Kansas, police detective who will be discussed later in the chapter on criminal cops, was federally indicted for accepting payoffs from sex traffickers who ran their operation out of an apartment complex (Lowe, November 14, 2022). The now-retired detective is also charged with putting an innocent man in prison, rape, sexual assault, and kidnapping during his decades-long reign as a criminal cop.

Legitimate Businesses Operating Outside the Law. Legitimate companies that operate outside the law or outside their license pay corrupt police officers for protection. In the 1970s, the NYPD Knapp commission found that it was routine for construction companies to pay the police to block traffic, violate pollution guidelines, destroy city property, and illegally block sidewalks. Some legitimate cabs, and now Uber drivers, pay the police to operate outside prescribed routes and areas. The jitney cabs in my department paid the downtown detectives in charge of legal taxicab regulations to operate. My partner and I arrested a jitney driver operating on our beat and were told in no uncertain terms not to do that again. Our sergeant said there was nothing he could do. He said we would be walking a beat in the boonies if we did it again. We were messing with the chief's money.

NYPD Karaoke Bar Protection Scandal. A recent NYPD karaoke club protection scandal, in a department with a history of police protection scandals going back to the 1800s, was still reverberating in New York in 2019. In December 2015, the Queens district attorney alleged that a lieutenant and a detective, along with several uniformed officers out of the 109 Precinct in Flushing, were involved in a bribery protection scheme (Weiss, March 29, 2016). The detective, a ten-year veteran, allegedly had accepted $2,000 a month since 2013. He was charged with accepting bribes and obstruction of government administration. The 109 Precinct has a sizeable Asian population with karaoke clubs, bars, and room salons that sell high-priced drinks. The officers accepted money payoffs to tip off Queens karaoke clubs to police raids and to protect customers from being arrested for using drugs. It was alleged that, on several occasions, the lieutenant and the detective had intervened in several arrests of drug-using customers from clubs that paid the protection bribes. They convinced the arresting officers to release the suspects. The investigation revealed recordings and surveillance tapes of the lieutenant and detective convincing other officers not to raid certain clubs and to release handcuffed prisoners.

By March of 2016, there were twenty-three NYPD officers suspected of being involved in the protection scandal in some manner. The list of alleged conspirators included two captains, three lieutenants, three sergeants, three detectives, and numerous uniformed officers. Police commissioner William Bratton, in his second term as commissioner, publicly acknowledged the corruption investigation but quickly denied the alleged number of officers possibly involved. A sergeant whistleblower who worked undercover for internal affairs claimed at least one hundred officers were involved. He also claims that Commissioner Bratton subjected him to internal investigations and barred him from promotions. The whistleblower was quoted in a newspaper article, saying that "the whole internal investigation is a big joke."

In 2017, the case sputtered to an ignoble end. The lieutenant was fired and allowed to plead guilty to a misdemeanor charge of attempted official misconduct. He received a conditional discharge, meaning he would have his record expunged if he stayed out of trouble for six months. He kept his pension because he had over twenty years of service. The fired detective was allowed to plead guilty to a misdemeanor charge of obstruction of government administration and was granted a conditional discharge. In 2018, the police whistleblower who uncovered the protection conspiracy sued the NYPD for harassment and claimed the NYPD turned a blind eye to corruption, drugs, and hookers. The suit alleges that he was subjected to "a persistent campaign to harass, defame, threaten, intimidate, extort, and endanger his life."

Furthermore, the suit claims that Commissioner Bratton may have been involved in the scandal. There was no substantiation provided for the last claim. A 2019 article in the *New York Daily News* reports that an unknown number of cases from this scandal are working their way through the internal discipline system. Two officers have been fired. One officer fired in March 2019 was found guilty at a department trial for associating with known criminals and failure to report corruption.

Pattern: The Fix

Barker identified two patterns of the fix: 1) taking up of traffic tickets, and 2) the quashing of prosecution proceedings once charges have been placed. Although these patterns of police corruption were once common in police agencies, they are almost nonexistent today. Uniform and numbered tickets in most departments have made this corrupt behavior extremely risky. In today's open-source media exposure of the operation of the criminal-justice operations, quashing a prosecution or fixing a trial is almost impossible for a police officer to do, except in misdemeanor cases in small jurisdictions. In the 1960s and 1970s, criminal cases, even murder cases, were "sold." I am aware of numerous criminal cases that were "fixed" during that time period. Evidence had a habit of disappearing in my department. Not today. However, fixes are used as a corrupt technique to affect other patterns of police corruption. For example, in 2011, a Rialto, California, police officer and a criminal attorney were charged with committing perjury to fix a criminal assault case. A criminal defendant through his lawyer paid the officer $2,500 to give perjured testimony (FBI, June 6, 2011). A Long Island, New York, police chief and three other officers were charged with fixing traffic tickets for local businessmen (Pegones and Estanowich, May 1, 2019). In the early 1980s, almost ninety-two Chicago public officials, including police officers and judges, were caught up in fixing criminal cases—Operation Graylord.

The following police-corruption patterns do not involve a criminal exchange between police officers and citizens. The acts range from opportunistic thefts that could involve any officers, from those known as grass eaters to criminal cops involved in direct criminal activities. As stated, a grass eater would be an officer with weak self-control who would encounter a tempting opportunity in a setting that he or she perceives to be safe. As the sisters always told us while we were growing up, "avoid the near occasion of sin." That is hard to do in police work where the occasions of sin are all around.

Pattern: Opportunistic Thefts

Acts. There are no corruptors in this pattern of corruption. Criminal police officers come to work with the idea that they will look for theft opportunities during routine patrol. They will be discussed in detail in a later chapter. For now, opportunistic thefts are thefts from unsuspecting persons or businesses as the opportunity presents itself. I was told by a veteran police officer about fifty years ago that "Crime happens when the opportunity and desire come together and there is little risk of getting caught." He said that's what the sisters taught him in the second grade. The sisters told me that sin occurred in the same manner when I was in the second grade and every grade after that. Of course, the sisters were right, and the social scientist "fancied" up that bromide and called it the "rational choice theory of crime."

The victims of these opportunistic thefts are people and businesses. This includes arrestees, traffic-accident victims, and unconscious or dead crime victims. Officers investigating business, residence, and vehicle burglaries steal money or valuables left behind by the original thief. Officers take money from unprotected sites they encounter during their routine patrol. This pattern of corruption has existed to some extent since the watch and ward colonial patrols. The behavior is easily rationalized by police officers when it is occasional, of low value, and does not involve a person. However, it is stealing and involves a slippery slope that leads to serious thefts and other criminal activities. The thefts often progress from an occasional incident to direct criminal activities.

Some police officers—meat eaters—routinely keep a portion of the money and drugs found during searches and seizures. Even worse, some police officers steal from unconscious and dead crime victims, especially if the victims were involved in criminal activities. Robert Leuci, a bestselling author and an admitted corrupt NYPD officer, described a disgusting opportunistic theft practice in his 2004 bestselling crook book *All the Centurions*. He escaped imprisonment by "ratting out" his coconspirators. Leuci said NYPD officers would soap down the fingers of dead persons to remove their rings. Other officers from departments throughout the United States have told me that some officers in their departments steal from the dead. I was teaching a police ethics seminar when an officer said, "Doc, we have an officer in our department who you would not want investigating a traffic accident that you or your family was involved in." One of the other officers joined in and gave his name. I replied, "If you know he does this, why don't you turn him in?" In chorus, they replied, "Hell, Doc, you know why we don't." I replied, "I sure do, but as long as some cops have their hands in someone's pocket and other cops know about it and do nothing, policing will never be a profession." We moved on to another topic.

Opportunistic Theft to Murder. In 2014, a Jefferson Parish, Louisiana, deputy sheriff was sentenced to ninety-two years in federal prison for a series of crimes that began with an opportunistic theft incident on August 2, 2007 (DOJ, November 10, 2014). On that date, the deputy sheriff stole the debit card of an unconscious accident victim and began purchasing merchandise and withdrawing funds from the victim's bank account. According to court documents, the deputy, between August 2 and August 9, made total withdrawals and purchases in the amount of $7,627.12. When the victim got out of the hospital and canceled the debit card, the deputy forged checks and cashed them using the victim's checking account. The victim was issued a replacement card. Then the victim disappeared on or about October 2, 2007, and was never seen again. However, the deputy continued to use the victim's debit card and "zeroed out" the victim's savings account. The investigation into the disappearance and the bank fraud revealed that the deputy and the victim had become friends after his release from the hospital. In 2014, after a four-day evidentiary hearing, a federal judge found that the deputy was responsible for the death and disappearance of the opportunistic theft victim and sentenced the deputy to ninety-two years in prison. The sentence was affirmed on appeal in *United States v. Hebert*, which was decided on December 23, 2015.

Other Recent Examples of Opportunistic Thefts:

- A lieutenant with the Mayes County, Oklahoma, sheriff's office, who was supervisor of the property room, pleaded guilty to stealing drugs (DOJ, April 3, 2019).
- The Homeland Security Investigation resident in charge of the office in Portland, Oregon, pleaded guilty to stealing government property and selling it on eBay (DOJ, October 11, 2019).
- The narcotics supervisor for the Mayes County, Oklahoma, sheriff's office was sentenced to six months of home supervision for stealing drugs for his personal use (DOJ, August 2, 2019).
- A sergeant with the Harvey Cedars, New Jersey, police department was sentenced to two years of probation and banned from public employment after stealing a donated all-terrain vehicle (Goudsward, June 20, 2019).
- A Normal, Illinois, police officer was charged with stealing, and then trying to return, $12,000 in cash from the residence of an overdose victim (Denham, December 1, 2019).
- A Louisville police officer working at a UPS shipping and storing facility as a drug interdiction officer was sentenced to five months in prison and five months of home detention for stealing $74,745 (DOJ, April 26, 2017).
- A DeKalb County, Georgia, police officer was charged with stealing from a crime scene (Dillon, March 7, 2017).
- In 2017, a Dekalb County, Georgia, police officer resigned and was arrested for stealing $241 from the scene of a drug raid. He was charged with theft by taking, tampering with evidence, and violation of oath of office.
- A seven-year veteran of the Baltimore Police Department was arrested and charged with taking an envelope with $111 in it from a business. He was called as a backup for an unsecured business and a surveillance camera caught him putting the envelope in his pocket (Fenton, September 25, 2023).

Pattern: Direct Criminal Activities

Acts. In this pattern, law-enforcement officers directly commit crimes against persons or property for material reward or gain. These criminal officers are like the notorious NYPD officer Michael Dowd, a "gangster cop" who spent twelve years in prison for running a drug-trafficking ring. They are "gangsters with badges." Later chapters discuss these "gangsters with badges" thoroughly. However, two mind-boggling examples of direct criminal activities should be mentioned here. The most egregious direct criminal activities in recent memory by law-enforcement officers are those of the NYPD "Mafia cops" and those of the FBI special agents who sold secrets to the Soviet Union.

Mafia Cops. NYPD detectives Louis Eppolito and Stephen Caracappa, both gold shield first-grade detectives—in the highest detective rank—are known as the "Mafia cops" because of their involvement with organized crime families in New York City. Looking at his prehire background, one must wonder why Eppolito ever became a cop. He was the grandson of a "made" man in the Mafia, the son of a Gambino soldier, and the nephew of a Gambino captain. There are also questions in Caracappa's background. A felony conviction before he was hired mysteriously disappeared from his record. Both detectives retired in 1992, and moved to Las Vegas. In 2006, the retired detectives were tried for and convicted of labor racketeering, extortion, narcotics trafficking, and eight counts of murder and conspiracy to commit murder during their careers with the NYPD in the 1980s and early 1990s. These two criminal cops acted as hitmen for the mob in two murders.

FBI Spies. FBI Special Agent Robert Hanssen, a former police officer, joined the FBI in 1976 and began spying for what was then the Soviet Union in 1979. After the breakup of the Soviet Union, he spied for the Russian intelligence service. In 2001, he was arrested and pleaded guilty to fifteen counts of espionage and conspiracy in exchange for no death penalty. He was sentenced to life in prison without the possibility of parole. A second FBI special agent, Earl Pitts, spied for the Soviet Union and Russia. He was arrested in 1995 and sentenced to twenty-seven years in prison. These two rogue FBI agents will be discussed more fully later.

Conclusion

Police corruption is the misuse of the officer's official position for personal gain. There are a variety of schemes, including quid pro qua actions where a police officer receives some material gain for not doing what he should do, that result in police corruption. Even the acceptance of gifts and gratuities, a common practice in policing, is not a trivial issue that can be ignored. There are consequences that come with all police quid pro quo acts. The officer does not make an arrest, does not write a ticket, or does not report a crime. Or the officer, who may serve at any level of government, in the worst-case scenario, uses his or her camouflaged identity, privileged knowledge, and access to steal and commit other profit-motivated criminal acts. The real costs of police corruption are (1) the degradation of the police-work occupation (police work will never be a profession while one cop is taking a material gain, and other cops know it and do nothing); (2) the use of discipline and supervision are compromised (how does the sergeant discipline his subordinates when they break the rules or takes money?); and (3) police corruption leads to some police officers becoming criminal cops. The next chapter addresses criminal cops.

Discussion Questions

1. Why is the corruption of authority a serious problem in American police work? Support your answer with examples not mentioned in the text.
2. Does your local police agency have the reputation of not allowing police corruption? Do you agree with that assessment? Why or why not?
3. Read the following interview taken from the author's research. How does it fit into this chapter's discussion?

WHO GIVES A SHIT?

The following is an excerpt interview from a more extensive study on police misconduct and crime, which I conducted. Officer Y agreed to an interview about police corruption in his police department on conditions of anonymity, no taping, and no questions about his involvement. Officer Y is a twenty-six year veteran of a large municipal police department in the Southwest of the United States, in an area with a majority-Hispanic population. The interview took place in 2017 at a neutral location.

> Interviewer: When I say police corruption, what comes to your mind?
>
> Officer Y: Well, as I understand it from my experience, training, and college classes. Police corruption occurs when a cop takes money not to do something he should do. It also means taking cash or something of value not to do something he should do. Right?
>
> Interviewer: That's a good definition. Does that go on in your department?

Officer Y: Well, that depends on what substation you're talking about.

Some of the substations are full of opportunities for corruption, and the cops take advantage of them. Other substations don't have the temptations. I have worked at both kinds of substations. You know what I mean. You were a cop. You can ride around the city and pick out the corruption areas. Ain't no secret. Read the damn newspaper.

Interviewer: I know that, but I want you to tell me what makes the substations different in opportunities for corruption. Pretend I don't know anything about police corruption.

Officer Y: OK. Let's pretend you don't know shit, and you ain't no cab driver, bus driver, first responder of any kind, or the DA or a judge. They all know. First, some substations are predominately populated by illegals, blacks, the poor, and the homeless. You have a lot of crime because the victims and the criminals live next to each other. Now, illegals are safe targets. A cop can "hit a lick" on them, and they ain't gonna report it. He is safe, and he knows it.

Interviewer: What do you mean by "hit a lick?"

Officer Y: That's right. You don't know shit. I mean, these illegals don't have any documents. They still drive, drink, and walk around. So a cop stops them for some real or made up offense and takes "a lick," you know money, to let them go. Some cops get a blow-job from the women. They get sex and money. You complain, and your ass gets deported. They know that.

Interviewer: Anything else? You know, like systematic payoffs?

Officer Y: Hell, yeah. They have these drinking and gambling places, you know cantinas, in some substations run by illegals and catering, if that's the right word, to illegals. The cops collect the rent from these places.

Interviewer: What do you mean by collecting the rent?

Officer Y: Oh. I forgot you don't know shit. Man, I've heard you talk about the "Pad" in New York City and the "Money Car System" in your department. It's the same thing here. They have to pay rent to stay in business. There are regular weekly collections of the rent by cops at these drinking, gambling, and whorehouses for illegals. They're in the neighborhoods. Drive around on the Southside on the weekends. Be careful; somebody don't shoot your white ass. There are even some in the black areas, but not as many. By the way, I go to police meetings here in the state and some regional meetings and hear about the same thing from other cops. Its always been that way.

You should hear the "old heads" talk about it. If there is money to be made, some bad cop is going to take it. I know cops you don't want to come to your burglarized business or residence. They will steal your shit. Even if you're involved in an accident or dead, they will steal from you. Everybody knows who they are.

Interviewer: If everybody knows, why doesn't the chief put a stop to it?

Officer Y: Are you kidding? He's a politician, not a police chief. He don't want a scandal. He has his head in the sand, and it don't come out unless it hits the newspaper or TV. His hammer, you know the deputy chief, keeps the lid on it. As long as the crooked cop is careful, he ain't got nothing to worry about. And, you know what the head shed does if they hear about some cop taking money?

Interviewer: What?

Officer Y: They transfer him to one of the bad substations where he can't hurt some respectable citizen. Or, if it's really bad, they let him resign and go to work for some really corrupt border police department. Some of them cops are gang members.

Interviewer: Do you see anybody trying to change things?

Officer Y: Who gives a shit? The illegals don't vote, and nobody believes them when they complain. *Who gives a shit?*

CHAPTER 8

Criminal Cops

WHEN THE BAD GUYS WEAR BADGES

Key Terms:
    Criminal cops
    Direct criminal activities
    Profit-motivated police crime
    NYPD Lieutenant Charles Becker
    Prohibition
    The Outfit
    Wickersham commission
    Patrick Murphy

Chapter Objectives:
    After reading this chapter, the reader should be able to do the following:

1. Identity criminal cops and their patterns of behavior
2. Trace the link between Prohibition and organized crime and criminal cops
3. Explain profit-motivated police crime

A Brief History of American Criminal Cops

American criminal cops have engaged in serious crimes as individuals, groups, and systematic organized gangsters since the early nineteenth century. The working relationship between criminal cops and gangsters in American cities is an American historical tradition (see Hopkins, 1931; Rubinstein, 1973; Fogelson, 1977; Reppetto, 1978; Lindberg, 1991; Rousey, 1996; Russo, 2001; Ousley, 2008; Barker, 2011; and others too numerous to list). On the West Coast, police brutality against minority groups, such as the Chinese, and police corruption were rampant. In 1906, China's ambassador to the United States handed federal authorities a list of brutal and corrupt officers in Oakland, California, and the Bay Area (Winston and Bondgraham, 2023). Nothing was done about it. In Chicago, individual police officers engaged in corrupt and criminal acts before, during, and after Prohibition. The first known American law-enforcement officer executed by the state for an on-duty murder occurred on the East Coast in 1912. NYPD Lieutenant Charles Becker was executed for murdering a gangster to prevent him from disclosing Becker's corrupt cabal of cops and gangsters (Barker, 2020b). He was not the first or the last US police officer engaged in organized crime and murder for criminal enterprises.

After Prohibition, American crime became organized and centralized "when state actors [public officials] criminally leveraged their positions of power for financial gain." Organized crime groups controlled illicit vice markets in collusion with corrupt state actors, politicians, and public servants. Police officers, or the ones they could buy, were the muscle behind the gangsters and crooked politicians before, during, and after Prohibition.

PROHIBITION

Prohibition—America's great social experiment—went into effect on January 16, 1920, and faded into history as a failed experiment on December 5, 1933. The moral-policing law made the manufacturing and distribution of alcohol illegal, but it still could be consumed. Bootlegging alcohol became a cottage industry and expanded the opportunities for illegally making money for criminals, politicians, and law-enforcement officers at all levels of government. During the next two decades, large cities, such as Kansas City, Chicago, and New York, and small cities, such as Newport, Kentucky, Galveston, Texas, and others, became "open cities" where local ethnic gangs became organized crime enterprises. The sale of liquor was so open that even drug stores were divided into three parts in these open cities—soda fountain and sundries in the front, craps and card games in the middle, and bootleg liquor in the back. The profits of these mob-controlled drugstores and "throw away the key" clubs, which never closed, depended on a compliant political system and a cooperative police agency.

Public corruption existed before Prohibition and became embedded in the political structure during Prohibition as gangsters gained in strength and wealth; but individual criminal police officers still engaged in corrupt and criminal acts (Joseph and Smith, 2021). The "noble experiment"—America's venture into morality by law—proved that police officers and law-enforcement agencies at all levels of government could be as corrupt and incompetent as any. One of the most tragic examples was a South Dakota sheriff, Verne Miller, who went from being a war hero and respected lawman to a wanted outlaw and a "killer cop" (www.bbyfacenelsonjournal.com, Smith, April 2021, and Wikipedia accessed November 11, 2023, Reppetto, 1978). Miller, living as an auto mechanic in Huron, South Dakota, joined the Army in 1917; saw combat in France; and was promoted to sergeant and decorated for valor and bravery. When he returned to Huron after the war, Miller joined the Huron police department and then was elected county sheriff. Several years later, he was arrested for embezzling money from the county and served at least two years in prison. His story becomes complicated after his parole. Then he went bad. Some attribute his change of behavior to heavy drug use and advanced syphilis; others discount this.

In any event, he left his wife, took up with another woman, and became a bootlegger. Then he began robbing banks and associating with organized criminal gangs. In November 1932, he participated in a bank robbery in Minneapolis, Minnesota. The robbery went awry, and two police officers were killed. Miller became a wanted outlaw. In June 1933, Miller was a member of an organized group of hitmen that were trying to free a mob crime figure from federal custody on his way to prison. They ambushed the agents and the prisoner at Union Station in Kansas City, Missouri. The shootout, known as the Kansas City Massacre, left four police officers dead and two wounded. Miller and two shooters escaped. Two days later, his mutilated dead body was found along a road. The speculation is that the criminals killed him to keep him from ratting them out. Miller was only one of many American law-enforcement officers who went bad during Prohibition.

POLICE EVERYDAY CORRUPTION

Police officers before and after Prohibition engaged in "everyday" traditional patterns of corruption, such as conducting door-to-door raids, collecting bribes, shaking down violators, and opportunistically stealing from individuals, businesses, and unprotected property. Eventually and incrementally, organized crime groups seized political control and, in due time, control of the police. Organized crime in its basic form needed the police to ensure payments, collections, bribes, and coordination for the protection of illegal markets. And then the social experiment ended, and the country never went back to normal; or maybe it did.

When the thirteen-year-long hangover was over, the former disorganized urban criminal gangs were highly organized crime enterprises, with their tendrils in politics and legitimate industries throughout the American nation (Behr, 1996). During Prohibition, law-enforcement corruption and crime multiplied astronomically as Prohibition agents and local police protected the gangsters with money and influence and victimized the poor and recent immigrants without power and political influence. The rich and the bootleggers were virtually immune from arrest and prosecution. Prohibition ended with the promise that its repeal would end the horrific depredations that occurred during the United States' brief experiment with moral policing. It had the opposite effect. Instead of ending organized crime, it was the beginning of American organized crime and systematic police corruption and crime. A quick look at the history of American police graft and crime reveals how normal the existence of criminal cops is in some America cities. However, that is not true in the entire American policing experience. Some American police departments were then and are now "relatively" free of criminal cops.

St. Paul, Minnesota, threw off the yoke of American gangsters after Prohibition ended. The city came under control of a reform-minded group of progressives that appointed a reform-minded police chief in 1935. For the next six years, he fought against corrupt officers with ties to organized crime (Steinberg, March 7, 2018). There were other cities that followed suit. Nevertheless, there is a constant battle to eliminate them from the police occupation.

Police Graft in America: The Beginning

The earliest form of systemic organized police malfeasance—police corruption and criminality among cops—in New York City in the nineteenth century consisted of collections of protection payments in each police precinct by the wardman. This political appointee picked up the tribute from individual saloons, houses of prostitution, and gambling establishments. The wardman in turn gave what he collected to the politically appointed police captain. The police captain was responsible for the graft distribution within the police department and among the politicians. Individual police officers patrolling their beats were free to shake down certain unprotected criminals, liquor sellers, prostitutes, and gamblers. The marginalized poor, drunks, and recent immigrants who could not speak English were lumped together in the dangerous classes and added to the list of safe targets. Some but not all urban American police officers engaged in opportunistic thefts, robberies, and burglaries of unconnected persons and businesses. The "honest" policemen were safe and kept their jobs if they abided by the rules—no arrests or raids of protected persons—and kept their mouths shut. Variations of this systematic form of police graft existed in Chicago and other US urban cities (Key, 1935). This fragmented system of small groups of corruptors in each police district became centralized during and after America's "great social experiment." Vice and its production, supply, distribution, and production became "big business" in America. This phenomenon was most evident in the "big business" of illegal liquor.

BIG BUSINESS OF ILLEGAL LIQUOR

The illegal liquor business, after Prohibition ended, required an extensive organization for the manufacture, importation, and distribution of illegal liquor to thousands of illegal saloons in America's metropolitan areas. The now-organized groups needed a body of armed men to protect their customers and territory from rivals. This syndicate and organized criminal enterprise are best represented by Chicago's Capone syndicate—the remnants are now known as "the Outfit." Capone's criminal organization spread its tendrils into legitimate businesses as its illegal liquor customers were forced to buy towels and table linens, tobacco products, ginger ale, and pretzels from "subsidiaries" of the crime enterprise (Key, 1935). A competing crime group—Colosimo—controlled prostitution in Chicago. One "madam" controlled two hundred houses of ill repute. In addition to her protection payoff and political contributions, she had to patronize certain grocery stores and she and her girls had to go to designated doctors. The "police graft" guaranteed no arrest and prosecution, and the police raided independent crime competitors. As was customary, individual criminal police officers below the supervisory officer's level were allowed to freelance shakedowns, thefts, and other crime on unprotected persons and businesses if they didn't create a scandal or "shoot their mouths off." Even as bad as it was, not all the police in these cities were connected. Only those "who could be trusted" were assigned to specialty squads, like the vice squad and the gambling squad. The other "honest" officers were assigned to a territory with few or no illegal protected establishments. Key (1935) quotes the police reformer, August Vollmer, on why "honest" officers allow corrupt and criminal officers to operate with implicit and explicit support. He responded as follows:

> It is an unwritten law in police departments that police officers would never testify against their brother officers. Viewing it from the inside, it is soon found that as a general rule policemen believe that the average citizen is opposed to them and they must fight their battles against their common enemy. (August Vollmer quoted in Key, 1935, p. 636)

POLICE PROBLEMS AT THE TIME OF PROHIBITION

The National Commission on Law Observance and Enforcement (the Wickersham commission) was established by President Hoover on May 20, 1929. The eleven-member group was charged with surveying the US criminal-justice system under Prohibition and making recommendations for public policy. Their recommendations had lasting relevance (Wickersham Report, 1931):

1. The chief evil, in our opinion, lies in the insecure, short term of service of the chief or executive head of the police force and his being subject while in office to the control by politicians in the discharge of his office.
2. The second outstanding evil of such poor police administration is the lack of competent, efficient, and honest patrolmen and subordinate officers. . . . That is only to say that the personnel of the police force at its inception and in it continuance has not the character and qualities which its duties require.
3. The third great defect of our police administration is the commission and description of the criminals may be quickly spread over a wide territory and as a part of that, the necessary equipment in motors to pursue traces of the criminals making their escape.
4. The well-known and oft proven alliance between criminals and corrupt politicians which controls, in part, at least, might well be taken as a primary cause of police inefficiency, since it rules the head and every subordinate and lays a paralyzing hand upon determined actions against major criminals.
5. But the inefficiency of our police in failing to detect, arrest, and prosecute the gang criminals cannot all be laid to insufficient equipment, incompetence, and corrupt politics. The Commission stated that "The excessively rapid growth of our cities in the past half century, together with the incoming of millions of immigrants, ignorant of our language, laws and customs, and necessary adhering in their racial segregation in large cities, to the language and customs of their native lands, has immensely increased the difficulties of the police in detecting crime among foreign born in such localities and arresting criminals. . . . Added to the difficulties concerning the foreign born, the influx of large numbers of Negroes to our northern cities has measurably added to the difficulties of police administration." Does this sound similar to current explanations of urban crime?
6. There are too many duties cast upon each officer and patrolman. This is the outcome of the transition from rural or small-town policing to city communities.

POLICE PROBLEMS AFTER PROHIBITION

The organized crime groups in America's urban cities, flush with cash and thirsty for profit after Prohibition, moved into the now-legitimate liquor businesses and found new targets for their protection rackets. New York's underworld bosses became the "invisible government" as they moved in on bakeries, restaurants, laundries, construction companies, limousine services, the garment and jewelry industries, and the New York Fulton Fish Market. The same or similar criminal organization expansion occurred in Chicago, Kansas City, Atlantic City, New Orleans, Cincinnati, Newport (Kentucky), Philadelphia, Detroit, and other American cities. A national meeting of representatives of American criminal organizations occurred in Atlantic City, New Jersey, on May 13, 1929, in an attempt to form a national crime syndicate. Crime bosses from Chicago, Boston, Cleveland, New Jersey, New York, and Kansas City attended the three-day meeting. There were lessor crime figures from St. Louis (Missouri), East St. Louis (Illinois), New Orleans, and Hot Springs (Arkansas). These organizations did not coalesce into a national crime syndicate, but the meeting demonstrated the development of American organized crime (Ousley, 2008). Once engrained in American cities, the sordid tradition of organized crime, accompanied by criminal cops, continued into the modern era. This became painfully clear in the 1950s, when the US Senate Special Committee to Investigate Organized Crime in Interstate Commerce, chaired by US Senator Estes Kefauver, was formed. It was known as the Kefauver committee.

KEFAUVER COMMITTEE, 1950 TO 1951

US Senator Estes Kefauver, a senator from Tennessee, fearing the rapid national growth of organized crime syndicates, such as the reputed Italian Mafia in the Northeast and Midwest, and the growth of legalized gambling in Nevada, introduced Senate Resolution 202 in January 1950 (Moore, 1974). The Senate resolution called for a national investigation of organized crime syndicates involved in interstate commerce and engaging in organized crimes, such as illegal gambling, prostitution, drug trafficking, and extortion. He and four other senate committee members believed that the crime syndicates had established legitimate businesses to lauder their ill-gotten gains and had gotten so powerful that local police agencies were unable to control the gangsters and their criminal enterprises. During the fourteen months of its existence, for the first time in American history, the committee held televised and radio broadcast hearings in fourteen cities, including Miami—the first—Chicago, Detroit, Kansas City, and New York City. An estimated thirty million tuned in to watch the hearings in New York City in March 1951. Frank Costello, the head of the largest gambling syndicate in the country, testified in person. The sensationalized hearings exposed corrupt politicians, criminal police officers, and "legitimate" businessmen. The Miami investigation found gambling everywhere, from restaurants to cigar stands. Bribery and other forms of corrupt practices were uncovered throughout the Chicago police department. The entire world got a look at American organized crime and its effect on politicians and law enforcement. Other than publicity—a few politicians were forced to resign—the outcomes of the committee investigations were modest.

Twenty years later, the patterns of those involved in police corruption remained the same. Only the names had changed. The history of corrupt and criminal cops revealed itself again in the massive American police scandals of the 1970s and 1980s here and in the United Kingdom. According to Harper (2022), the collusion between individual police officers and organized crime existed in police agencies in the United Kingdom in the 1970s. The UK police commissioner from 1972 to 1977 prosecuted, sacked, or forced out 450 Scotland Yard officers, many for colluding with organized crime members.

American Systematic Police Corruption and Crime in the 1970s and 1980s

NYPD KNAPP COMMISSION: POLICING'S DARK SIDE EXPOSED

The NYPD has been a petri dish of police malfeasance—corruption and crime—since it was chartered and organized in 1844 (Chevigny, 1969; Miller, 1973; Lardner and Reppetto, 2000; Johnson, 2003; Barker, 2011; and others too numerous to list). The early patrolmen were appointed by corrupt politicians. Consequently, there were systematic police corruption scandals in 1913, 1930, and 1950, roughly establishing a twenty-year cycle of scandal, investigation, and "reform"; however, what happened in 1970 was different. The 1972 Knapp Commission Report on Police Corruption in the NYPD, the largest police department in the world, set off a firestorm of controversy and public condemnation throughout America and the world. For the first time in history, the national and international public saw corrupt American police officers testifying in public hearings on TV. Several unique features of the Knapp commission amplified its role in exposing the dark side of American policing. Contrary to traditional thinking and accepted common sense, policing was viewed as a secret brotherhood, whose members would never divulge the bad behavior of fellow "brothers in blue." But there they were on TV, telling all.

There is a lot of truth in the police brotherhood secrecy "myth." Most occupations do protect their misbehaving members from public transparency up to a point. The #METOO movement, doctors concealing "bad" doctors, and religious establishments concealing pedophile priests and pastors are examples of this. However, some forms of occupational proscribed behaviors are risky and condemned (Barker, 2011). As stated earlier, there are a variety of factors that go into peer support for police corruption patterns and criminal behavior. Every occupation, even or especially politics, has pariah workers who are not tolerated by the other workers. For example, Minneapolis police officers testified against Derek Chauvin, who was convicted of the murder of George Floyd. There is no honor among thieves or crooked cops when personal or group "red lines are crossed" or prison sentences are mentioned. The path of the whistleblower is not easy in any occupation, but it is sometimes followed.

Knapp Whistleblowers

In the Knapp commission example, the first attempt to report and expose police corruption by the two police whistleblowers was stonewalled and ignored by the police department hierarchy (Knapp Commission, 1972). Renowned former commander of detectives with the Chicago Police Department, police historian, and author of numerous books on American police, Thomas Reppetto, says that the two whistleblowers were told by the department's brass that they might end up floating in the East River. The bosses said they would get back to them. They never did (Reppetto, 2012, p. 118). Undeterred, the two disgruntled officers took the unprecedented action of going outside the department for action. They went to a *New York Times* reporter and complained about the NYPD's systematic corruption and the refusal of supervisors to take any action. In April, a *New York Times* front-page article described widespread police corruption and the department's failure to take any action, arousing the public and causing the mayor to create the Knapp commission by executive order in May 1970. The sitting NYPD police commissioner resigned in August 1970 and was replaced by the well-known police reformer Patrick Murphy. NYPD whistleblowers still exist in the NYPD but it doesn't get any easier (see textbox 8.1).

Textbox 8.1. NYPD Whistleblower: He Must Be Crazy

Adrian Schoolcraft, a Texas native and the son of a Texas police officer, moved to New York City after a tour of duty with the US Navy. He joined the NYPD in 2002 and left in 2010. According to Wikipedia and newspaper accounts (Goodman, September 29, 2015; Tempey, September 30, 2015), the trials and tribulations of an NYPD whistleblower had not improved twenty years after the Knapp commission's report. Schoolcraft, observing what he believed to be official misconduct, including mismanagement of crime statistics by precinct commanders, the existence of a quota system, overtime misuse, and police abuse in stop and frisk arrests, leading to wrongful convictions, began secretly recording conversations in the precinct, at roll call, and during false arrests from 2008 to 2009. He took these recordings to NYPD investigators. He was promptly relieved of his weapon, reassigned to a desk job, and sent to see two department psychiatrists. Then things got worse.

Schoolcraft's father contacted David Durk, a retired NYPD detective and a Knapp commission whistleblower. Durk contacted an officer with the NYPD internal affairs bureau, and Schoolcraft was subjected to "forced" internal affairs monitoring. In 2010, Schoolcraft went public with his recordings and allegations, and they were published in *The Village Voice* in a series titled "The NYPD Tapes." The NYPD brass exploded. One evening, Schoolcraft took off early after feeling sick, went home, took some Nyquil, and went to bed. He was awakened by a mass of heavily armed Emergency Service Unit officers, led by an NYPD deputy chief. They had gotten a key from the landlord by saying that Schoolcraft was suicidal. Schoolcraft was forcibly removed, taken to a hospital psychiatric ward, and handcuffed to a bed. He stayed there for six days. After Schoolcraft was discharged, he was suspended without pay. He sued the NYPD for $50 million. In 2015, he settled his suit for $600,000, back pay, and benefits.

Police Corruption Was a Way of Life

Police corruption had become a way of life in the NYPD and other American police agencies by the 1970s (personal experience and my early research). A rookie NYPD officer described how it was in his department in the 1970s: "I had come to believe that taking money was a part of the everyday life of a patrolman" (Droge, 1973). He felt that, if you didn't take money, you were ostracized and looked on as an oddball who couldn't be trusted. A fellow officer expressed the NYPD norm at the time: "Sure I took money, everybody did, it was the custom" (Knightly, January 8, 2012). Taking money was a police tradition, a habit, and very common. That way of thinking and acting occurred in police agencies throughout the United States (personal experience and unstructured interviews with working police officers from numerous US police agencies). However, the "real" money and the corruption problem occurred in the special vice units. In the NYPD, the special units were plainclothes officers.

Plainclothes officers targeted gamblers and whorehouses who were "on the pad"—paying regularly for protection. Each plainclothes man received $500 in an envelope every month if he was assigned to the fifteenth division in Queens; $800, in the thirteenth division in Brooklyn; $800, in the first and third divisions in Manhattan; and $1,500, in Harlem (Knightly, January 8, 2012). Following the revelations and publicity of the Knapp commission, the public knew about the pad also. Commissioner Murphy, a Brooklyn native and former NYPD deputy chief, was determined to destroy the "everybody does it" tradition.

NYPD Commissioner Patrick Murphy, 1970–1973

Patrick Murphy was one of a small cadre of college-educated police executives who moved from police department to police department as reform agents (Wikipedia; Dombrink, 1988; and Reppetto, 2012). The former WWII Navy pilot joined the NYPD in 1945. While "on the job," he earned a bachelor of arts degree and a master of public administration degree from St. John's University. He rose quickly through the ranks. In 1963, Murphy took an eighteen-month leave of absence to become the chief of police in Syracuse, New York. The police department was in the throes of a police-corruption scandal involving systematic payoffs from gamblers, prostitutes, and liquor-law violators. The Syracuse Police Department (SPD) detectives were "tipping off" criminals and associating with organized crime members. Murphy knew about this behavior. It was occurring in the NYPD, but he was not yet in a position to do something about it. That would come later. His brief time as SPD chief led to many reforms and solidified his reputation as a police-department reformer. Murphy returned to the NYPD. Two years later, in 1965, President Lyndon Johnson appointed Murphy, now an NYPD deputy chief, to be the assistant director of the Law Enforcement Assistance Administration (LEAA) located within the Department of Justice.

Law Enforcement Administration. Creation of the LEAA was one of the most significant efforts to reform American state and local agencies in American history up to that time. LEAA provided funds to state and local agencies to conduct research and to provide educational programs to American police officers. Hundreds, maybe thousands, of police officers attended colleges and universities on LEAA grants and loans. The author and his brother were two of those officers. The creation of LEAA and its emphasis on local police reform were part of the Johnson administration's "war on crime."

The LEAA office was in Washington, DC. The Metropolitan Police Department in Washington, DC, was a corruption-ridden police agency. In 1967, LEAA Assistant Director Patrick Murphy was appointed the District of Columbia's first director of public safety and put in charge of both the police and fire departments. His reform efforts in Washington, DC, led to his appointment as the reform commissioner of the Detroit, Michigan, police department in 1969. In 1970, New York City Mayor John Lindsay saw his aspirations of running for president running down the drain with the growing police-corruption scandal and the Knapp commission revelations. He was advised to call the former NYPD deputy chief and proven police reformer back home to clean things up—which he did.

According to most accounts, Commissioner Murphy had some successes in reforming the NYPD in his short tenure (Dombrink, 1988; Reppetto, 2012). John Lindsey did not run for another term. He had already served two terms—eight years. The new mayor appointed his own police commissioner.

However, Murphy's system of supervisor accountability changed the thinking in the command structure. Supervisors were strictly held accountable for the behavior of their personnel. The "rotten apple" excuse did not exonerate the supervisor. If there was a pad or abusive police conduct in a precinct under the supervisor's command, the supervisor had to explain why it was there and why he or she hadn't taken some action. Murphy introduced "defense of life" shooting policies that recognized the sanctity of life. The "fleeing felon" rule was out. Internal affairs, instead of reacting to complaints, became proactive and searched for evidence of police corruption. Integrity tests and field associates—rookie police officers reporting to internal affairs—became routine. There were massive transfers of supervisors and rotation of officers in corruption-prone assignments, such as vice units.

Media Attention

In the immediate years following the Knapp revelations, there was a plethora of "crook" books by corrupt officers and "honest" books by police officers who resisted the temptations of the morally dangerous policing occupation. The two NYPD whistleblowers, Frank Serpico and David Durk, became instant celebrities. The movie, *Serpico,* starring Al Pacino as Frank Serpico, was nominated for an Academy award. Descriptive terms that described corrupt officers—grass eaters and meat eaters—patterns of corrupt behavior—pad, rent, score, bagman—became a part of the popular culture, still in effect. The publicity and general interest in police corruption stimulated new scholarly interest on the part of sociologists and other academics who had ignored police research in the past (Roebuck and Barker, 1974).

Criminal Cop Groups

Then, in 1986, the "shit hit the fan" in the NYPD's seventy-seventh precinct, with the exposure of a group of criminal cops. They engaged in robbery, burglary, and drug dealing and called themselves the "buddy boys." Their exposure led to a new interest in patterns of police crime that had been in existence since the advent of the police occupation but that had received little attention—law enforcement officers engaging in direct criminal activities, literally criminals wearing badges.

Criminal Cops Defined

Technically, any police officer who commits a crime and is convicted is a criminal cop. That broad definition is unacceptable for several reasons. Police officers, like all occupational criminals, commit crimes when they are "off the job" that may be related to their occupational status. However, defining off-duty police job-related crimes is complex. For example, a police officer driving his car home while he or she is not "on duty"—is the officer off duty? Some would say yes, and others would say no. It certainly makes a difference if the officer is intoxicated or had an at-fault accident with injury. Some point out that the public considers any police officer driving a police vehicle as being "on duty" and, therefore, would classify DUI as on-duty crime. That view was not shared by some departments. The same problem exists with domestic violence. Is it an on-duty crime or an off-duty crime? This is more than a semantic debate. Commissions of DUI and domestic violence are serious violations when committed by police officers, individuals who have sworn to uphold the law. Police officers and other criminal-justice officials, whether it is fair or not, are held to a higher standard of behavior. Are police domestic-violence offenders or DUI drivers criminal cops? Probably not. Furthermore, not all police misconduct is criminal. Violations of administrative rules and regulation or ethical standards are typically not criminal but may violate police department policies and could get the officer terminated. DUI and simple and aggravated assaults by intoxicated police officers are the most common off-duty crimes.

Alcohol-related crimes are most likely to be committed by off-duty cops. Numerous police officers are fired or suspended for off-duty behavior that represents "conduct unbecoming an officer," according to department policy. The definition of criminal cop must go beyond policy infractions.

Direct Criminal Activities

Barker identified serious or felonious police corruption acts as "direct criminal activities"; these include robbery, burglary, and the sale of and trafficking in drugs. Police officers engaged in these activities are crooks in uniform. In other words, their felonious actions are profit-motivated. He was defining criminals who happen to be wearing badges for material gain. For example, all police breaking and entering are not criminal—executing a search warrant, for example, is not criminal—but some police breaking and entries are burglaries, just like those of any other criminal. Some articles, cash, and property taken from the scene of a crime by a police officer are evidence of police criminal behavior. And some of these incidents are thefts. Therefore, police crimes are *criminal* acts that involve the abuse of police power with felonious intent. He later included intentional law-enforcement-caused homicides. All police homicides (the killing of a human being by another human being) are not criminal, but some are— murder and manslaughter.

Police criminal behavior is defined as committing illegal acts whose definitions require felonious intent to do real harm or are profit oriented. If the officer is acting in an official capacity while off duty when the officer committed the act, the officer is a criminal cop. An officer can be found to be acting in an official capacity if the officer is using knowledge gained "on the job" to commit or facilitate the crime or is using his or her service weapon or identifies himself or herself as a police officer. This can become complex at times. Suppose the drug trafficker is a retired law-enforcement officer using his former police status and knowledge to engage in crime. It happens. In January 2023, a retired Rocky Mount, North Carolina, police officer was stopped for multiple traffic violations (Journey and Donahue, January 13, 2023). According to the newspaper accounts, he identified himself as a retired officer, which is usually enough to be released on "professional courtesy." However, his actions raised reasonable suspicion of criminal activity. The deputies called for a K-9, and the retired officer got belligerent and was arrested. The K-9 alerted the deputies to the presence of drugs, and 198 grams of cocaine with a street value of $20,000 was found in the retired officer's car. A search warrant was executed at his home, and more drugs, four pistols, scales, and drug paraphernalia were found. He was subsequently arrested for trafficking in cocaine, maintaining a vehicle and dwelling for the purpose of narcotics, and resisting arrest. He is a criminal cop.

A retired San Diego police officer and three others ran a criminal enterprise, an illegal massage business offering commercial sex. The criminal defendants bought storefronts and used them as supposed massage parlors that catered to mostly Chinese customers. They recruited undocumented Chinese immigrants and forced them to work in the businesses and put them in guarded houses. The criminal enterprise secured credit-card machines for charge transactions. The Department of Justice said that the retired police officer was a detective with the vice squad and used his experience and skills to further the conspiracy (DOJ, October 13, 2023). He was convicted and sentenced to thirty-three months in prison.

Off-duty arrests of police officers committing crimes are usually not that serious; however, they can be (see below and textbox 8.2).

Textbox 8.2. Robber Cop

On April 4, 2022, a Las Vegas Metropolitan Police Department (LVMPD) officer was indicted for the alleged robberies of three casinos. The alleged robberies netted a total of $164,000. The robberies occurred on November 12, 2021, January 6, 2022, and February 2, 2022. In the last robbery, the off-duty officer ran into the Rio Hotel casino sports book and yelled, "Get away from the money. I've got a gun [his service weapon] I will shoot you." He grabbed $78,898 and ran toward the parking lot. Casino employees triggered the robbery alarm. In the parking lot, a casino security tackled him, and the LVMPD officer threatened to shoot him. His exact words were, "Are you willing to be shot over this? I'm going to shoot you! Go ahead and shoot me now," he said. The bumbling robber was restrained by other security officers until LVMPD officers arrived (Charns, March 7, 2022). He wore black latex gloves and body armor on each robbery. He was caught on each casino's "eye in the sky" surveillance cameras with a distinct walking gait—kicking his left foot and leg out as he walked. He also appeared to have trouble with his leg while running. During the search of his house, paperwork was found indicating that he had injured his leg in 2019. He pleaded not guilty and is awaiting trial.

What is the Nature and Extent of American Police Crimes?

What is the nature of police crimes? What do they have in common? As stated, police crimes are criminal acts that involve the abuse of police power with the felonious intent to commit serious law violations. The extent of the national police crime problem is not known. There is no central database that collects information on police crime. However, data is beginning to appear in scholarly and public literature, and the results are disturbing.

NYPD Study of Dismissal for Cause

Kane and White's (2013) study presented the dilemma of defining police crime when they identified the eight examples of behavior that resulted in the termination of 1,543 NYPD officers from 1975 to 1996 (see Textbox 8.3).

Textbox 8.3. Police Misconduct Resulting in NYPD Terminations 1975–1996

1. Profit-motivated crimes—All offenses, other than drug trafficking and whether or not on-duty or off-duty, in which the end or apparent goal of officers' wrongdoing was a profit.
2. Off-duty crimes against persons—All assaultive behavior, except for profit-motivated robberies by off-duty officers.
3. Off-duty public order crimes—All offenses, other than drug trafficking or possession, against public order, including driving while intoxicated and disorderly conduct.

4. Drugs—Possession and sale of drugs. and related conspiracies, as well as failing or refusing to submit to department drug tests.
5. On-duty abuse—All offenses by on-duty officers involving use of excessive force, psychological abuse, or discrimination based on citizens' membership in a class (e.g., gender, race, ethnicity, sexual preference).
6. Obstruction of justice—Conspiracy, perjury, official misconduct, and all offenses in which the apparent goal is the obstruction or subversion of judicial proceedings.
7. Administrative failure to perform—Failure to abide by departmental regulations concerning attendance, performance, obedience, reporting, and other conduct not included in other offense types
8. Conduct-related probationary failures—All misconduct-related terminations of probationary officers in which misconduct in types 1–7 is not specified, and excluding simple failure in training programs.

Rank Order of Dismissals	Charge Percent	Number
Administrative/failure to perform	20.1	742
Drugs	19.0	468
Profit-motivated crime	15.7	387
Off-duty crime against person	11.6	286
Obstruction of justice	10.8	266
Off-duty public order crime	5-8	144
On-duty abuse	4.8	119
Conduct on probation	2.2	53
Total	100.0	2,466
Source: Kane and White, 2013.		

FIRST NATIONAL STUDY OF AMERICAN POLICE CRIME

An academic, who was a former police officer, and his colleagues examined nonfederal police crime reported in newspapers through a Google and Google Alert search over a thirty-six-month period—January 2005 through December 2007 (Stinson, Liederbach, Buerger, and Brewer, 2016). Their search identified 6,724 criminal cases, involving the arrest of 5,543 sworn police officers. These nonfederal state and local officers were in 1,205 counties and independent cities in all fifty states and the District of Columbia. The police crimes were divided into five key types: 1) sex-related police crime; 2) alcohol-related police crime; 3) drug-related police crime; 4) violence-related police crime; and 5) profit-motivated police crime (see Table 8.1 and Table 8.2). These are not mutually exclusive categories. Stinson and his colleagues, in the first national study of police crime,

Table 8.1.   Arrests Recorded

Police Crime	Number of Arrest Cases	Number of Officers
Violence-related	3,328	2,586
Profit-motivated	1,592	1,396
Sex-related	1,475	1,070
Alcohol-related	1,405	1,238
Drug-related	739	665

Source: Stinson et al., 2016, p. 22.

provided a broad definition of police crime that includes police crimes that cause intentional harm and are profit-motivated (see Table 8.1).

We discussed sex-related police crimes in a previous chapter. We discussed police corruption in Chapter 7 and finished the discussion with direct criminal activities as the last pattern of police corruption. Therefore, we will expand the discussion of profit-motivated police crime and save law enforcement–caused homicides for a later chapter.

PROFIT-MOTIVATED POLICE CRIMES

Stinson and his colleagues concluded that, contrary to popular rhetoric and long-standing scholarship, profit-motivated police crime is common in American police agencies, large and small. Profit-motivated misconduct is easy to recognize since there are no legal circumstances where officers can receive a material reward except from their paycheck. In the Kane and White NYPD study (2013), bribe taking was the single most common dismissal charge, followed by grand larceny—felony-level stealing—insurance fraud, burglary, petit larceny, and receiving property. Moneymaking police crime is not exclusively a big city problem. Barker found that out in his late 1970s studies in small southern cities (Barker, 1977). Data from the existing research and public information suggest that there are a "substantial" number of criminal cops taking advantage of the occupation's opportunities for individual and group crime. However, it is seldom mentioned that some federal law-enforcement officers are also criminal cops. An illustrative, not exhaustive, list of police liars, thieves, and gangsters from Barker's files of local and federal lawbreakers for 2019 includes local law-enforcement officer drug trafficking—ten incidents. Four incidents involved local police agencies—Philadelphia, McAllen (Texas), Detroit, and Miami; and six incidents involved federal agencies: the US Customs and Border Protection (CBP) agency (four), the US Drug Enforcement Agency (one), the TSA (one), and the Department of Health and Human Services (one). The list included three incidents in which federal law-enforcement officers were lying. In addition,

Table 8.2.   Most Serious Charges in Each Category of Police Crime in 2016

Police Crime		Number of Charges	Percentage (%)
Sex-Related	Forcible Fondling	352	23.9
	Forcible Rape	322	21.8
	Statutory Rape	100	6.8
	Unclassified Sex Crime	98	6.6
	Forcible Sodomy	95	6.4
	Pornography	86	5.8
Alcohol-Related	Driving Under the Influence	817	58.1
	Simple Assault	149	10.6
	Aggravated Assault	103	7.3
	Weapons Violation	47	3.3
Drug-Related	Drug/Narcotics Violations	308	41.7
	Robbery	60	8.1
	Driving Under the Influence	38	5.1
	All Other Larceny	33	4.5
	Theft from a Building	28	3.8
	Burglary—Breaking and Entry	26	3.5
Violence-Related	Simple Assault	870	26.4
	Aggravated Assault	570	17.1
	Forcible Fondling	352	10.6
	Forcible Rape	322	9.7
	Intimidation	200	6.0
	Murder/Nonnegligent Manslaughter	99	3.0
	Negligent Manslaughter	43	1.3
Profit-Motivated	Unclassified Theft/Larceny	255	16
	False pretenses/Swindle	199	12.5
	Drug/Narcotics Violation	189	11.9
	Robbery	103	6.4
	Theft From Building	92	5.8
	Extortion/Blackmail	85	5.3
	Embezzlement	77	4.8
	Burglary/Breaking and Entry	72	4.5
	Bribery	56	3.5
	All other offenses	49	3.1

Source: Stinson et al., 2016.

the list included three incidents in which a detention officer was smuggling contraband into a jail or corrections facility. Under the category of individual federal criminal behavior, there were two incidents of armed robbery; two incidents of espionage (involving the Central Intelligence Agency and the Defense Intelligence Agency; three FBI agents have been convicted of espionage); and one incident of conversion of government property. One study reports that, from 2006 to 2014, thirty CBP applicants admitted during polygraph tests that they had been sent by Mexican cartels to join the CBP (Jancsics, 2019).

DRUG-RELATED POLICE CRIME

Police drug-related crime differs from the other forms of police corruption subsumed under the pattern of protection of illegal activities, such as the vice crimes of gambling, prostitution, and others. Police drug-related crime includes individual armed criminal police officers committing direct criminal activities—engaging in robberies and drug dealing, escorting drug dealers in marked cars, and engaging in elaborate payoff conspiracies protected by groups of police officers or drug units (see Textbox 8.4).

Textbox 8.4. Police Drug-Dealing Examples

Robbery and Extortion
Chicago 1996—Seven officers of the tactical unit of the fifteenth district were indicted in December 1996 on federal charges for allegedly using their positions, skill, and experiences to rob and extort money and narcotics for drug dealers on Chicago's west side.

Protecting Drug Traffickers and Murder
New Orleans 1994—For six months, New Orleans police officers protected a cocaine supply warehouse containing 286 pounds of cocaine. As a result of an FBI undercover investigation, eleven officers, who were paid nearly $100,000 by undercover agents, were convicted. The undercover part of the investigation was terminated when a witness was killed under orders of a New Orleans police officer.

Facilitating Drug Trafficking
Savannah, Georgia, 1994—As a result of an undercover operation, ten officers were convicted for protecting drug dealers. Officers took guns and drugs from drug dealers on the street and sold them to undercover agents portraying drug dealers.

Washington, DC, 1994—As a result of an undercover operation, twelve officers were arrested and convicted for protecting an undercover agent portraying a drug dealer who was transporting hundreds of kilos of cocaine into Washington, DC.

Source: General Accounting Office. Law Enforcement: Information on Drug-Related Police Corruption. GAO/GGD=98-11. May 1998.

Stinson and his colleagues' (2013) study of 221 police drug-related arrests found that 48.9 percent of the cases—n = 195—involved on-duty police officers involved in drug trafficking—selling or dealing drugs or both. This behavior is "direct criminal activities" by criminal cops. The second most common police drug-related crimes were the shakedown and theft of drugs from a dealer during car stops. The last police drug pattern was facilitation: protecting, assisting, or hindering the prosecution of drug dealers. This included selling or providing information to the dealers about investigations or arrests. The 1994 Mollen commission, a 1998 General Accounting Office report, and a 1997 Chicago report on police crime found that police drug-related crime was systematic group crime by police officers actively committing crimes, not passively ignoring crimes or protecting criminals (Stana and Roleff, 2003).

Other Examples of Drug-Related Police Corruption

- In 2011, a former Fulton County, Georgia, sheriff's deputy was sentenced to six years in prison for corruption relating to drugs. On at least two occasions, he protected drug dealers while he was on duty, in uniform, and in a marked police vehicle. He received a payoff of $2,000 each time.
- Three Jackson, Mississippi, police officers were sentenced to ten years in federal prison in 2013 for agreeing to provide armed protection to a shipment of cocaine coming into the city. The officers were to be paid $10,000. There was a problem with the payoff arrangement. The supposed "drug dealers" were undercover FBI agents.
- The same year, a deputy sheriff in the Pierce County, Georgia, police department pleaded guilty to providing "security" for protecting methamphetamine trafficking. The sheriff learned that the deputy was providing security while on duty, in uniform, and in a marked police vehicle. He alerted federal authorities. They set up a sting with undercover agents and caught the deputy in the act.
- A BTTB female officer with the Baltimore, Maryland, police department was engaging in two patterns of corruption—protection of illegal activities and misuse of official information—at the time of her arrest and conviction for extortion and aggravated identity theft. She was charged with helping a heroin dealer by providing armed, uniform security for drug transactions, giving

advance information of search warrants, and using police databases to check for informants. At the same time, she committed aggravated identify theft by providing police database information to a tax preparer to be used to obtain fraudulent tax returns. She pleaded guilty and was sentenced to five years in prison (DOJ, February 6, 2014).

Individual police officers of all ranks provide protection and information to drug traffickers for money or the equivalent. A 2014 decision from the US Court of Appeals for the Third Circuit provides an example of protection payoffs for drug dealers.

United States of America v. Donald Abraham Solomon. Donald Solomon was the chief of police for the small borough of East Washington, Pennsylvania. He often bragged that he was the "best cop money can buy" (Mayo, June 14, 2013). The borough is only 0.45 square miles and is surrounded on three sides by the city of Washington. The city of Washington is 3-1/3 square miles, with a population of 13,663.

Federal authorities learned from an anonymous tip that Chief Solomon was involved in criminal activities related to drug trafficking and decided to conduct an undercover operation "to probe Solomon's criminal tendencies." On June 30, 2011, and July 1, 2011, a confidential informant met with Solomon and asked him to provide security services for a third party. Solomon agreed to run a criminal records check on the third party and asked the informant if the third party wanted him to provide security protection. The informant told Solomon that was the idea and that he would be paid at least "a grand" for the security work. Chief Solomon replied, "Tell him [the third party] I'm the best cop money can buy." On July 8, 2011, Solomon and the informant met to discuss the chief providing security for a four-kilogram cocaine deal. Each of them was to be paid $500 per kilogram. On July 27, Solomon and the informant met with the third party, identified as Joseph. Joseph was an FBI agent posing as a drug dealer.

Solomon agreed to provide protection for the multikilogram cocaine deal. The chief would wear his uniform and sit in his marked police vehicle while the drug transaction took place. On August 17, 2011, the informant gave Solomon $1,000 as a "good faith" payment for the pending drug deal. The staged drug deal occurred on August 31, 2011. Solomon sat in his marked police vehicle as the drug deal happened in a church parking lot. Joseph paid Solomon $1,500, and he agreed to provide security for future shipments. Joseph and Solomon exchanged phone numbers.

On September 11, 2011, Solomon agreed to provide security for a ten-kilogram cocaine shipment on September 26. On September 26, the staged drug deal occurred, and Solomon was paid $5,000. On October 26, 2011, Solomon was indicted and arrested. On January 4, 2013, Solomon pleaded guilty and received an eleven-year sentence that was later reduced to seven years and three months.

- A female El Paso, Texas, police officer was sentenced to two years in prison for helping her stepfather distribute cocaine out of his house (Moreno, January 25, 2023). She aided her stepfather by running counterintelligence and running license plates to identify undercover officers. She pleaded guilty to four counts of drug trafficking.
- On January 25, 2023, the chief of police of the Greensburg, Pennsylvania, police department was arrested and charged with six federal criminal counts (DOJ, January 25, 2023):
  1. Aiding and abetting the distribution of cocaine—November 2021
  2. Aiding and abetting the distribution of cocaine—February 2022
  3. Aiding and abetting the distribution of methamphetamine—January 2022 through February 2022
  4. Aiding and abetting the distribution of methamphetamine—May 2022
  5. Aiding and abetting the distribution of methamphetamine—July 2022
  6. Conspiracy to possess with the intent to distribute and distribute methamphetamine and cocaine—from June 2021 to October 2022

INTERNATIONAL POLICE DRUG PAYOFFS

The international Mexican drug-trafficking cartels are known to affect American police corruption. A recent US federal conviction of Genaro Garcia Luna, the *former* secretary of *Public Security* in Mexico—the equivalent of the director of the in the United States—serves to show how police corruption in our southern neighbor affects the United States (Sanchez and Santana, February 21, 2023). Luna, who lives in luxury from an ill-gotten fortune, moved to Miami in 2012 and applied for naturalization in 2018 and lied about his past criminal acts. He was convicted of engaging in a criminal enterprise with the Sinaloa drug cartel. Specifically, his corrupt acts included having Mexican police agents act as bodyguards and escorts for drug traffickers and attack rival drug traffickers. He and his agents alerted Sinaloa members of raids and supplied them with public security uniforms, credentials, and vehicles. He faces a mandatory minimum sentence of twenty years in prison and a maximum of life imprisonment.

Kent, England, Police Study, 1998 to 2001. Caless, a British police scholar examined 122 police-corruption cases from the Kent, England, police service and found some interesting findings that contrast with what is known about American police corruption and that demonstrate that corruption may vary by work setting and opportunity. First, the 122 officers were divided into ranks (see Table 8.3).

The reported rank orders were surprising, especially in that among the criminal officers were more detectives than "on the street" working constables. Forty-one (37 percent) of the alleged criminal cops, including five senior police

Table 8.3.   Kent, England, Criminal Cops

Type of Criminal Cop	Number of Cops
Police Constables	31
Detective Constables	50
Police Sergeants	3
Detective Sergeants	16
Detective Inspectors	17
Detective Chief Inspector	3
Chief Superintendent	1
Detective Chief Superintendent	1

officers, were supervisors. The nature of the alleged criminal acts is interesting. The traditional American categories of police corruption, such as shakedowns, opportunistic thefts, and kickbacks, incidents of which occur in police–citizen contacts, were absent or in the minority. The crimes of the officers were weighted heavily toward contacts or collusion with criminals (see textbox 8.5).

Textbox 8.5. Alleged Criminal Behavior

- Twenty-seven officers alleged to have formed a relationship with criminals
- Twenty-one passed confidential information to criminals
- Twenty-one perverted the course of justice
- Thirty-one were implicated in thefts
- One was involved in blackmail
- Three were involve in forgery
- Eight were involved in drug dealing or selling seized drugs
- Four were involved in violence or threats of violence

The last findings are more in line with what Americans would expect from police occupational deviance. The findings substantiate the ubiquitous nature of police crime and police criminals. A finding of note was that the highest incidence of criminal activity occurred in officers with sixteen to twenty-five years of service. This suggests, as is often said, that police officers become corrupt and criminal after long exposure to opportunities and peer-group support for misconduct or criminality. Only a few join as criminals. Yet, the first knee-jerk reform effort is to improve vetting and hiring practices to weed out the "bad apples," without paying proper attention to the organization and culture that is making "bad apples." Caless speculated that, as officers mature, they may be subject to less supervision and their association with criminals goes unnoticed. That is certainly a factor that should be examined.

Another factor that this research made clear is that there is a real need for restricting confidential information on criminals to a strict "need to know" basis. Too many officer knew too much about the inner workings of criminals and criminal organizations. A later chapter returns to that issue along with the issue of tenure in assignment.

Conclusion

Criminal cops are historical examples of those who engage in American police occupational/workplace deviant behaviors. Prohibition introduced organized crime into America, and it spread to systematic police corruption, as exemplified by what was found by the Knapp commission. Following the Knapp commission, groups of criminal cops emerged, resulting in law-enforcement officers intentionally engaging in serious criminal behavior, ranging from theft to criminal homicides. These police officers are predators looking for and responding to available opportunities; they are not officers who occasionally yield to the temptations. American criminal cops who cause serious harm or engage in direct criminal activities for profit act variously as individuals, groups, and agencies, depending on their organization's nature. These categories are interrelated and can exist in any police department singularly or together in the same department—a rare but possible phenomenon.

This chapter should not leave the impression that all that is needed to produce criminal cops is the presence of officers with the predisposition to commit corruption and crime and their intersection with the inherent opportunities of the police occupation. It must be stressed that there are other factors at work within any workplace setting, factors that affect the nature and extent of occupational workplace deviance. Among those factors are, or could be, limited tenure in corruption-prone assignments, obtrusive supervision, regular integrity audits, and other countermeasures. Later chapters explain how the risk and countermeasures can balance the opportunity and predisposition or inclination. The next chapter addresses police crime and the influence of BTTB cops, also known as criminals with badges, and examines their individual and group behavior.

Discussion Questions

1. Are there other police occupational crimes that have been created by new technologies? What about crimes in other occupations? A hint—the medical-care occupations.
2. Why would a law-enforcement officer not intervene when he or she sees another officer commit a crime? Does an officer have a duty to do so?
3. Why are whistleblowers so dangerous to police executives?

CHAPTER 9

"Bad to the Bone" Killer Cops and Criminal Cop Drug Dealers

Key Terms:
> Criminal cops
> Bad to the bone cops (BTTB)
> Killer cops
> Serial sex-motivated killer cops
> Rape plus murder killer cops
> Law enforcement–caused homicides
> Crack epidemic
> Drug-related crimes by cops

Chapter Objectives:
> After reading this chapter, the reader should be able to do the following:

1. Identify the major challenges to American policing in the twenty-first century
2. Explain the historical development of law enforcement–caused homicides
3. Explain the relationship between the crack epidemic and criminal cops

Police officers using their official position for personal gain or self-fulfillment is one of the world's oldest deviant police practices (Bayley and Perito, 2011). That self-fulfillment includes engaging in illicit sex and abuse of authority. Bayley and Perito opine that a broad definition of police corruption includes perjury, physical abuse of prisoners, sexual misconduct, and racial profiling. In other words, any police deviant conduct for personal reasons, not for public benefit. This book uses narrower definitions of police deviant behavior that confine police *corruption* to behavior seeking personal material gain, that confine police *misconduct* to patterns of behavior usually handled in an administrative trial process, and that confine serious police *criminal* behavior to behavior that is subject to criminal prosecution (see Cubitt, Gaub, and Holtfreter, July 28, 2022). Roebuck and Barker (1974) and, later, Punch (2000) opined that there were three categories of police deviance: misconduct, corruption, and crime. Police crime could include murder, drug dealing, robberies, and burglaries. Police crime in the form of murder and drug dealing extended the nature of criminal police deviance from the rare individual behavior, done by so-called "rotten apples," into group deviance occurring in the workplace. The systematic nature of group police criminal behavior meant that neophyte officers had to be initiated into the nature and techniques of police crime, the rationalizations, the group's definitions of what would be supported and what would be condemned, and the risk posed (of discipline or other sanctions). This was police occupational/workplace deviance. This police deviance was not confined to the United States or to English-speaking police organizations.

Barker and Punch were among the first scholars to explain that police criminal behavior is not confined to developing, autocratic, or non-English forms of government. Police crime is, in most instances, an occupational phenomenon. Wherever criminal cops exist, they make a mockery of the rule of law and destroy the trust that the public has in the existence of procedural law, which is intended to provide equal and fair treatment for all. Bayley and Perito (2011) caution that eliminating police corruption in all its forms, using a broad or narrow definition, "is required for *any country* that has establishing the rule of law as a national objective" (italics added). Citizens of the United States, like citizens of all other democratic societies, believe that the "rule of law" is a national objective. The existence of individual criminal cops and groups of criminal cops belies our national objective of the rule of law.

Criminal Cops: A Historical Fact

Criminal cops are a historical fact in democratic societies where publicly paid citizens act as society's primary means of social control (Punch, 2000; Barker, 2011). The predominate "varieties'" of police crime, such as accepting bribes, procedural abuses that pervert the course of justice, and the excessive use of force, appear to some extent in all democratic societies (Waddington, 1999). There have been police-crime scandals in the United States, France, Spain, Britain, Belgium, Germany, Australia, and the Netherlands (Punch, 2000). Criminal cops are the unintended consequences of creating a policing occupation. The power of the position and the inherent opportunities for misuse of that power makes it an inevitable conclusion that some will use their authority for personal gain or, intentionally, accidently, or with malice, not adhere to the rules or ethical standards of the police occupation. The worst of these violators are "killer cops" and cops who commit drug-related crimes. These two categories of cops stand outside the usual or common definitions of criminal cops or "rotten apples" or "rogue cops." They are often outside the supposed "blue brotherhood" or the police peer group, even in a corrupt and deviant police agency. For that reason, they are defined as "bad to the bone" (BTTB) cops. They stand out as deviant cops even among other corrupt and criminal cops. They are rare, and their existence is denied by most police professionals. However, they exist in the dark side of policing and must be acknowledged and dealt with. One of the worst killer cops I ever met was a state trooper who killed his fiancée, also a cop I knew, for the insurance money (see Barker, 2020b). I taught him when he was a local police officer in the regional police academy. I recall that you could look in his eyes and see that nobody was home. The obvious questions at that time were and now are *How could this happen? Were there any clues to his eventual deviance? Was he an aberration in police work?*

The short and quick answers to these questions are disturbing. The American fragmented policing system, without national standards and oversight, "encourages" and "facilitates" police occupational/workplace deviance, and that includes the development of killer cops and cops who commit drug-related crimes—"BTTB cops." External oversight of police agencies, with an emphasis on accountability and integrity, is the most obvious check on police behavior and power. In the United States, with an estimated eighteen thousand local agencies, that has proven to be a nightmare control suggestion.

National and International Police Occupational Problems

KILLER COPS ARE AN AMERICAN NATIONAL POLICE OCCUPATIONAL PROBLEM

The latest example is five former members of the Street Crimes Operation to Restore Peace in Our Neighborhoods unit of the Memphis Police Department being charged with second-degree murder and federal civil-rights violations for the beating death of Tyre Nichols (Associated Press, September 12, 2023). One accused officer has already pleaded guilty and appears to be ready to testify against the others. Killer cops are also an international police occupational problem. In the United Kingdom, a police murder and rape of a kidnapped woman and two recent murders of black men by white officers are igniting riots and social protests (Stickings, September 12, 2023).

KILLER COPS: LAW ENFORCEMENT–CAUSED HOMICIDES

The 2014 police slaying of Michael Brown in Ferguson, Missouri, and the subsequent mishandling of his body raised police-caused homicides to a national social issue with possible racial implications. The resultant riots and disturbances fueled the debate as social activists demanded justice and a reexamination of police violence against the citizens they serve. The brutal death of Tyree Nichols in Memphis, Tennessee, in 2023, by black officers signaled that police murders may be more of a workplace problem than a racial problem. Killer cops are historical examples of officers who engage in American police occupational/workplace deviant behaviors that have affected diverse groups defined as members of the dangerous classes by the social and political elites.

Police Violence against the Dangerous Classes

The United States has a sordid history of police-caused homicides—murder and manslaughter—going back to the slave patrols in the southern states before the Civil War (Barker, 2020b). This violence against its own citizens affected the entire American republic and was more centered on social status and the absence of political power than race. In the North, police killed white civilians in the 1834 Anti-Abolition Riots, the 1849 Astor Place Riots (New York City), and the 1863 New York City Draft Riots (Barker, 2020b). The brutal NYPD police killed over sixty people, including women and children, in the Orange Riots, 1870–1871. During what is known as the Great Strike of 1871, American police officers in Chicago and Pittsburgh fired into crowds of peaceful protestors until they ran out of ammunition. In 1877, in what is known as the Lattimer Massacre, Lattimer, Pennsylvania, police officers killed nineteen immigrants from southern and eastern Europe (Barker, 2020b). During the 1909 Presses Car Street Strike, officers with the Pennsylvania State Police killed an estimated eleven to twenty-six strikers and a deputy sheriff. The 1937 Memorial Day Massacre in Chicago resulted in an out-of-control group of Chicago police officers killing at least ten demonstrators after firing point-blank into the crowd. This violence against certain vulnerable groups without political or economic power continued into the 1960s.

1960s Police Violence against Social Activists. There is no accurate account of how many blacks and white social activists were killed by police officers during the 1960s civil-rights struggle. I was a member of the search party looking for the remains of the slain white and black civil-rights protestors in Mississippi in 1964 and was a southern police officer in the late 1960s. I was "on the job," but not in Selma, Alabama, when the Bloody Sunday March in Selma (on May 7, 1965) occurred. The violent response resulted from the murder of a black Vietnam veteran by an Alabama state trooper. The trooper pleaded guilty to manslaughter decades later, in 2007 (Barker, 2020b). Other racial and ethnic groups have experienced American killer cops.

American Police Violence against other Defined Dangerous Groups

Texas Rangers v. Mexican Americans. Today's highly respected and professional Texas Rangers have a vile past when it comes to law enforcement–caused homicides against Mexican Americans. In 1918, a company of Texas Rangers rode into Provenir, Texas, looking for Mexican bandits. The Rangers tied up all the men and boys, removed them from the village, and shot them. Later it was confirmed that those killed were innocent farmers, not bandits. No one was ever prosecuted for these murders (Barker, 2020b). The estimates of native Mexicans and Mexican Americans killed by the pre-1915 Texas Rangers ranges from several hundred to five thousand (Barker, 2020b). The tradition of American law-enforcement officers killing citizens under questionable circumstances continues.

Killer Cops in the Twentieth Century

Some BTTB police killer cops have the usual motives of revenge, hatred, and profit. In the 1980s, two NYPD detectives known as the "Mafia cops" murdered at least nine people for Mafia crime families (Barker, 2020b). In 1989, an FBI special agent strangled to death a female informant who was pregnant with his child to keep the affair secret. He claimed that the strangling was accidental and occurred in a heat of passion (Barker, 2020b). The evidence suggests otherwise. In 1991, a BTTB LAPD police officer, William Leasure, one of several LAPD officers declared as the most corrupt officers in LAPD history, was sent to prison (Barker, 2020b). He received two fifteen-year-to-life sentences for crimes ranging from running a multimillion-dollar yacht-theft ring to participating in three contract murders. The most bizarre account of a stone-cold killer cop involves a female officer whose case reads like fiction. A female LAPD detective killed the wife of an ex-lover and kept it a secret from 1986 to 2009 (see textbox 9.1).

Textbox 9.1. Killer Cop: LAPD Detective Stephanie Lazarus

On February 24, 1986, Sherri Rasmussen, a bride of three months, was found brutally murdered. Autopsy results revealed Sherrie was shot three times in the chest; each shot was a fatal wound. She was supposed to be at work but called in for a sick day that morning (Barker, 2020b). The forensic evidence, except for the DNA swab and blood evidence, was put in the secure LAPD evidence locker and forgotten. No suspects were identified, and no arrests were made. The case went cold.

The official murder theory of a surprised burglar was unquestioned by the authorities, even though the murdered woman's family vigorously objected for twenty-three years to the original findings and suggested a "likely suspect" for the murder—an unnamed jilted LAPD female police officer, who had been stalking and harassing Sherri. Members of the police department all the way up to the chief of police met the murdered girl's family's repeated requests for a complete investigation with scorn and indifference. Thus began allegations of a police cover-up. No member of the LAPD was going to recognize that a female LAPD officer was the possible murderer. In 2004, when cold-case homicide detectives were routinely examining unsolved murders and surreptitiously reexamined the Rasmussen case, the shit hit the fan.

The evidence gathered at the Rasmussen crime scene was gone. The forensic evidence taken at the original crime scene—hair, fiber, and blood samples—mysteriously disappeared in 1996. According to official records, an LAPD detective, giving a bogus name, appeared at the property room and checked out all the forensic evidence for the Rasmussen case and never returned it (Barker, 2020b). However, one piece of evidence was still available. A deep bite, almost to the bone, on Sherrie Rasmussen's arm had left a DNA sample. The DNA evidence was safe because it was stored in the coroner's freezer, not the evidence locker, all those years. The DNA testing discredited the original theory.

Then the detectives discovered an entry in the "murder book" that read, "Verified S. Lazarus is the former girlfriend. P.O." Did it mean police officer? They checked the files of LAPD officers and found one match: Stephanie Lazarus, Detective II assigned to the Commercial Crimes Division, Art Theft Detail. She had worked in the office right across the hall from Officer Rasmussen. Lazarus was arrested.

She remained in jail for two and one-half years before her trial began on February 6, 2012. The evidence from fifty-one state witnesses piled up, revealing a cold calculated murder done by a jealous and jilted lover who carried a badge. The final witness, an FBI profiler, testified that someone with police experience had staged the burglary scene, and that someone was Stephanie Lazarus. The trial ended that day, the twenty-fifth anniversary of the death of Sherrie Rae Rasmussen. After a day of deliberation, the jury found Lazarus guilty of second-degree murder.

LAPD Chief of Police Charley Beck issued a written statement, expressing the sense of betrayal the department felt with the murderer being one of their own. He apologized for the long time achieving justice took. On May 11, 2012, Lazarus was sentenced to twenty-five years to life, plus another two years for the firearms enhancement. This killer cop will die in prison.

There are two former New Orleans Police Department officers sitting on death row—a man and a woman, both black officers. The man, Len Davis, is on death row for arranging the murder of a woman who filed a brutality complaint against him. The murder was a direct result of Davis's ties to organized crime. Davis operated a police drug-trafficking protection ring, and he feared the murder victim would expose his crimes (Barker, 2011).

In 1995, the woman on death row, a New Orleans Police Department officer, Antionette Franks, walked into a Vietnamese restaurant with her eighteen-year-old gangbanging lover and murdered three people, including an off-duty officer working security. After these murders, the body of her father was found in a small grave under her house, but she was not prosecuted for this murder because she was already on death row. Franks had serious mental issues that she did not divulge in her application. During the vetting process, Franks failed two personality evaluations. The examining psychologist rated her as "not recommended for hiring" (Barker, 2020b). He said she was not suitable for police work. That decision was overruled because of pressure to hire a black female. In the 1990s, the understaffed New Orleans Police Department was under pressure to hire more minorities.

Twenty-first Century Killer Cops

In 2011, a Washington, DC, police officer was sentenced to fifteen years in prison for a 2009 murder that occurred during his involvement in an attempted robbery of a drug dealer (Barker, 2020b). In 2021, an on-duty Memphis Police Department officer allegedly killed his girlfriend's current lover (Kennin, June 9, 2023). According to the newspaper account, the officer admitted to kidnapping the man and killing him in the backseat of his police vehicle. He then drove to a secure location and hid the body. The former officer is out on bond awaiting trial.

Retired Briarcliff Manor, New York, police officer Nicholas Tartaglione is without a doubt an example of a BTTB police officer. He retired from the police department in 2008 and supplemented his income by selling cars and trafficking in drugs (Lieberman and Bandler, April 6, 2023). In 2023, the muscle-bound retired cop, who was Jeffrey Epstein's cellmate for a brief period in 2016, was convicted of four murders over a drug debt. Tartaglione was a brutal and violent man during his whole police career (Schwartz, 2023). He should never have been hired or allowed to wear a badge.

Law Enforcement Officers Kill Their Own. Sidney Dorsey was a respected former law-enforcement officer in Atlanta, Georgia, and the first black man to be elected as sheriff of DeKalb County, Georgia, when he entered a murder conspiracy to kill another black man, Derwin Brown, who had just defeated him in his reelection bid. Brown had run a successful election campaign on the promise to eradicate the well-known corruption occurring in the sheriff's office (Associated Press, June 18, 2002; Dziemianowicz, March 24, 2023; and Wikipedia, accessed August 6, 2023). In a dramatic runoff, Brown was elected, and he made known whom he was going to fire. Sheriff Dorsey met with four sheriff's department employes and plotted Brown's assassination in the hope that a special election would be called, and Dorsey would be reelected.

On December 15, 2000, three days before he was to take office, Brown was shot eleven times in his driveway and died in the hospital. The main shooter was later identified as a deputy who had been discovered filing false overtime reports for extra pay. He eventually was granted immunity and flipped on Sheriff Dorsey. Dorsey was tried and convicted in 2002. He received life without parole for the conspiracy to commit murder. Twenty-two years were added to his sentence for racketeering and violation of oath of office. Dorsey admitted his part in the murder conspiracy in 2007.

Selected Illustrative, not Exhaustive, Recent Examples of Law Enforcement–Caused Criminal Homicides—Murder and Manslaughter

Notorious homicides receiving large publicity, such as the cases of George Floyd and Tyree Nichols, have been omitted from the following examples:

- A white Eutawville, South Carolina, police chief was charged with murder for killing a black man who complained to him about a daughter's traffic ticket. The first trial ended in a hung jury. He was tried again with the same result—a hung jury. A third trial was avoided when the police chief pled guilty to misconduct in office and received a one-year home-detention sentence (CBS News, September 1, 2015).
- Reckless police pursuits are responsible for numerous police-caused homicides every year. A Garland, Texas, police officer was charged with manslaughter after firing forty-one times at the driver of a high-speed pursuit. The pursuit reached speeds over 100 miles per hour.
- The following homicide occurred after a pursuit ended. A Del City, Oklahoma, police captain was sentenced to four years in prison for manslaughter after fatally shooting an eighteen-year-old man after a short high-speed pursuit (Dinger, February 5, 2014). The police captain was under the influence of hydrocodone when he shot the teenager in the back as he ran away.
- Two Albuquerque, New Mexico, police officers were indicted for first-degree murder after shooting a homeless mentally disturbed man who was illegally camping in 2014 (Barker, 2020b).
- A white Norfolk, Virginia, police officer was indicted for voluntary manslaughter for shooting a mentally ill black man twice in the back. The man allegedly threatened him with a small knife (Barker, 2020b).
- A former Fairfax County, Virginia, officer pleaded guilty to involuntary manslaughter for a 2016 fatal shooting during a domestic disturbance call (Jackson, April 18, 2016). The officer was originally charged with murder.

- Two Wilson, Oklahoma, police officers were convicted of second-degree murder after they used a Taser on a naked man they found in a ditch. They answered a domestic disturbance call and found the man in the ditch, but they claimed he would not comply with their commands. The body was riddled with Taser probes, and the coroner said he died of multiple heart attacks because of the Taser use (Vigdor, November 8, 2021). Their use of the Taser violated all their training protocols.

- In an unusual police shooting case that was widely criticized for the sentence, a San Diego deputy sheriff, who had been on the job for eighteen months, was sentenced to three years' probation and one year in jail for shooting a mentally ill man in the back multiple times as he ran away (CBS 6 Staff, February 7, 2022). He was originally charged with second-degree murder. The charge was reduced to voluntary manslaughter. The judge cited the defendant's young age—twenty-three at the time of the shooting—his lack of police experience, and his lack of a prior record as the reasons for the charge reduction and light sentence. The victim's family responded by saying it shows that a law-enforcement officer can shoot someone in the back and only get a year in jail.

- In a case that received national attention, a white female Brooklyn Center, Minnesota, police officer was found guilty of first- and second-degree manslaughter for the fatal shooting of a black man during a traffic stop (Halter, December 23, 2021). The officer claimed she mistakenly drew her pistol instead of her Taser.

- Three Sharon Hill, Pennsylvania, police officers negotiated a plea to reckless endangerment in exchange for having manslaughter charges dropped (Associated Press, November 11, 2022). The three police officers, while working security at a high-school football game, fired into a crowd after hearing gunfire. One of their shots hit and killed an eight-year-old girl from a family who had immigrated from Liberia to escape the violence. The deputy district attorney said they had engaged in "a horrible amount of recklessness," even if it was unintentional (Nation, May 6, 2023). The officers were placed on five years' probation—the first eleven months of it on house arrest.

- A Nelsonville, Ohio, police officer and a Hocking College police officer answered a domestic disturbance call. The suspect got in his car and tried to leave the scene, causing the city officer to try to break the window. The college officer fired multiple shots into the car although he was told that the suspect's four-year-old son was in the car. The suspect was killed, and the city officer was injured. The campus officer negotiated a misdemeanor plea of negligent manslaughter, punishable by up to six months in jail, and agreed to permanently surrender his Ohio Peace Officer training certificate (Forster, March 31, 2022). He can never become an Ohio police officer again.

- The most recent murder by a police officer occurred in a mass-murder incident in a biker bar in Trabuco Canyon, California, on August 24, 2023.

As already said, police officer is a master social status that forever identifies the holder of that social position. The mass murderer was John Snowling, a retired sergeant from the Ventura Police Department in California. Snowling retired from the police department in 2014. He and his wife filed for divorce in 2022. On the day of the shootings, Snowling entered the bar and shot and wounded his wife and the person she was sitting with. He killed two other patrons in the bar and fired on the responding police who killed him (Staff, August 24, 2023).

COPS WHO COMMIT DRUG-RELATED CRIMES

In the 1960s and 1970s, there appeared to be a distinction between "clean" and "dirty" criminal cops, a distinction pertaining to police misconduct for profit motives. Clean corrupt acts involved payoffs and shakedowns from gamblers, liquor violators, and prostitutes. In other words, police corruption related to moral policing against sin was acceptable within limits. The burgeoning drug market was off limits. That was "dirty" money, like stealing from the church. Supposedly, even the Mafia considered drug trafficking a no-no. In the 1980s, that changed. The change began with what is known as the 1980s crack epidemic. According to one police expert of the time, the opportunities for and the nature of police corruption and crime shifted in the 1980s (Dombrink, 1988).

1980s Crack Epidemic

Prior to the 1980s, cocaine was the drug of the elites and those who could afford the expensive powdered form. Marijuana was the drug of choice for the poor and marginalized classes. That began to change in the 1970s and early 1980s with the crack cocaine epidemic (Barker, 2011; D. Turner, August 8, 2023). The form and nature of police corruption and crime changed with the manufacture and distribution of crack cocaine, or crack. Drug-related police corruption and crime became the second-most persistent challenge to twenty-first-century American policing.

Crack cocaine is the result of converting powdered cocaine into a smaller form that can be smoked. The name "crack" comes from the sound it makes while being smoked. Dissolving cocaine hydrochloride into water with baking soda produces solid masses of cocaine crystals that, when smoked, give an immediate euphoric effect that is highly addictive. The small crystals were cheaper to produce and therefore easily available and cheaper. It has been estimated that, from 1982 to 1985, the number of crack-addicted users increased by 1.6 million (D. Turner, August 8, 2023). Crack first appeared in Miami, which was flooded by immigrants from Cuba, through the Cuban Mariel boatlift, and from other

Caribbean countries. Crime increased in urban cities, such as Miami, New York, Philadelphia, and Chicago, and in rural areas as drug trafficking expanded throughout the United States. Some officers encountered the opportunity to make a year's salary in one shakedown of a drug trafficker. Police involvement in drug-related corruption, profits from which were once considered "dirty" money, increased exponentially. Officers were faced with more opportunities for corruption and crime, and many turned to criminal behavior. I recall police officers I had trained in the police academy or former students of mine being arrested for drug robberies, burglaries, and use. The change was made clear in the 1985 Miami police scandal.

The Strange Case of the Miami River Cops

In 1985, three incidents occurred, leading to what was at that time considered to be the worst police scandal in Miami history (Sechrist and Burns, 1992). The three events were as follows: First, in May 1985, police seized 850 pounds of cocaine hidden in a boat on the Miami River. The police department began an investigation when one of the smugglers said that there had been over one thousand pounds of cocaine on the boat. The implication was that the police had stolen the missing cocaine. The second event occurred on the night of July 13, when ten Miami police officers, some in uniform, raided a boat with 400 kilos of cocaine. The police threw the smugglers in the water and confiscated the drugs. Then, on July 28, 1985, eight Miami officers, some in uniform, boarded a boat with 350 kilos of cocaine. Six smugglers jumped off the boat, and three drowned. Police officers from the last incident tried to sell the stolen cocaine to a federal undercover agent. It became clear that many of the same officers were involved in all three drug-seizure incidents. The investigation revealed that there was a large police drug-dealing enterprise in the Miami Police Department. By the end of 1988, nineteen "river cops" involved in these three incidents were arrested and convicted. Three were convicted of murder, and six received sentences of thirty years or more. Six of the eight officers among the original eight river cops received an average of twenty-four years in prison.

The Back Story to the Miami Police Scandal. The police criminal enterprise began to come together in the early 1980s when Miami became awash with illegal drugs and an increase in drug dealing. Miami became known as the "illicit drug capital of the United States" (Dombrink, 1988). Homicides and robberies increased dramatically, and the city relaxed its police hiring standards due to affirmative-action suits to increase minority hiring. Many of those recruited had drug use in their background. The department was also having a supervision problem. Many of the experienced first-line supervisors—sergeants—had left or retired. The officers who eventually formed the criminal enterprise began their criminal careers by shaking down and robbing drug dealers and then selling drugs. The police would have informants reveal the location of million-dollar loads of cocaine, and they would steal it and sell it. The same phenomenon was occurring in other urban American cities in the 1980s, particularly New York City and Philadelphia.

In 1985, the largest complaints of police misconduct were drug-related, including police drug use and accepting protection payoffs from drug dealers (Dombrink, 1988). According to Dombrink, officers with less than five years on the job were responsible for 89 percent of the drug charges and 2 percent of the police complaints. Then a police scandal occurred in New York City, and the Mollen commission settled the controversy. The form and nature of American police corruption and crime had changed forever. American police in the twenty-first century faced new challenges and skepticism.

NYPD Criminal Cops: The Mollen Commission

Since its inception, the NYPD has experienced a twenty-year cycle of police corruption, scandal, reform, backslide, and then a new scandal (Baer and Armao, January 1995). In 1992, the previous NYPD police scandal had occurred in 1971 and resulted in the appointment of the Knapp commission. Following the twenty-year cycle, it was time for a new scandal and another commission. One was coming, but it was unlike past scandals, and it would change the form and nature of how police professionals, the academic community, and the public viewed police occupational/workplace deviant behavior and policing as a profession.

The signal event occurred in May 1992, when six NYPD officers from two precincts were arrested by nearby Suffolk County, New York, for engaging in drug dealing. The leader of the group of criminal cops, Michael Dowd, was no stranger to NYPD internal affairs. However, Dowd was not with his criminal crew when they were arrested. He was on duty at the time, so he was arrested at an NYPD precinct. At the time of his on-duty arrest, he was stoned from cocaine and drunk on vodka and had a bag of crack cocaine in his pocket. He, like most criminal cops, had a history of civilian complaints. In the previous six years, he had been the subject of fifteen unsubstantiated allegations.

Reeling from the embarrassment of another police jurisdiction arresting a group of NYPD criminal cops, the New York City mayor appointed the Mollen commission to investigate the nature and extent of police corruption in the NYPD. Its findings were stunning, even to many police-misconduct experts in the police occupation and academic community, including me. Or, maybe it would be more accurate to say that the findings confirmed what some had suspected. After all, in 1985, a corruption scandal in the seventy-seventh precinct foreshadowed what was coming.

Some NYPD officers in the seventy-third precinct, known as the "buddy boys," were engaged in a criminal enterprise of robbing drug dealers and selling the stolen drugs. This was considered an aberration, and, once again, the "rotten apples" bromide was raised. That was quickly dismissed. The Mollen commission revealed that the nature of police crime and corruption had changed.

The two-year commission investigation led to criminal charges against seven officers in Brooklyn's seventy-third precinct and fourteen officers in Manhattan's thirtieth precinct. There was substantial evidence of corruption and police crime in other precincts in Brooklyn, Manhattan, and Queens. There was substantial evidence that the distinction between "clean" and "dirty" money had disappeared. The commission found that police corruption and crime were primarily related to the drug trade. Police officers were users, partners with drug traffickers, and dealers themselves. The reforms put in place after the Knapp commission were in shambles.

The commission found that "The distinction between the criminal and the corrupt cop had disappeared. Corrupt cops no longer used their authority to exact payoffs; they actually engaged in criminal activity" (Baer and Armao, January 1995). Specifically, NYPD police officers were selling confidential information, escorting drug traffickers, and harassing rival drug dealers. Police officers were involved in direct criminal activities, such as robbing drug dealers and their customers, burglarizing drug dens and stash houses, stealing drugs and money, and selling confiscated drugs and guns. The cops were as bad as or worse than the criminals. In addition to individual cops "scoring" a shakedown, groups of criminal cops calling themselves "crews" searched out opportunities for larceny, theft, extortion, and robbery. These crews were "akin to street gangs: small, loyal, flexible, fast moving, and often hard hitting" (Baer and Armao, January 1995). The nature of police occupational/workplace deviant behavior had changed. That was evident in the main character of the Mollen investigation—NYPD Officer Michael Dowd.

Michael Dowd: Bad to the Bone Criminal Cop

Michael Dowd's story reads like bad fiction. He is the epitome of BTTB criminal cops. In fact, when asked by the Mollen commission whether he was a drug dealer or a cop, he answered "both" (Colins, May 16, 2015). He is one of those NYPD officers who earned the title of "NYPD's most corrupt cop." It appears that, in every twenty-year cycle, the NYPD identifies the "most corrupt cop in NYPD history." However, it appears that Michael Dowd may keep that title in perpetuity. He was truly a criminal with a badge. Even so, the commission was quick to point out Dowd was not an aberration or a "rotten apple" in an otherwise corruption-free police department. Although the majority of the NYPD officers were honest, they found that police corruption and crime related to drug crime existed in varying degrees in precincts throughout the city. It was a serious problem for the NYPD and other American police departments, and it still is.

Dowd's Backstory. Dowd graduated from the NYPD police academy in 1982 while the American crack epidemic was in full bloom. He was assigned to a precinct, and, during his first year, he accepted his first bribe (Margaritoff, December 1, 2021). He shook down a motorist for $200. That began his criminal career, which ended in 1992, when his police coconspirator "ratted" him out and wore a wire. As I have repeatedly said, police criminals are not unlike criminals in general. There is no honor or code of silence that exists once long prison sentences are mentioned. Dowd's coconspirator or accomplice, Ken Eurell, never spent a day in prison (Guzzo, September 6, 2016). Even though Eurell sold kilos of cocaine while in uniform and acted as security for drug dealers, he walked while Dowd went to prison.

Dowd was arrested in July 1992, based on information from his trusted accomplice, Ken Eurell, and was one of sixty-three NYPD officers indicted for crimes ranging from murder to drug-related offenses. He stood out from the rest because of his brazen acts of drug dealing and his lavish lifestyle (Margaritoff, December 1, 2021). He and Eurell worked for a cocaine trafficker for $8,000 per week. They also sold cocaine and robbed rival drug dealers. Dowd recruited other cops to work in his criminal "crew." In 1994, Dowd was convicted of racketeering and conspiracy to distribute narcotics. He was sentenced to twenty-six years and served twelve years and six months.

Philadelphia Police Department Criminal Cops in the Early 1980s

Police corruption and crime events in Philadelphia in the early to middle 1980s also signaled the changing nature of police as criminal actors. Thirty-one police officers were indicted for precinct-wide vice extortion rings, including narcotics offenses. Those indicted and convicted included a chief inspector, the deputy commissioner, four lieutenants, and a captain (Dombrink, 1988). The Philadelphia task force investigation of departmental corruption and the Citizens Crime Commission of Delaware Valley concluded that the "rotten apple" theory should be abandoned because it reinforces the silence and acts against systematic police reform. They suggested that there should be limited tenure in specialized vice and narcotics units and proactive instead of reactive probes of possible corruption (Dombrink, 1988). Almost predictably, police crime in Chicago became a scandal.

The 2007 Chicago Special Operations Section Scandal

As the crack epidemic expanded and crime increased, the "war on drugs" went into high gear, with the creation of task forces and elite special units being the police response to organized drug-trafficking enterprises. The unintended consequences of creating these specialized units are still being experienced. Witness the out-of-control behavior of the Street Crimes Operation to Restore Peace in

Our Neighborhoods unit of the Memphis Police Department and its members' fatal beating death of Tyre Nichols on January 7, 2023. Creating specialized corruption-prone units must be done with proper vetting and recruitment principles and increased supervision and accountability. If not, the unintended consequences can be disastrous. This is what happened with Chicago's Special Operations Section (SOS) unit.

Obviously, there were groups of American criminal cops operating as criminal enterprises in the nineteenth century before, during, and after Prohibition, but these police criminal groups were different. In 2013, a fifty-year study of Chicago police misconduct found three hundred Chicago cops had been convicted of serious crimes. One-third of the convictions involved illegal drug trafficking, weapons sales, and gang activity (Associated Press, January 30, 2023; see Textbox 9.2). The SOS unit was one of those cited.

Textbox 9.2. Chicago's Criminal Cops

1. The Marquette Ten was a group of criminal cops working in the city's Marquette District. They were paid by drug dealers to notify them of raids and beat up their rivals.
2. The Austin Seven was a group of criminal tactical-unit members in the 1990s who shook down drug dealers. The tactical-unit members from the Austin District also committed robberies and home invasions. The collateral damage from their crimes caused 120 narcotics cases to be dropped.
3. In 2001, police officer Joseph Miedzianowski, a candidate for the most corrupt Chicago cop in history, was the epitome of a BTTB cop. He was a member of the specialized Gang Crimes Unit. He was convicted of running a national interstate drug-trafficking enterprise between Miami and Chicago. He also fixed criminal cases and hid a man wanted for murder.
4. The BTTB cop Jerome Finnegan and his crew are discussed below.
5. In 2011, two BTTB cops were indicted and pleaded guilty to working with gang leaders to steal money and drugs during traffic stops and home invasions.
6. A Chicago police officer, Sergeant Mark Gibson, worked with drug traffickers to steal money and drugs from drug dealers.
7. In 2011, the Chicago Police Department was rocked by a scandal of epic proportions. The department's chief of detectives was arrested and pleaded guilty to helping run a nationwide gang of jewel thieves.

Source: Modified from CBS Chicago, January 17, 2013.

The setting for SOS, an elite drug and gang unit, was the "war on drugs" that resulted from the crack cocaine epidemic. The victims were powerless vulnerable minority and marginalized persons. They were the ones that the unit was supposed to protect. According to the FBI, the officer in charge of SOS, Jerome Finnigan, and his fellow unit members routinely engaged in unlawful searches and seizures and stole cash from the places searched (FBI, April 7, 2011). In a 2004 incident, Finnigan and his unit made an unlawful stop of a man, a suspected drug dealer, and took the keys to his residence. They searched his residence without a warrant and stole $450,000 in cash, which they split among themselves. In 2005, Finnegan and his main coconspirator, Officer Keith Huerra, and other unit members unlawfully searched a residence and recovered two firearms, twelve kilos of cocaine, twenty-five pounds of marijuana, and approximately $88,000 in cash. They only inventoried $1,800 of the cash and split the rest.

In 2006, Finnegan and six members of the SOS unit were arrested and charged with robbing the homes of innocent persons and drug dealers, and the unit was disbanded (Associated Press, January 30, 2023). As usually occurs in these criminal cop prosecutions, one of the SOS members "flipped" on the ringleader, Finnigan. His trusted accomplice Keith Huerra wore a wire and captured Finnegan arranging a hit on a police officer who was going to testify against him (Main, March 21, 2012). Finnegan was sentenced to twelve years in prison for the murder-for-hire scheme and income-tax evasion. In an interesting twist to this case, Finnegan offered to "rat" out other Chicago cops for an early out of prison (Main, September 15, 2016). He was turned down. There is no honor or loyalty among criminal cops.

Conclusion

What, if anything, is known about criminal cops? First, individual BTTB criminal cops with serious personality issues, such as the police sexual serial killer, Gerard John Schaefer Jr., and the female mass murderer, Antionette Franks, and some alleged drug dealers and gang members hired by American police agencies with lax or no background checks could be considered "rotten apples"; however, such individuals are extremely rare, and their cases do not represent the American criminal-cop problem. Criminal cops are the result of workplace opportunities, occupational norms, peer support, and the overall police culture. The evidence indicates that most police officers do not come to the job with criminal intentions, but low self-control and weak supervision in the workplace causes *some* to break and bend rules and laws. It is a slow and escalating process.

Punch (2000) characterized the process as climbing a *ladder of deviance* where police officers make conscious decisions to take a step higher, stop, or back up. This idea has merit because ethnographic studies and my experiences have revealed police officers who progressed to BTTB status, where crime is their major activity. They are criminals with badges. Other who are not so committed to being criminal cops have stepped down the ladder, reformed their behavior, and become reformers or even whistleblowers. Obviously, the more serious the crime, the less likely it is that this will happen.

Discussion Questions

1. How can a police agency ensure that potential criminal cops are not hired?
2. If you were a police chief, would you establish specialized units to deal with drugs and serious crime? This is not a yes or no question; you must support your answer.
3. Why does the presence of killer cops and cops who commit drug-related crimes call into question policing as a profession? Or does it?
4. A frequent criticism of the discussion of BTTB cops is that there is too much attention on bad cops, leading to an unbalanced negative impression of the American policework occupation. Do you agree with this criticism? Support your opinion. If you agree, then provide the number or percentage of BTTB cops whose presence would create a crisis in a police agency.

CHAPTER 10

Federal and Corrections Law-Enforcement Occupational or Workplace Deviance

Key Terms:

Law-enforcement officers
Corrections officers
Deviant case analysis
SMU
PREA
Corrections officer–caused homicide

Chapter Objectives:

After reading this chapter, the reader should be able to do the following:

1. Be familiar with the law-enforcement occupations of corrections and federal workers
2. Examine the misconduct and crime of corrections and federal workers

Law-enforcement officers in the American federalist system are publicly paid federal, state, local, and special-district officials who are responsible for social control. They have general powers of arrest above those possessed by every citizen in a democracy. Societies' defined law-enforcement officers perform one or more of the *direct* police services of traffic, patrol, crime investigation, or detention in their defined jurisdiction. The terms law-enforcement officer and police officer are often used interchangeably. Up to this point, this book has focused on the police occupational/workplace deviance of local police officers. They are the police most easily recognized by the public, the police who answer 911 calls and investigate crimes. However, there are other American law-enforcement officers that most of us have limited contact with. They are corrections and federal law-enforcement officers, and they also commit police occupational/workplace deviance.

Correctional officers and federal law-enforcement agencies' uniformed officers and ununiformed special agents are, by tradition and statute, law-enforcement officers. The Department of Justice investigates allegations of constitutional violations by them, which include use of force, sexual misconduct, theft, false arrest, and deliberate indifference to serious medical needs or substantial risk of harm to those in their custody (www.justice.gov). The Department of Justice is a designated federal law-enforcement institution, and its rules extend to its employees' conduct while they are on and off duty, "as long as he/she is acting or claiming to act, in his/her official position." Who are they and what do they do?

Correctional officers are responsible for the custody, supervision, and regulation of persons incarcerated in state and federal prisons, local jails, and lockups. Their arrest powers are defined by the appointing agency and statute. Local general-purpose American law-enforcement officers have the most expansive arrest powers as they perform their assigned duties of proactive and reactive traffic regulation, patrol, criminal investigation, and detention in the community and other social settings as assigned. On the other hand, corrections and federal law-enforcement agencies have limited arrest powers, defined by statute, in limited social settings or jurisdictions. Correctional duties are primarily reactive, but they can be proactive, such as when they search visitors, inmates, and cells for weapons and contraband.

Correction and federal law-enforcement agencies are scandal-prone and sexual-abuse-prone entities, and their officers engage in misconduct, malfeasance, and murder. As with all occupational/workplace deviance, the nature and extent of misconduct, malfeasance, and murder in correctional and federal work settings is the result of inclination, opportunity, and risk.

Corrections Agencies and Corrections Officers

There are local, state, and federal corrections agencies, defined as jails, lockups, and prisons. The workers in these agencies are not all law-enforcement officers. The definition of who is a corrections officer is sometimes difficult to understand. For example, the US Bureau of Labor Statistics defines corrections officers as those who "Guard inmates in penal or rehabilitative institution in accordance with established rules and regulations. Many guard prisoners in transit between jail, courtroom, prison, or other point. Includes deputy sheriffs, and police who spend their time guarding prisoners in correction institutions (US Bureau of Labor Statistics, May 2022). Their 2022 estimate was 363,250 persons are employed as corrections officers, making a mean wage of $26.33 per hour or $54,760 per annum. The position requires having a high-school diploma or GED.

According to the American Correctional Association (ACA), a corrections officer is anyone who works with offenders. They are eligible for ACA membership if they are, "actively working in the corrections profession." (https://aca/ ACA). The ACA Certification Handbook lists four types of adult certifications with law-enforcement powers: 1) certified corrections officers, who work directly with offenders; 2) certified corrections supervisors, who work with staff and corrections officers and supervise and implement policy; 3) certified corrections managers, who manage corrections staff; and 4) certified corrections executive individuals, who are at the highest level. There are staff members, such as nurses, chaplains, and others, who deal with inmates and who are not law-enforcement officers, and they may commit misconduct and crime. For example, a federal prison chaplain at the Federal Correctional Institution, Dublin, women's prison in California was sentenced to eighty-four months in prison for repeatedly sexually assaulting inmates and lying about it (DOJ, August 31, 2022). On occasion, he performed custody duties, handcuffing inmates, and referring inmates for disciplinary actions. He told his victims that reporting him would not be taken seriously because he was a chaplain, and they were inmates. That is classic sexual predator behavior.

CORRECTIONS OFFICERS' MISCONDUCT

Corrections officers, as law-enforcement officers performing custodial duties, oversee individuals who have been arrested and convicted or who are awaiting possible conviction. These criminal-justice workers in unique carceral workplace settings have a variety of duties and responsibilities in a dangerous and coercive environment. They must, at a minimum, maintain safety and security in their workplace and inspect all incoming persons, including staff, visitors, inmates, suppliers, and any others, for weapons and contraband. The list of items in the contraband definition includes anything that could aid in escape, such as a map or lock picks; drugs—legal and illegal; anything that could be used in drug taking, such as syringes or pipes; cell phones; tattooing equipment; alcohol and tobacco products; weapons; pornographic materials; and anything else designated by the facility as contraband. Corrections officers must safely transport inmates between institutions and process inmates into and out of the institution.

On the human side, corrections workers resolve disputes between inmates and safely supervise inmates during daily events. No other occupation at the local or state level, except police work, allows for so much power and control of others with the minimum hiring standards of a high-school diploma or GED and no serious criminal record (Barker, 2011; Burton, Jonson, Petrich, and

Miller, 2023). Federal corrections agencies require at least a bachelor's degree or a combination of college credits and experience.

There is a lack of empirical research of deviant behavior in the correctional workplace; however, a review of the literature revealed three studies that are relevant to the study of law-enforcement occupational/workplace deviant behavior by corrections officers.

FELLMAN, MASTER'S THESIS, 2017

April Jean Fellman, in her master's thesis, succinctly outlined the types of deviant behavior committed by federal corrections officers and correctly identified one of the causative factors of corrections officers' misconduct in US jails and prisons—ineffective supervision (Fellman, 2017). As stated in the law-enforcement officers occupational deviance causal equation: opportunity + inclination + low risk = police occupational/workplace deviance. Ineffective supervision results in a low-risk work setting, which contributes to occupational deviance. Fellman points out the Federal Bureau of Prisons internal affairs policy categorizes corrections officer misconduct into three classifications:

- Classification 1 includes violations of the Prison Elimination Act of 2003 (PREA), which forbids sexual misconduct and requires each agency to have and enforce policies on correction officer sexual misconduct. Physical assaults, drug trafficking, making false statements, facilitating escape, and aiding or abetting criminal activity with inmates are also included in this classification. These malfeasance acts are committed by corrections criminal officers and are BTTB criminal behavior.
- Classifications 2 and 3 are primarily violations of rules and regulations and are disposed of internally.

Fellman opines that a proactive approach to corrections officers' misconduct is the best weapon against correctional officer misconduct. She correctly points out that a strengthened hiring and vetting process and increased supervision would prevent misconduct. The next study examines "rotten apples."

DEVIANT CASE ANALYSIS: ROTTEN APPLES

Previous chapters identified a group of criminal cops who are akin to what some called "rotten apples," identified as BTTB cops, who are true outliers. These BTTB cops are criminals with badges and a real problem in a law-enforcement agency when they come together in groups or criminal enterprises. Burton,

Jonson, Petrich, and Miller (2023) identify corrections worker "bad apples" as being BTTB criminal officers in the corrections occupation/workplace. In answering the question, "Why do individuals choose to become corrections officer?" they opine that some, a small minority, become corrections officers for "nefarious and disconcerting reasons."

The authors opine that the results of their study suggests that some "bad apples" choose to become corrections officers for bad reasons, in addition to the normal reasons for choosing the correctional officers occupation, such as pay, benefits, a new opportunity in the criminal-justice field, and helping others. Their reasons are potentially "problematic for the safety or well-being of all living and working in the prison" (Burton et al., 2023, p. 1513). In other words, this "deviant" class or BTTB group already possesses the inclination to engage in workplace deviance. Thirty-eight of their 673 new officer sample gave responses that indicated this potential. Respondents in the "bad apple" subsample expressed attitudes that centered on the opportunity to use force or weapons or attitudes that valued being in a position to punish or inflict sanctions on the dogs (inmates) or animals (moral offenders). One-third of the "bad apple" applicants said that having power over those serving time was their primary reason for choosing corrections as an occupation.

According to the study's authors, this is the first study of corrections officers' intent in becoming a member of the occupation; therefore, it needs replication and further study. It is possible that potential BTTB corrections officers join for the deviant opportunities. Custodial staff and other corrections employees' frequent engagement in sex scandals, drug trafficking in prisons and jails, and excessive use of force against inmates receives 24/7 media coverage. Therefore, the occupation and its opportunities for deviant behavior would be known by potential employees. The number of "secret" deviants drawn to one of society's "dirty work" occupations because of these opportunities is unknown as is their "modeling effect" on fellow workers. More research of this kind is needed.

WORLEYS' INSTITUTIONAL CORRECTIONS OFFICERS DEVIANCE, 2009

Robert and Vidisha Worley's descriptive study of corrections officers' misconduct is a seminal study of how occupational deviance is transplanted into institutional or workplace deviance (Worley and Worley, 2011). Their study recognized that at least three forms of corrections officer occupational deviance existed. Some officers engage in the brutal use of force or allow inmates to assault one another with impunity. This can, and does, result in murder. Other prison employees, including guards, smuggle in contraband, such as drugs and alcohol. Lastly, they recognized the problem of sexual assault and harassment against inmates. They opined that a prison guard subculture, like the police subculture, exists in correctional settings and initiates guards into the accepted and condemned forms of misconduct and the strictures of being a "rat" on other guards.

The lead author was a seven-year veteran Texas prison guard while he pursued his graduate studies. He and his coauthor (his wife) developed and pretested two Likert-style scales—self-reported deviance and perceptions of deviance committed by coworkers—and administered the scales to 501 guards attending in-service training. As expected, the self-reported deviance scores were low. However, the perceptions of deviance scores of prison guards they worked with indicated that they believed that fellow workers broke the rules, called in sick when they were not, engaged in sexual misconduct with inmates and other guards, brutalized inmates, and committed crimes. More descriptive research of this nature is needed.

Taken together, the three studies examined show the existence of correctional officer occupational/workplace deviance and the need for more scholarly examination in this area. Workplace deviance is a critical twenty-first-century problem in the criminal-justice industry at all levels of government, including the federal level. An Associated Press investigation found that more than one hundred federal prison workers had been arrested, convicted, or sentenced for crimes from 2019 to 2021 (Balsomo and Sisak, November 14, 2021). The list included a warden indicted for sexual abuse, an associate warden charged with murder, numerous guards smuggling contraband, and a prison chaplain who accepted bribes for smuggling drugs.

Federal Corrections Officers

The US Bureau of Labor Statistics in May 2022 reported that there were 14,710 federal corrections officers. That statistic represented 0.071 percent of the US corrections and jailers' industry. According to the latest article on the US Bureau of Prisons (BOP) website, there are 138,271 inmates in the federal system (www.bop.gov, accessed September 28, 2023). Some of these inmates are placed in restricted housing "to ensure the safety, security, or the orderly operation of Bureau facilities, or protection of the public." In plain language, these are dangerous inmates. The designated inmates vary in their threat level and so do their restricted housing definitions. Those who present the greatest threat are housed in the BOP's administrative maximum facility in Florence, Colorado—about 328 extremely BTTB inmates.

Almost 8 percent (7.7 percent) or 11,113 inmates are housed in special housing units (SHUs) within the prison facility (www.bop.gov/about). These inmates are under investigation for misconduct and/or criminal behavior. Some such, as former police officers or known snitches, are in protective custody. Another type of restrictive housing is special management units (SMUs). Events in an SMU in Thomson, Illinois, led to the worst federal corrections officer "culture of torture" scandal in recent history.

Physical and Psychological Abuse at the Thomson SMU. In 2018, the BOP announced that it was moving the SMU from the high security prison, the US Penitentiary (USP), Lewisburg, located in Lewisburg, Pennsylvania, to a newly retrofitted facility, the Administrative US Penitentiary (AUSP), in Thomson, Illinois. USP, Lewisburg, had a sordid history of prisoner abuse and corrections officer misconduct since its opening in 1932. Its last major prison riot occurred in 1995. In 2009, an SMU was created within the penitentiary to hold violent and disruptive prisoners. The BOP transferred the SMU to the federal penitentiary at Thomson, Illinois, in 2020. The SMU problems of inmate abuse and corrections officer misconduct went with the transfer to the USP, Lewisburg, according to the report, *Cruel and Usual: An Investigation Into Prison Abuse At USP Thomson*, by the Washington Lawyers' Committee for Civil Rights & Urban Affairs, Uptown People's Law Center, and Levy Firestone Muse LLP (2023). The eighteen-month investigation involved more than forty lawyers and staff members. They found evidence of extreme physical and psychological abuse involving 120 inmates.

The investigation revealed that guards placed inmates in dangerous four-point restraints while the inmates lay on a concrete slab. This involved shackling all four limbs and on occasion adding a belly chain. This painfully stretched the body in four different directions. This torture often caused temporary paralysis or numbness and left permanent scars known as "Thomson tattoos." Sometimes inmates were left in this restraint for days, without food or water and access to a toilet. Inmates were beaten and sexually assaulted in these restraints.

Psychological abuse included extended solitary confinement. Sometimes, prisoners in solitary confinement were double celled (two inmates were held in a cell designed for one) for up to twenty-three hours a day. As punishment, inmates who had conflicts with each other, such as rival gang members, or inmates who were sexual abusers were double celled together. This resulted in beatings and sometimes deaths. The staff at the Thomson SMU refused to provide mental-health care, even though BOP regulations said that persons with mental-health problems were not to be assigned to an SMU. Staff responded to suicidal and self-harm attempts with brutal beatings, restraints, and extreme isolation.

Sixty-one percent of all federal corrections officers are white, and racism was rampant in Thomson SMU, with the frequent use of the term "boy" and the "n____" to blacks. There is a BOP grievance process for inmates, but the forms for filing a grievance had to be provided by and submitted to corrections officers, who would either not provide the forms or tear up the completed forms. Then the corrections officers retaliated against the complainers with beatings or solitary confinement. The corrections workers even disrupted meetings with lawyers. The report documented 165 corrections officers who engaged in inmate abuse and concluded that it was not a matter of "bad apples" but a matter of a "culture of torture."

The abuse evidence and scandal caused the BOP to close the Thomson SMU in February 2023 and to transfer all prisoners and staff elsewhere. Based on a selective, not exhaustive, search of my files, the Internet, and Google, American corrections officers at all levels of government have been arrested for, charged with, and convicted of a variety of acts of misconduct and crime.

CORRECTIONS OFFICERS' CRIMINAL CONDUCT

Corrections Officer–Caused Homicides (Murder and Manslaughter)

This section reports on corrections officer–caused homicides with the caveat, once again, that reporting on this matter is difficult in the absence of reliable official data. The Government Accounting Office has admitted that the Department of Justice has no idea of how many persons die in American jails, prisons, and law-enforcement custody (Government Accounting Office, September 20, 2022). Although the 2013 Death in Custody Reporting Act requires all states receiving certain federal funds to report these deaths, in 2021 only 30 percent of the states had completed records. Therefore, our examples come from open-source data. There could be hundreds, maybe thousands, of unreported in-custody deaths of persons held in law-enforcement custody (Corey, September 20, 2022). My personal SWAG (scientific wild ass guess) would say there are from three hundred to one thousand unreported in-custody deaths. There is a need for research on this issue.

2023 Federal Cases

- A federal BOP lieutenant pleaded guilty to violating the civil rights of an inmate by showing deliberate indifference to the inmate's serious medical needs, resulting in his death. He personally observed the inmate showing signs of serious medical problems and failed to notify any medical personnel. The next day he was notified that the inmate had fallen to the ground and was motionless. He let the inmate lie there for an hour and a half before summoning medical help. He had previously, in 2021, failed to summon help for a suicide victim. He waited over an hour before letting anyone enter the cell and perform life-saving attempts (DOJ, July 12, 2023).
- A federal BOP lieutenant and a prison nurse at the Federal Correctional Institution at Peterburg, Virginia, were indicted for violating the civil rights of an inmate by showing deliberate indifference to his serious medical emergency, resulting in his death (Associated Press News, June 7, 2023). They committed BOP misconduct by lying on their reports of the death.

2023 State Cases

- Nine black Memphis, Tennessee, jail deputies were indicted in the death of a black man who was having a psychotic episode in the jail (CBS News, September 2, 2023). Jailers punched, kicked, and knelt on the inmate's back when he burst from his cell naked and ran. He was stuck with handcuffs, rings of jail keys, and pepper spray containers. His death was listed as a homicide and came after the beating death of Tyre Nichols in January.
- The Tragic Case of the Injury and Death of Larry Earvin. Larry Earvin, a sixty-five-year-old black man died from his injuries at the hands of three Illinois Department of Corrections officers in 2018; however, the criminal incident was not resolved until 2023. Mr. Earvin's injuries and death are a textbook example of misconduct and crime by American corrections officers. The hapless mentally ill man, who struggled with schizophrenia and bipolar disorder, was four months away from parole on a six-year petty larceny sentence when he was viciously beaten by corrections officers; he died six weeks later.

According to newspaper accounts, Earvin was late in reporting for outdoor yard time and was ordered back to his cell for that rule violation (Associated Press, March 22, 2023). The inmate became combative, and an "officer in distress" call went out. Three corrections officers, including a lieutenant, a sergeant, and an officer, responded to the call and were transporting the handcuffed Earvin to the segregation unit. When the inmate reached the segregation vestibule, where there were no surveillance cameras, the inmate was thrown headfirst into a wall and the three corrections officers began kicking, punching, and stomping him. According to the sergeant who later cooperated and testified against his codefendants, one of the other corrections officers jumped up in the air and landed on the prone inmate with both knees.

Staff members picked up Earvin, who was incoherent and bleeding from the head, and carried him into the segregation unit's holding cell. Earvin's vomiting and low blood pressure prompted prisons officials to airlift him to Springfield, Illinois, for emergency surgery. His injuries were fifteen broken ribs, a punctured colon, and other serious abdominal injuries. He died on June 25, 2018. A forensic examiner ruled the death a homicide resulting from blunt force trauma (Vigdor, March 9, 2021).

Following the classification of the death as a homicide due to blunt force trauma, an investigation was conducted by the FBI. At first, the three officers that escorted Earvin to the segregation unit denied the beatings and filed false reports. At least six other correctional officers who had witnessed the prison guards and the inmate's travel denied seeing any excessive use of force. Later they would attribute their false statements to three common cultural factors among prison workers at the facility (Vigdor, March 9, 2021; O'Connor, October 31, 2022). First, there was a culture of violence that prescribed that disruptive prisoners were to be beaten before they were placed in segregation or solitary confinement. The same treatment is common among police officers who "tune up" or "adjust the attitudes" of persons who resist arrest or "piss off the police." Second, corrections officers, just like the police, divide their workplace setting into "us" against "them." "Them" are to be controlled by any means necessary. Lastly, corrections workers, like other law-enforcement officers, see themselves as being in a brotherhood that observes a code of silence. One corrections worker who later testified against the brutal officers said that "You're part of a brotherhood out there, and you don't want to be the guy that snitches" (O'Conner, October 31, 2022). As I have repeatedly said, my experience and most research shows that, if two or more people are involved in a crime, one will flip on the other. Omerta, codes of silence, and the "blue wall of silence" are more rhetoric than reality if the stakes of silence are big enough. That is what happened in this incident.

Following the investigation, all three corrections officers were charged with conspiracy to deprive civil rights, deprivation of civil rights, obstruction of an investigation, falsification of documents, and misleading conduct. As the old saying among criminals goes, "the first rat gets the best deal." The corrections sergeant who was deeply involved in the savage beating pleaded guilty to civil-rights violations and obstruction of justice and agreed to testify against his two codefendants in exchange for a six-year sentence. The lieutenant and the other corrections officer were convicted of all charges and sentenced to twenty years. Six of the witnesses who had originally lied to the authorities received no misconduct discipline after they testified against their "brothers." Justice was served, or was it?

- A female captain serving at the Manhattan Detention Complex in New Yok City was convicted of criminally negligent homicide for barring a subordinate from preventing a mentally ill inmate's suicide (Crane-Newman, May 3, 2023). The newspaper account reports that the inmate threatened to commit suicide, and the female captain stopped a male corrections officer from entering the cell. Ten minutes passed, and the inmate tied a noose around his neck, affixed it to a light fixture, and jumped off a stool. The captain and guards entered the cell as the inmate swung back and forth. The captain ordered everyone out of the cell and closed the door. She said the inmate was faking suicide. Fifteen minutes later, they entered the cell. The inmate was dead. She was sentenced to six months in jail. The inmate's family objected to the light sentence.
- A California prison guard, Sergeant Brenda Villa, learned the hard way of the supposed efficacy of the "code of silence" in the setting of attempts to cover up assaults that lead to death of inmates. She was convicted of perjury for

her testimony in a grand-jury investigation into use of excessive force and an inmate's death. She was not present when the incident occurred, but she left out the name of an officer who was because of his prior presence in excessive-force incidents (US Attorney's Office, July 18, 2023).

CORRECTIONS OFFICERS' SEXUAL MISCONDUCT

Sexual misconduct between correctional staff and incarcerated persons is a historical problem in American correctional facilities. That includes police lockups, jails, and prisons. According to federal law and most states' laws, any sexual contact between correctional staff and incarcerated persons is illegal and constitutes sexual abuse. The physical setting and inherent power imbalance negates the legal right to freely give consent. Therefore, consent is not a valid defense. Historically, inmates who survived earlier sexual violence, inmates who have marginalized identities such as those identifying with a group that is part of the LGBTQ+ constellation, and inmates who have special mental-health-care needs disproportionally experience sexual abuse in corrections institutions (Marcellin and McCoy, May 2021). One study found that persons with mental illness were 80 percent more likely to be sexually victimized by inmates and corrections staff (Marcellin and McCoy, May 2021). In the twenty-first century, the nature of correctional officers' sexual encounters include male-on-female, female-on-male, male-on-male, and female-on-female.

Although correctional staff sexual misconduct is one of the most pernicious forms of occupational/workplace deviance, the extent and nature of this occupational/workplace deviance in the United States is often unknown. Analysis of it, like analysis of all other forms of law-enforcement deviance, suffers from a lack of official data sources. Prior to the Government Accounting Office 1999 report, there was no attempt to gather national data on staff sexual misconduct committed against women inmates (Government Accounting Office, June 1999).

The 1999 Government Accounting Office report on the three largest US correctional jurisdictions holding women inmates—the BOP, Texas, and California—and the District of Columbia found 506 allegations of staff-on-inmate sexual misconduct from 1995 to 1998. It should be mentioned that the four jurisdictions did not have readily available data. The Government Accounting Office had to help the institutions come up with data through interviews and records checks. The BOP had 236 allegations; California, 117 allegations; and Texas, 153. Ninety-two, or 18 percent, were sustained. Texas had 48 sustained allegations, and the BOP and California had 22 each. The BOP indicated that a small number of these allegations could include female staff and male inmates, female staff and female inmates, or male staff and male inmates (Government Accounting Office, June 1999, p. 8). The Government Accounting Office said that the low rate of sustained allegations could be due to a lack of physical evidence—the "he said, she said" nature of the complaint. In any event, the twenty-two sustained allegations resulted in eighteen staff resignations, three staff dismissals, and one staff reassignment.

PRISON RAPE ELIMINATION ACT OF 2003

Following the release of the 1999 Government Accounting Office report, media attention, and several prison and jail scandals, Congress unanimously passed the Prison Rape Elimination Act (PREA) in 2003. The stated purpose of the act was to "provide for the analysis of the incident and effects of prison rape in federal, state, and local institutions and to provide information, resources, and recommendations and funding to protect individuals from prison rape" (National Prison Rape Center, www.prearesourcecenter.org). The act would require research from the Bureau of Statistics and the National Institute of Justice. The Act established the National Prison Rape Elimination Commission to develop standards for addressing prison sexual abuse. These standards were developed in 2012. The standards required the institution to adopt zero-tolerance policies on sexual violence, train correctional staff on prevention and response, offer victims numerous ways to report incidents, provide medical and mental-health care to victims, and ensure that victims had access to confidential communication with community-based victims' advocates. Unfortunately, the standards were often hard to understand and expensive to implement. A criticism leveled at the standards is that they were not developed in partnership with persons incarcerated or working in correctional facilities. Staff from professional associations and organizations were the main standards developers.

The PREA would be funded by the Bureau of Justice Assistance and the National Institute of Corrections. Data would be collected from all US corrections facilities, including prisons, jails, juvenile facilities, military, and Indian country facilities. That mandate included ICE facilities.

Data collection would rely on four measures: 1) the Survey of Sexual Victimization; 2) the National Inmate Survey; 3) the National Survey of Youth in Custody; and 4) the National Former Prisoner Survey. According to the Bureau of Justice Statistics (BJS), the published reports are "based on a random sample or other scientifically appropriate sample" (DOJ, June 2023). If the data are accurate, the data collection success would be remarkable. However, those statistics are based on the states that provide official information. The number of institutions on which the data are based is not mentioned. A 2017 *Prison Legal News* article reports that nineteen states were in compliance with the PREA standards, thirty-eight states filed assurances but no audit data, and Utah and Arkansas refused to comply (Gilna, November 8, 2017). According to the PREA, 100 percent of the persons sampled in 2020 and completed in 2022 from the BOP, state prison systems, and state juvenile justice systems completed the survey (DOJ, June 2023, NCJ 306488). The other response rates were 95 percent of sampled local jails and 97 percent from other adult correction facilities.

The last BJS report on substantiated sexual-victimization reports from adult correctional authorities covered the period from 2016 to 2018 and was published on January 31, 2023 (BJS, January 23, 2023). There were 2,229 substantiated staff-on-inmate sexual-misconduct incidents. Corrections officers or supervisory personnel were responsible for the majority (64 percent) of the inmate incidents. Maintenance or support staff were responsible for 13 percent of the inmate incidents, and medical or health-care staff committed 10 percent of the staff-on-inmate sexual misconduct. These findings support the causal relationship between occupational/workplace deviance and opportunity. The finding that half of the sexual assaults happened in areas not under video surveillance factors in on the real or perceived risk of sexual misconduct on a person with credibility problems. Forty-four percent of the staff complaints led to discharge or termination.

PROBLEMS WITH THE PREA

The passage of the PREA is a worthy bipartisan signal that America will no longer tolerate rape and sexual assaults in its prisons and jails, but implementing the PREA has been difficult so that it has not lived up to its potential. Many critics say the law is virtually toothless in enforcing its requirements (Gilna, November 8, 2017). Correctional institutions that do not comply would forfeit 5 percent of their federal corrections-related grants. The penalty is grossly inadequate. For many facilities, the cost of compliance exceeds the federal funds they receive, if any. For that and other reasons, as of 2016, forty states had not complied with the PREA standards. In the future, more states may comply but, for now, sexual misconduct continues.

SELECT EXAMPLES

The Federal Rape Club: The US Federal Correctional Institution is a low-security female facility with the nickname "The Rape Club" (Balsamo and Sisak, February 6, 2022). The pervasive sexual abuse by BOP corrections workers, including the warden and the prison chaplain in 2021 and 2022, added to the credibility of the appellation. Sexual abuse of inmates by the corrections officers and staff was the norm and has been so for decades. In 2019, an inmate allegedly reported that a maintenance worker in the prison repeatedly raped her. She was put in solitary confinement for three months and transferred to a prison in Alabama. According to the Associated Press report, there were 422 complaints of staff-on-inmate sexual abuse in the BOP system in 2020.

In 2020, several women reported sexual abuse to the Inspector General. Their complaints went public and led to eight members of Congress demanding an investigation (Burbank, March 7, 2022). These members of Congress—male and female—pointed out that most of the complaints that went public had been reported to authorities at least five years earlier and nothing had been done. They reiterated that the complaints included allegations against correctional workers and staff, such as the chaplain and a recycling technician. "This is unacceptable considering PREA (Prison Rape Elimination act Standard 51 (b)', requires a means to anonymously report such acts to a public entity outside the agency and have it investigated. The resulting investigation had serious repercussions.

The former warden was convicted on four counts of abusive sexual contact against three female inmates and lying to federal agents (Galicza, June 14, 2023). He was sentenced to five years and ten months in prison. The director of the BOP was forced to resign. Eight correctional officers (guards) pleaded guilty to sexual offenses and/or lying to federal agents and are serving their sentences. A cook supervisor pleaded guilty to sexually abusing three female inmates he was supervising and lying to a federal agent. The civil suits are still ongoing. At least five former inmates have twelve lawsuits against Dublin corrections officers and the BOP.

- 2021—Associate Federal Warden—A former federal associate warden was charged with sexually abusing several female inmates. He groped the women and forced two to strip naked as he took pictures of them (Associated Press, September 29, 2021).
- July 31, 2019—Federal Corrections Officer—A BOP lieutenant was sentenced to twenty-five years in prison for five counts of sexually abusing inmates at the federal Metropolitan Detention Center in Brooklyn, New York (DOJ, July 31, 2019).
- March 16, 2018—Federal Corrections Officer—A federal corrections officer at the BOP Federal Correctional Complex, Victorville, in California, was arrested and charged with sexually abusing two female inmates (DOJ, March 16, 2018).
- June 2017—Female State Prison Guard—A Georgia state prison guard was sentenced to five years in prison for repeatedly having sex with an inmate. She became pregnant and had his baby before her sentence. Her rationale was "I was young and made a mistake" (Gilna, November 8, 2017).
- July 2017—Male County Detention Officer—A Hardin County, Kentucky, detention officer (guard) was arrested for raping a female he was guarding in the hospital. He gave her dipping tobacco and then had sexual intercourse

with her in a bathroom (Gilna, November 8, 2017). He pleaded guilty to sexual misconduct and was sentenced to a year in jail.

- September 2017—Male Jail Guard—A Bernalillo, New Mexico, jail guard was convicted of raping a female prisoner in the courthouse elevator. The jail's staff and the guard had a history of sexual misconduct. He had been told by a supervisor not to be alone with female prisoners because he had a history of hitting on them (Gilna, November 8, 2017). He had been fired once before because of "consensual" sex with an inmate but was rehired because he showed remorse.
- 2017—Corrections Worker—A female librarian in an Arkansas state correctional facility was fired and charged with sexual misconduct for having sex with a prisoner in the prison library (Gilna, November 8, 2017).
- 2017—Corrections Worker—A prison chaplain in an Arkansas prison was convicted of having sex with five prisoners and was sentenced to five years in prison (Gilna, November 8, 2017).
- 2023—Fox in the Hen House—A male nurse working at Oregon's only prison for female inmates was convicted on seventeen counts of nonconsensual sexual abuse of female prisoners before and after the prisoners' medical treatment or while the prisoners were working as orderlies. He was sentenced to thirty years in prison. He would manufacture reasons to get the orderlies alone in medical rooms, janitor's closets, or behind privacy curtains and would sexually abuse them. He would make his position of power over them clear and would tell them they would not be believed if they complained (DOJ, October 18, 2023).

Corrections Officers' Criminal Conduct

Corrections officers, like all American law-enforcement officers at all levels of government, may engage in criminal conduct, depending on the available opportunities and real or perceived support that exist in their workplace setting. This can be seen in the selected examples.

- February 2023—Three South Carolina Corrections Officers Arrested—Three guards (one male and two female) at the Richland County Alvin S. Glenn Detention Center have been arrested and charged with misconduct in office. The specific charges deal with smuggling contraband into the facility and warning the inmates of cell searches (Hughes, February 7, 2023). The facility has been under investigation by the South Carolina Department of Corrections and local attorneys because of four suspicious death in the jail over the last twelve months.
- 2023—Federal Supervisor Obstructs Justice—A BOP lieutenant wrote false reports to cover up two beatings of inmates. He was a supervisor at the US

Penitentiary Big Sandy in Inez, Kentucky. Two corrections officers who engaged in the beatings pleaded guilty to the assaults and testified against him (DOJ, March 14, 2023). So much for the myth of brotherhood and the code of silence.

- January 2022—Federal Corrections Officers—Two federal corrections officers at the privately run maximum-security Leavenworth Detention Center pleaded guilty to smuggling contraband into the institution. The female officer smuggled contraband and solicited other corrections officers to engage in her smuggling scheme. The male officer smuggled tobacco, cell phones, and drugs into Leavenworth (DOJ, January 28, 2022).
- 2021—Corrections Officer and Inmates Crime Cabal—a federal corrections officer and two inmates at the US Penitentiary in Atlanta were charged with bribery, smuggling, and drug-related offenses for a scheme to smuggle the contraband into the maximum-security prison (December 20, 2021).
- 2019—Corrections Criminal Enterprise at Maryland Correctional Institute, Jessup—One of the largest instances of corrections officer misconduct in Maryland history became public in 2019, when twenty defendants, composed of correctional officers, employees, contractors, inmates, and outside "facilitators" were indicted for bribing officers and staff members to smuggle contraband into the corrections institution. The smuggled contraband included narcotics, cell phones, flash drives, tobacco, cash, and money orders. The corrections officers, staff, and contractors hid the contraband on their persons and delivered it to the inmates in their cells, in the medical facility, and at prearranged "stash" locations (DOJ, April 16, 2019).
- 2023—Georgia Warden Arrested—A Georgia warden at the Smith State Prison in Glennville, Georgia, was arrested and charged with engaging in a criminal enterprise with a prison gang in his facility (Hughes, February 12, 2023). A multimillion-dollar smuggling ring, Yves Saint Laurant Squad, was smuggling cell phones, drugs, and other contraband into the prison for at least the last ten years. The criminal gang was revealed after the attempted murder of a guard who could not be corrupted or intimidated. The assassins went to the wrong house and killed an innocent man. The Georgia Bureau of Investigation discovered the criminal enterprise during their investigation. A former female guard who was caught smuggling contraband was killed two years earlier to keep her from "ratting" out the gang.

Federal Law-Enforcement Agencies

As stated in Chapter 2, in 2016 there were eighty-three federal law-enforcement agencies (Brooks, October 2019). In 2021, there were seventy-three federal government agencies employing full-time law-enforcement officers who were authorized to carry firearms and make arrests (Longley, February 16, 2021). Employees in these agencies conduct investigations, execute search warrants, make arrests, and carry firearms. The largest front-line federal agencies are, in order, the CBP, the BOP, the FBI, ICE, the US Secret Service, the Administrative Office of the US Courts, and the DEA.

The largest agency is the CBP (dealing with customs and border control), and it is the most corruption-prone US law-enforcement agency, with almost thirty-nine thousand officers. The smallest federal agency is the Bureau of Reclamation, with twenty-one law-enforcement officers. However, in 2008, there were sixteen federal agencies with fewer than 250 law-enforcement officers. An easily recognized uniformed federal law-enforcement agency is the US Capital Police, which employs more than 1,600 officers. The Capitol Police has a history of police misconduct, particularly sexual misconduct and drug-related misconduct (Marquette, September 2020). BOP officers and Federal probation officers also have arrest and firearms authority (Longley, February 16, 2021). They also have histories of police misconduct.

Forty-one of the federal agencies are not typical in-the-field agencies. They are agencies with the Office of Inspector General, which oversees the federal agencies and their activities. The remaining forty-two federal law-enforcement agencies range from the CPB with 43,724 full-time officers to the fifty-three-member Tennessee Valley Authority Police. The largest federal departments with the most agencies are the DHS (six agencies), the Department of the Interior (six agencies), and the Department of Justice (five agencies). There are egregious examples of law-enforcement criminal behavior by federal law-enforcement officers, including serial killing, murdering for hire, spying for the Soviet Union, and engaging in sexual misconduct.

FEDERAL SPECIAL AGENTS AND THEIR OCCUPATIONAL DEVIANCE

American law-enforcement officers at all levels and in all jurisdictions have opportunities for misconduct, malfeasance, and murder unique to their type of agency. Therefore, there will be some—a minority—deviant, norm-violating, and criminal law-enforcement officers in all levels of government. That includes the highly respected FBI.

FBI Misconduct, Malfeasance and Murder

In 2020, a *Politico* article reported that an Associated Press investigation found that there had been at least six sexual allegations against senior FBI officials in the previous five years—from 2015 to 2020. The allegations involved an assistant director and special agents in charge of field offices and ranged from unwanted touching to sexual advances (Associated Press, December 10, 2020). The article reported that an investigation by the Office of Inspector General from 2009 to 2012 found 343 sexual "offenses" within the FBI. The following year, in response to the sexual-misconduct allegations, the FBI's deputy director said, "Individuals who engage in this type of misconduct don't belong in the FBI and they certainly should not have supervisory oversight of others. Period" (Mustain and Tucker, June 11, 2021). According to one 2022 report, there were 665 FBI personnel who resigned or retired between 2004 and 2020 following misconduct allegations. The number of sexual-misconduct incidents in the FBI or any other American law-enforcement agency is unknown; however, it happens.

A curious twist to FBI misconduct reports occurred following the January 6, 2021, US Capital breach. A former thirteen-year FBI special agent and supervisor was indicted for civil disorder and assaulting, resisting, and impeding police officers. He allegedly told Washington, DC, Metropolitan Police officers, "You guys are disgusting. I'm former law enforcement. You're disgusting. You are the Nazi. You are the Gestapo. You can't see it. Shame on you! Shame on you! Shame on you!" (DOJ, June 1, 2023).

FBI Malfeasance

The FBI has a malfeasance problem. Recall that malfeasance is unlawful misuse of the official position for personal use. There were two FBI spies for the Soviet Union. Special Agent Robert Hanssen, a former police officer, joined the FBI in 1976 and began spying for what was then the Soviet Union in 1979. After the break-up of the Soviet Union, he spied for the Russian intelligence service. In 2001, he was arrested and pleaded guilty to fifteen counts of espionage and conspiracy in exchange for no death penalty. He was sentenced to life in prison without the possibility of parole. A second FBI special agent, Earl Pitts, spied for the Soviet Union and Russia. He was arrested in 1995 and sentenced to twenty-seven years in prison. There are other examples of FBI corruption.

Ben Vo Duong Tran, FBI agent. At the time of his arrest in 2008, Ben Tran was not an FBI special agent. He had been with the bureau in the Chicago office from 1992 until 2003, when he was fired. Tran had been suspended from the FBI in 2001 for trying to bribe a Vietnamese official while on a personal trip to Vietnam. While on suspension, he was arrested by Chicago police for impersonation of a police officer and was subsequently fired by the FBI. The next year, Tran was arrested in Georgia for fraudulently obtaining firearms and silencers by claiming that he was a Georgia resident and an FBI agent (McCarthy, August 24, 2008). This case was dismissed because the evidence seized was ruled inadmissible. The ex-FBI agent moved to New Orleans and turned into a pure gangster.

Tran and a criminal accomplice traveled to Southern California to establish an armed home invasion crew to rob and kill, if necessary, members of drug-trafficking organizations and rob their stash houses. Tran, through his Vietnamese contacts, planned to meet two other robbery crew members in a hotel in Fountain Valley to begin their crime spree. Unbeknownst to Tran and his partner, the two new crew members were an undercover FBI agent and an FBI civilian informant. Tran and his partner were arrested after the meeting, and the police found a machine gun, a silence-equipped assault rifle, a .22-caliber handgun equipped with a silencer, 630 rounds of ammunition, thirty separate magazines, two bulletproof vests, camouflage clothing, and electrical zip-ties (DOJ, March 18, 2009). Tran and his partner were found guilty and sentenced to thirty years each.

Robert G. Lustyik, FBI Special Agent, 2015. Lustyik, a twenty-four-year FBI special agent was sentenced to ten years in prison for his participation in a bribery and obstruction of justice scheme. The disgraced federal law-enforcement officer pleaded guilty to conspiracy to commit bribery and obstruction, eight counts of honest services wire fraud, obstruction of a grand jury investigation, and obstruction of an agency proceeding. Lustyik used his position as an FBI counterintelligence officer to obstruct a criminal investigation into an American businessman's kickbacks to obtain Department of Defense contracts worth $54 million (DOJ, March 30, 2015).

Charles F. McGonigal, FBI Special Agent, 2023. McGonigal was the former FBI special agent in charge of the New York field office. He was arrested for receiving $225,000 dollars from an individual who had business interests in Europe and had worked for a foreign intelligence service (DOJ, January 23, 2023). He concealed the material facts of his involvement with foreign agents and made false statements about them. He has since pleaded guilty.

Babak Broumand, FBI Special Agent, 2023. Broumand, a twenty-year FBI veteran was responsible for national security investigations and assigned to the FBI field office in San Francisco when he was arrested in 2018 (DOJ, February 27, 2023). The agent was convicted of supplying sensitive law-enforcement information to an attorney with ties to Armenian organized crime. From January 2015 to December 2018, Broumand received $150,000 in cash and checks, private jet flights, a Ducati motorcycle, hotel stays, escort services, meals, and other valuables in exchange for database searches and investigation information on Armenian organized crime enterprises. In 2016, Broumand interfered with an FBI investigation into a corrupt HIS special agent with ties to an Armenian crime boss. The HIS special agent was convicted and sentenced to ten years in prison. In 2023, Broumand was convicted and sentenced to seventy-two months in prison, to pay a $30,000 fine and to forfeit $132,309.

FBI Murder

This book later discusses two FBI special agents who were murderers—John Connolly Jr. and Paul Rico—who engaged in murders in support of organized crime. However, the first FBI agent to be charged with a criminal homicide was Special Agent Mark Putman in 1989. Putnam killed an attractive dirt-poor coal miner's daughter in Pikeville, Kentucky (Barker, 2020b). The young woman was his informant with a "loose" reputation, looking for a way out of Eastern Kentucky. She envisioned that Putnam was her ticket out of Kentucky coal country poverty. They began having sex within months of meeting each other. The young woman became pregnant and threatened to tell his wife about the affair. He claimed that in a fit of rage he accidentally killed his lover. He concealed the body. A year later the body was found. Putnam negotiated a plea to first-degree manslaughter and received a sixteen-year sentence. The light sentence was denounced by the residents in coal country. Still is.

OTHER DEVIANT FEDERAL SPECIAL AGENTS

One of the most corruption-prone American law-enforcement agencies is the DEA (the Drug Enforcement Administration [see textbox 10.1]). This federal law-enforcement agency with approximately 4,500 special agents in the United States and foreign countries has a sordid past of corruption and scandal because of its mission of drug control (see below).

Textbox 10.1. Drug Enforcement Administration's Mission

The mission of the Drug Enforcement Administration is to enforce the controlled substances laws and regulations of the United States and to bring to the criminal- and civil-justice systems of the United States, or any other competent jurisdiction, those organizations and principal members of organizations involved in the growing, manufacture, or distribution of controlled substances appearing in or destined for illicit traffic in the United States; and to recommend and support nonenforcement programs aimed at reducing the availability of illicit controlled substances on the domestic and international markets.

Presenting the entire history of crime and corruption of DEA special agents is outside the scope of this book; therefore, this section presents selected recent examples of DEA special agent malfeasance.

DEA Special Agents' Malfeasance

Veteran DEA Agent Nathan Koen. In 2016, a fourteen-year veteran DEA agent, Nathan Koen, was assigned to the DEA office in Little Rock, Arkansas, as the group supervisor (DOJ, May 11, 2022). Two years later, the FBI began investigating Koen following allegations of corrupt behavior. An informant claimed that he made protection payments to Koen to facilitate the trafficking of heroin, methamphetamine, marijuana, and cocaine in Florida, California, and Arkansas. The informant agreed to set up a payoff arrangement monitored by the FBI. A $9,000 payoff was videotaped and recorded. Koen was charged with conspiracy to possess with intent to distribute heroin, cocaine, and methamphetamine, and one count of bribery of a public official. He pleaded guilty to bribery in exchange for dismissal of the drug charges and was sentenced to 135 months in prison.

The Epitome of Criminal Federal Special Agents: DEA Agent Jose I. Inzarry. Jose Inzarry is considered to be one of the most corrupt agents in the history of the DEA (Nadeau, November 15, 2022). He had served as a federal air marshal and a border patrol agent before joining the DEA in 2009. Inzarry pleaded guilty to nineteen felony counts for acts committed while he was serving as a DEA special agent. He was sentenced to 145 months in prison (DOJ, December 9, 2021). According to the Department of Justice press release following his conviction, Inzarry and his organized coconspirators—violent Columbian drug cartels—stole $9 million from DEA undercover investigations. He received at least $1 million from bribes and kickbacks. He used the money to purchase jewelry, luxury cars, and a home. He and his coconspirators engaged in identity theft to open bank accounts and launder drug sale proceeds. His lavish lifestyle drew attention to him, even from fellow corrupt law-enforcement officers. He was a BTTB criminal cop even among rogue cops. One of his trusted confidants "ratted him out" to keep from going to prison.

It is well known among criminals and crooked cops that "the first rat gets the best deal." The saying "Three can keep a secret, if two of them are dead" has been attributed to both the Hells Angels Motorcycle Club and the Mafia. My law-enforcement experience and research convince me that the statement is true. Crooked cops fall all over themselves to be "the first rat" when prison is mentioned.

In 2022, a current and a former DEA agent were indicted for a large-scale bribery scheme. Manuel Ricco was a former DEA agent who had retired as the special agent in charge for the Miami field office in 2018. He then operated his own business, which allegedly provided private investigative services for criminal defense attorneys. The indictment alleged that he contacted DEA Special Agent John Costanzo, who was the group supervisor for the Miami field office. Allegedly, the two supplied confidential information on who were DEA targets and on anticipated arrests and raids in exchange for cash bribes (DOJ, May 20, 2022).

ATF Special Agents. A thoroughly BTTB ATF special agent and a BTTB Tulsa, Oklahoma, police officer pleaded guilty to trafficking in methamphetamine, cocaine, and marijuana. They also admitted to falsely arresting two suspected drug dealers—a man and a woman—on fabricated drug-trafficking charges. The two law-enforcement officers falsely testified in court, leading to the conviction of their victims, who were sentenced to prison. The falsely accused and convicted victims had their convictions vacated, and they were released from prison (DOJ, May 6, 2010).

ATF Special Agent Chad Allen Scott, who was referred to as the "white devil" by drug traffickers, oversaw a New Orleans–based federal drug task force (Miller, August 13, 2021). The seventeen-year ATF investigator was also a BTTB corrupt law-enforcement officer (Ciaramella, August 29, 2019). According to his indictment on federal charges, from 2009 to 2016, Scott and two other law-enforcement task force members stole money from suspects.

Discussion Questions

1. Were the interests of justice served in the trial of the three Illinois corrections officers who murdered Larry Earvin? If yes, why? If no, why not?
2. What are the common elements in the occupational workplace deviance of police, corrections, and federal law-enforcement officers?

CHAPTER 11

Twenty-First-Century American Policing

American policing is in a crisis mode once again. Policing, broadly defined, is the exercise of the state's authority over its citizens. In theory, that authority, in a democratic society such as the United States, should be legitimate, fair, and equitable for all. Every citizen should be treated the same. The rule of law presupposes procedural justice. For that to be implemented, police agencies and police workers should be beyond reproach. Unfortunately, that theory is not matched by the reality of what American police workers do. Police workers make their decisions based on extralegal factors that are hidden from view and supervision. Police workers often become so obsessed with justice that they hurt themselves and others in pursuit of what they perceive to be justice. Were their victims guilty? Surely, they were guilty of something, think some police officers, who may see themselves as "avenging angels dressed in blue." Often there is no "thin blue line" between cops and criminals. The line between good police and bad police is porous.

The Parkland School massacre showed the world that all American local cops are not heroes. Some are cowards. Publicly paid police workers don't share the same DNA. Some are thieves, robbers, child molesters, and murderers, just as some priests, preachers, politicians, doctors, schoolteachers, and members of every other occupation engage in deviance that varies by opportunity and social setting. The key to American local police reform is understanding that local police deviant behavior (rule breaking, criminal, and noncriminal behavior) has its roots in the nature of the occupation: the workplace setting, the inherent opportunities, and the agencies' culture. Police deviant behavior is not just an American problem, it is a worldwide problem that is exacerbated in English-speaking democracies where the publicly paid police are supposed to abide by the rule of law and be transparent and accountable to the public they serve and protect.

Police deviance involves more than corruption for personal gain. Police deviance includes rule violations, lying, stealing time, use of excessive force, sexual misconduct, racial profiling, and police crimes, such as identity theft, perjury, robbery, burglary, and intentional homicides. In other words, police deviance occurs in three categories—misconduct, malfeasance, and homicide—and it exists in developed societies, such as the United States, Australia, Canada, and the United Kingdom. where it is located in the occupation's dark side (Bayley and Perito, 2011). Police deviance—criminal and noncriminal—exists in all countries and societies with publicly paid police workers, and sometimes its presence is open to public view and well known.

According to Transparency International, a nonprofit nongovernmental association that monitors corruption globally in over 180 countries, police corruption was an open part of life in Nigeria and India and other developing countries such as Mexico in 2011(Bayley and Perito, 2011). Their latest list consists of 180 countries. Those with the most police corruption now include Afghanistan, North Korea, Yemen, Venezuela, Somalia, South Sudan, and Syria (Dyde, 2022). Similar open-visibility conditions or common knowledge that the police are corrupt exists, or has existed, in American police agencies (Barker, 2011). Barker defined them as "rogue" or deviant police agencies. In effect, police work is a morally dangerous occupation, leading to deviant individuals, groups, or organizations wherever it is found. For example, one of the best empirical indicators of the nature and extent of deviant police behavior in developed countries with a free press can be found by the number of "blue-ribbon" commissions of investigation that has been created in a police agency or country (see Table 11.1).

American Police-Work Occupation

The complexity and variety of the deviant behaviors of police workers is inherent in the American police-work occupation. Police deviance has its roots in a flawed occupational police culture, not individuals. American policing completed its evolution to a morally dangerous occupation when the British police model was transported to New York in 1845. In New York City, the politicians were in charge, discipline was lax, and the opportunities for graft were increased. In the United States, the politician-crime-police alliances grew in urban cities where the police were used to control elections, collect graft, and control the dangerous classes, as defined by the elites. The recurring police-politician-crime cabals stimulated calls for reform from those out of power. The first NYPD reform efforts called for a rational and legal bureaucracy that was impersonal, tightly controlled, and dedicated to efficiency and integrity (Repetto, 1978, p. 60). This clarion call set in motion the incremental profession movement among

Table 11.1.   "Blue-Ribbon" Police Corruption or Police Practice Commissions prior to 2011

Country	Commission	Date
USA	Lexow Commission, New York City	1895
	Curran Committee, New York City	1912
	Wickersham Commission, United States	1931
	Knapp Commission, New York City	1972
	National Commission on Criminal Justice Standards and Goals: Task Force on Police	1973
	Mollen Commission, New York City	1974
	Christopher Commission, Los Angeles	1992
	Chicago Commission on Police Integrity	1997
	District of Columbia, Washington, DC	1998
	Chemerinski Report, Los Angeles	2000
Australia	Beach Inquiry, Victoria	1978
	Lusher Committee, New South Wales, Australia	1981
	Neesham Inquiry, Victoria, Australia	1985
	Fitzgerald Commission, Queensland, Australia	1989
	Wood Royal Commission, New South Wales, Australia	1997
	Kennedy Royal Commission, Western Australia	2004
Canada	Vancouver Inquiry	1956
	Keable Inquiry	1977
	MacKensie Commission, Canada	1978
India	National Police Commission	1981
Ireland	Morris Tribunal	2008
Israel	Zeiler Commission	2007
Kenya	Kenya National Task Force on Police Reform	2009
Malaysia	Malaysia Royal Commission on the Police	2005
Northern Ireland	Patten Commission	1999
Uganda	Uganda Corruption Commission	2004
United Kingdom	Royal Commission on Police Powers and Practices, United Kingdom	1929
	Royal Commission on Police	1962

Note: Modified from Blue Ribbon Commissions Investigating the Police, Bayley and Perito, 2011, Table 1.

"progressives" in and out of the police-work occupation. The American policing advances of the twentieth century began in earnest with the establishment of the IACP (International Association of Chiefs of Police) in the 1920s. This professional organization established the first national crime database. Then, as the saying goes, "the sh___t hit the fan." The 1931 Wickersham commission was the first national law-enforcement commission to expose the sorry state of American policing behavior. Its report, Report on Lawless in Law Enforcement, stunned the nation and revealed an American police crisis. Reforms, mostly bureaucratic in nature or based on individual deviance, followed the revelations. Slow, inchoate reform efforts followed this report. Then the 1970s Knapp commission on corruption in the NYPD revealed the sordid police practices in the nation's largest police department. The police reforms that followed this public exposure included establishment of new police professional organizations, the establishment of the Community Oriented Policing Office (COPS Office) in 1994, and the involvement of the federal government in American police reform. Thus, began efforts to identify and thwart the inherent opportunities of the tainted morally dangerous occupation. That is where policing is today.

American policing in the twenty-first century is guided by the premise that, depending on their behavior, the police in a democracy can be either a blessing or a curse. They can be the defenders of our liberty or the oppressors of a free people. The American police's behavior, especially at the local level, as individuals, groups, and organizations can be a blessing and a curse. The litany of horrors committed by some American law-enforcement officers filled the pages of this book. Thankfully, the transgressors are in the minority; however, that gives no solace to the victims.

Furthermore, the fragmented nature of the American police-work system makes the examination and possible reform of police deviant actors difficult, if not impossible. There are no national police occupational standards. American local police are those who meet the "minimal state and local qualifications" and go on to fulfill the "minimal state and local training standards." These minimally qualified and trained American police applicants join local departments that may or may not have internal or external oversight. In time, it became "normal" that some American police officers would succumb to the temptations to engage in misconduct, malfeasance, and homicide. This is not being overly critical. It is being realistic.

The American police-work "system" consists of an estimated eighteen thousand local and independent police agencies and an alphabet soup of law-enforcement agencies at the county, state, federal, and special-district levels. This "system" precludes making universal and binding qualifications, standards, and expectations for the American police-work occupation. However, all these disparate agencies and organizations in a democracy have one thing in common. The public expects them to perform their official duties within the rule of law and procedural justice, treating all those they encounter the same and fairly. The public expects professional police behavior to be noncriminal and ethical.

Twenty-first-century police work in a democracy can be either a blessing or a curse. Police officers can be the defenders of our liberty or the oppressors of a free people.

Twenty-First-Century American Policing Behavior

PROFESSION OR PROFESSIONAL

In the twenty-first century, the historical debate over policing or police work resurfaced. Once again, professionals and scholars ask whether policing or police work is a profession or a skilled or semiskilled occupation? However, is the wrong question being asked? The distinction of who the police workers are and what they do and how they do it began in the 1700s in England. During the early twentieth century, police reformers were divided into two camps on this issue. The first camp of police reformers in the early to mid-1900s were upper middle class, Ivy League–educated public-administration–minded men who thought that the police chief executive officer must be college educated in the latest management techniques (Reppetto, 1978, p. 244). The unskilled but tightly supervised workers were thought to be different. College education for the menial police workers was not necessary and a waste of time. On the other hand, in the second camp were police practitioners like August Vollmer and those who followed his philosophy that all police officers should be highly educated and well-trained decision-making professionals dealing with social issues. Vollmer's philosophy of a profession of police workers, akin to social workers, required a college education of all the police workers. This idea was ironic for a man who only had a grade-school education and went on to become a college professor and establish or help to establish three law-enforcement college programs from 1905 to 1932. He became known as "the father of modern policing" (Reppetto, 1978; Gardiner, September 2017).

IS A COLLEGE DEGREE NECESSARY FOR ALL POLICE WORKERS?

Some years ago, I was heckled by a police chief at a professional meeting who kept yelling, "The only reason why you support a college degree for cops is because you are a dean of a college of law enforcement [the name was later changed to criminal justice at my insistence]." Finally, I got the chance to reply, "That is not true. I am a dean of a college of law enforcement, because I believe that all cops should be college educated with at least an associates degree." Furthermore, I knew at the time that no American occupation not requiring a college degree has ever been recognized as a profession (Barker, 2011). I am not aware that that has changed. I was, and still am, more interested in police behavior that is professional than the profession status of the police-work occupation.

PROFESSIONAL BEHAVIOR

Police practitioners and other police experts routinely describe police work as a profession whereby the law is the basis of all the police workers' official acts. That is, police workers should be professional in their behavior. The term profession is a noun describing a person, place, or thing. However, professional is an adjective describing the behavior of persons performing the occupational duties of police work or law enforcement. The temptations, opportunities if you will, to break the law or go outside the law in their official actions are always present in police work. This distinction leads to two different discussions.

If police work is to be recognized as a profession, someone must define who is eligible to be a member of the police profession and who is to recognize them as such. In 1905, August Vollmer said all American police should have a college degree and he outlined a course curriculum for this degree. Okay, has American policing made any progress on this requirement? The most recent report from the Fullerton Center for Public Policy reveals, 118 years later, only two local American police departments—those in Arlington, Texas, and Tulsa, Oklahoma—require all police officers to have a four-year college degree (Gardiner, September 2017).

The overwhelming majority of local American police agencies require a high-school diploma or GED for entry-level applicants. That was not always true. The 1967 President's Commission on Law Enforcement and Administration of Justice reported that only 70 percent of the nation's police departments required a high-school diploma. The commission went on to divide police officers, relabeled as community-service officers, into categories: police officer and police agent (The Challenge of Crime in a Free Society, 1967, p. 106). The police officer would have to have at least two years of college, preferably a bachelor's degree in liberal arts or social sciences. He would perform all police duties. The police agent would be an apprentice police officer under close supervision until he gained experience and got his two years of college. The 1973 National Advisory on Criminal Justice Standards and Goals made a series of recommendations: 1) every police organization should require at least one year of college of any applicant; 2) by 1975, the applicant must have completed three years of education at an accredited college or university; and 3) by 1982, every applicant must have four years of education (1973 NACJSA). Obviously, none of these recommendations were adopted.

However, the number of college-educated police officers is increasing. Many local police agencies state that applicants with college degrees are preferred, and 6.6 percent of American local/municipal police agencies require some college credit or a two-year degree. Many American police agencies require college degrees for promotion to senior positions. Other local police agencies (for example, those in California and Massachusetts) require master's degrees for the chief executive officer position (Gardiner, September 2017).

The latest statistics on educated police officers are encouraging. When I joined the Birmingham, Alabama, police department in the 1960s, only one officer had a college degree. There were no black or women officers. That has changed dramatically in Birmingham and throughout the country. Today, according to the 2017 Fullerton report, almost 52 percent of sworn municipal American police officers have at least a two-year degree. Thirty percent have a four-year degree, and over 5 percent have a graduate degree (Gardiner, September 2017). The states with the highest percentages of officers with at least a four-year degree are Massachusetts (49 percent), New Jersey (46.1 percent), Minnesota (42 percent), and California (39.5 percent). Massachusetts and New Jersey have the highest percentage of officers with a master's degree or higher (14.6 percent and 13.6 percent, respectively). Almost 29 percent of the chiefs and sheriffs have a four-year degree, and 32.1 percent have master's degrees.

The profession/occupation debate will continue along with the value of police education as an overall reform strategy; however, we should not divert attention away from examination of police deviant behavior. Educational requirements for positions in various police occupational levels do not affect deviant behavior. As pointed out, some law-enforcement officers with college degrees, like some other officers, commit police occupational/workplace deviance. Witness the behavior of federal law-enforcement officers.

Police work, because of its opportunities and workplace setting, is a morally dangerous occupation that brings out the best and the worst of some of its workers. The worst of their behavior is defined as occupational/workplace deviance. In some American police departments, there is no thin line between police workers and criminals. In other departments, the only difference between good and evil cops is the absence of opportunity in the workplace setting. Opportunities for deviance are a given with police work, but such opportunities are not spread evenly in departments or among departments. Some beats or assignments are more deviance prone than others. Police occupational/workplace deviance is still an American issue.

Déjà Vu All over Again

You may recall that in the Preface, I wrote about how my first experience with law-enforcement injustice was as a member of the US Navy's Shore Patrol at the Naval Air Station in Meridian, Mississippi, in 1964. As a member of the search party looking for the slain civil-rights workers murdered by the Klan and local Mississippi police officers, I encountered racial hatred that shocked me, even though I was raised in the South. I came to believe that American police racial hatred and brutality on that scale was over. It wasn't. American policing has come a long way since the civil-rights atrocities of the pre-1960s era. But there are still corrupt and criminal American police officers who, as individuals and in groups and organizations, act as outliers. The most egregious example of this happened again in Mississippi.

On August 3, 2023, six white former police officers with the Lexington, Mississippi, police department, calling themselves "the goon squad," pleaded guilty to federal civil-rights violations relating to beating and torturing two black men and shooting one of them in the mouth during a mock execution in January 2023 (Goldberg and Wagster-Pettus, August 3, 2023; Murdock, November 8, 2023; Daniels, November 8, 2023; and DOJ, November 8, 2023). The preliminary investigation linked the department to at least two murders and numerous acts of brutality and torture. According to newspaper accounts, the now-fired chief of police boasted of killing thirteen people. Two of the five officers in the racially motivated beating are also charged with a second count of civil-rights violations involving a white man whom they allegedly beat and repeatedly tazed to secure a confession. At this time, the former police officers are being civilly sued and facing state charges, and the department is being investigated by the US Department of Justice. The more things change, the more things stay the same.

Conclusion

The author said years ago that American police reform at the local level takes place slowly and often one agency at a time. The Lexington, Mississippi, example adds weight to that statement. There is no magic reform bullet that applies to all American local acts of misconduct, malfeasance, and police-caused homicides. And there is no central oversight agency to ensure that American law-enforcement reform takes place. There is reason to believe that will change. In the waning years of the twentieth century, the education level of police leaders meant everything and nothing.

Frank Rizzo, the controversial Philadelphia police commissioner (1968–1971) and mayor (1972–1980) and the reform police leader, Patrick Murphy, who worked in Syracuse (New York), Detroit, Washington, DC, and New York City, were both born in 1920. However, Rizzo lacked a high-school diploma and Murphy had a bachelor's degree and a master's degree. The times have changed. Danielle Outlaw, the first black female Philadelphia commissioner just resigned to take a position as a deputy chief security officer at the Port Authority of New York and New Jersey. Outlaw has a bachelor's degree in sociology from the University of San Francisco and a master's degree in business administration from Pepperdine University. She retired after twenty years with the Oakland, California, police department and then became the police chief in Portland, Oregon, before becoming the Philadelphia police commissioner.

The authors of the Fullerton report, which was based on the first national study of police education in forty years, concluded that American policing, "has evolved as a profession and officers are held to higher standards than ever before [professional behavior]" (Gardiner, September 2017, p. 2). They did offer a caveat that that is what they believe and what anecdotal evidence suggests. Indeed, the occupation is evolving. Police work has not achieved recognition as a profession, but it is closer than it was. Police history demonstrates that changing the occupation's culture is incremental and fraught with setbacks; yet efforts are ongoing.

The Fullerton study revealed that American police agencies are offering training on mental-health crisis situations (45.5 percent); procedural justice (35 percent), community policing (36.2 percent), implicit bias (37.1 percent), handling nonviolent protests/civil disobedience, and problem-solving policing (19.6 percent). Of the responding agencies, 99.5 percent practiced community policing. A finding that directly affects police fatal encounters is police response to mental-health incidents. Forty percent of the agencies had mental-health crisis response teams. Fifty-five percent of the teams included a mental-health professional. On the issue of police occupational/workplace deviance, almost 57 percent of American police agencies had early warning systems that identified potential and real problem officers. On the accountability issue, 13.5 percent had a citizen oversight committee or a civilian review board. These statistics should be higher, but it is a start.

Much of what was called police reform has been based on myths, common sense, and intuition. That has changed with the advent of what is labeled "evidence-based policing." The idea is that "what works" or is the best police practice in American policing should be subject to scientific or empirical evaluation and chosen based on verifiable results. August Vollmer and the early police professionals likely would agree with that. American police officers were doing a version of "hot spots" in the early 1900s (increasing visible patrols in areas with a high incidence of crime), and American police were doing "hots spots" policing in the mid-1960s, having learned it from the "old heads." That was part of being a beat cop. American police officers in the 1960s just thought they were catching safe burglars and robbers in the act because they were identifying their patterns. In the late 1960s, Chicago detectives were catching burglars with the aid of computer printouts of "high crime" areas. Twenty-years later, a scholar put a label on what experienced cops were doing. For that matter, the value of the 1972 Kansas City patrol experiment was well known before the evidence-cased-policing term was coined.

Recall that Sir Robert Peel in 1829 cautioned the English bobbies from committing "noble cause injustice" by committing acts that were labeled "testilying" in the twentieth century. That was common practice in American policing in the nineteenth century. Cops in England and the United States have been fiddling with, massaging, or inventing evidence to convict the "guilty" or punish the dirtbags for centuries. Cops, who called that practice "doing a hummer," laughed when that practice was given a fancy name by nonpolice scholars and "police experts." Defense attorneys called it perjury. No one believed them.

Whether or not police work is, can be, or should be recognized as a profession is not a settled issue in a fragmented system of local independent agencies in a democratic society such as the United States. The new scrutiny on American policing, stimulated by the current police crisis, promises to bring about more professional behavior. New research under the "evidenced-based policing" banner may accomplish what Herman Goldstein, the first American scholar accepted by the professional police community as an insider under the aegis of O. W. Wilson, hoped for: research results from studies of problems occurring in American police agencies, results that would have practical value in police administration (Goldstein, 1977, p. 68; Barker, Burton, and Woods, forthcoming.)

American citizens have not determined who the local police are and what they expect them to do. Are they crime fighters or social servants, both, or something else? The answer is "that depends." Americans are just not sure what the role is. American police reformers are not sure what effect additional police education will have. Will it make possible new terrorism strategies, new ways to adapt technology to police work, opportunities for discarding common-sense administration in favor of best practices identified by evidence-based research, creation of a cadre of police leaders who can make lateral entry into problem agencies, and identification of problem officers before they kill someone or cause a scandal? American police reformers don't know yet. Therefore, Americans and American police reformers keep perking along, buoyed by significant incremental changes in small, medium, and large American local police agencies, changes that create a culture of integrity.

This modest work is intended to aid interested police reformers in examining law-enforcement organizations; in identifying the threats (also known as the opportunities) in the workplace environment, including peer support for misconduct; and in devising appropriate early warning systems. Once an agency's behavior problems are identified, the agency must take the appropriate internal or external actions against them. The identification process should rely on empirical data and not intuitive reasoning. Reformers must continually ask whether American policing is a publicly paid occupation that requires prolonged training and formal qualifications until the answer is yes.

References

21st Century Solutions. (March 2023). *Building Public Trust in Policing.* 21CP Solutions, LLC.

Acosta, R. (November 16, 216). Ex-cop gets prison after raping children while on duty. *MLive.com.*

Ahern, J.F. (1972). *Police in Trouble: Our Frightening Crisis.* New York: Hawthorne Books.

Ahmad, S. (January 18, 2023). Off-duty Chicago cop interrupts robbery, shoots suspect in South Side, police say. *Chicago, Tribune.*

Anon. (December 20, 2022). Former CPD detective accused of assaulting women after being assigned to investigate an attack against her. *NBC News.*

Anon. (October 26, 2021). Police sexual misconduct "No place" for officers who abuse authority. *BBC.*

Anon. (April 13, 2023). Mpls City Council settles 2 civil cases against Derek Chauvin for nearly $9 million. *CBS Minnesota.*

Anon. (April 27, 2022). West Yorkshire Police officer who made child pornography avoids immediate prison time. *JTV News.*

Anon. (August 13, 2009). Johnson sheriff, DA call for probe into alleged misconduct. *WRAL.com*

Anon. (December 12, 2023). Former Iowa police lieutenant goes to prison for sharing nude photos with teen. *Des Moines Register.*

Anon. (December 17, 2002). 50 British police arrested in child porn operation. *The Irish Times.*

Anon. (February 13, 2020). 40 Maltese police officers arrested in overtime fraud probe. *Xinua News Agency.*

Anon. (February 18, 2022). Dozens of California Cops Charged over Fake Overtime Claims. *Bloomberg.com*.

Anon. (January 21, 2022). Bronx DA dismissing 133 convictions after former NYPD detective charged with perjury. *ABC/7 News*.

Anon. (July 2009). On the Beat: Police misuse records system.

Anon. (June 9, 2023). 42 Highway police officers transferred over overloaded truck bribery scandal. *Thai BBS World*.

Anon. (March 21, 2012). Paso Robles police chief Lisa Solomen relieved of command. *The Tribune*.

Anon. (May 31, 2023). NYPD officer cites "courtesy cards" as a source of widespread corruption. *Nation*.

Anon. (October 21, 2021). Fatal police violence by race and state in the USA, 1980–2019; a network meta-regression. *The Lancet*.

AP. (January 30, 2023). After Memphis Police SCORPION is disbanded, watchdogs take issue with Chicago Police specialized units. *AP*.

AP. (June 18, 2002). Former Sheriff Goes to Trial in Georgia in Successor's Death. *AP*.

AP. (June 7, 2023). Grand Jury indicts Bureau of Prisons employees in inmates death. *AP*.

AP. (March 22, 2023). Cooperating Ex-guard Gets 6 Years in Illinois Inmate's Death. *AP*.

AP. (November 11, 2022). Three ex-Pennsylvania police officers plead guilty in shooting of 8-year-old girl who was killed by a stray bullet. *Associated Press*.

AP. (September 12, 2023). Five former police officers charged in beating death of Tyre Nichols now face federal charges. *AP*.

AP. (September 29, 2021). US prison chaplain in California accused of inmate sex abuse. *AP*.

AP. (September 9, 2022). 5 Sentenced for Roles in Paterson Corruption Scandal. *Associated Press*.

Aronson, J.D. & Simon, A. C. (Summer, 2009). Science and the Death Penalty: DNA, innocence, and the debate over capital punishment in the United States. *Law and Social Inquiry*. 34(3): 603–633.

Ascoli, D. (1979). *The Queen's Peace: The Origins and Development of the Metropolitan Police*. London: Hamish Hamilton.

Balsamo, M. & Sisak, M.R. (February 6, 2022). AP Investigation: Woman's prison fostered culture of abuse. *AP*.

Balsomo, M. & Sisak, M.R. (November 14, 2021). Workers at federal prisons are committing some of the crimes. *AP*.

Barker, T. & Roebuck, J. (1973). *An Empirical Typology of Police Corruption*. Springfield, Ill.: Charles C. Thomas.

Barker, T. (1977). Peer Group Support for Police Occupational Deviance. *Criminology*. 15(3): 353–366.

Barker, T. (1996/2011). *Police Ethics: Crisis in Law Enforcement*. Springfield: Ill.: Charles C. Thomas.

Barker, T. (2006). *Police Ethics: Crisis in Law Enforcement*. 2nd edition. Springfield, Ill: Charles C. Thomas.

Barker, T. (2011). *Police Ethics: Crisis in Law Enforcement.* 3rd edition. Springfield: Ill.: Charles C. Thomas.

Barker, T. (2018). *The Outlaw Biker Legacy of Violence.* New York: Routledge.

Barker, T. (2020a). *Aggressors in Blue: Exposing Police Sexual Misconduct.* Cham, Switzerland: Palgrave Macmillan.

Barker, T. (2020b). *Law Enforcement Perpetrated Homicides: Accidents to Murder.* New York: Lexington Books.

Barker, T., Burton, C., and Woods, L. (2024). *Policing Reform: A Historical and Contemporary Analysis.* San Diego, CA: Cognella.

Barker, T., Hunter, R.D., and Rush, J.B. (1994). *Police Systems and Practices: An Introduction.* Upper Saddle River, N.J.: Prentice Hall.

Barlow, P. (April 19, 2023). Sussex Police officer downloaded child porn from Twitter while on duty. *The Argus.*

Bayley, D. & Perito, R. (2011). Police Corruption: What Past Scandals Teach about Current Challenges. *US Institute of Peace.*

Bayley, D.H. (May 1998). Police Overtime: An Examination of Key Issues. *Research in Brief. National Institute of Justice.*

Behr, E. (1996). *Prohibition: Thirteen Years That Changed America.* New York: Arcade Publishing.

Benoit, J-P, Dubra, J. (August 2004). Why do good cops defend bad cops. *International Economic Review.* 45 (3): 787–809.

Beyer, B.J. & Herndon, J. (March 14, 2018). Interrogative Specialists and False Convictions: Debunking the Con Artist Myth. *Journal of Police and Criminal Psychology.*

Bindler, A. & Hjalmarssom, B. (2021). The Impact of the First Professional Police Forces on Crime. *Journal of the European Economic Association.* 1916: 3063–3103.

Bittner, E. (1970). *The Functions of the Police in Modern Society.* Cambridge, Mass. Oelgeschlager, Gunn & Hain.

Bittner, E. (1980, reprint of 1970 publication). *The Functions of the Police in Modern Society: A Review of Background Factors, Current Practices, and Possible Role Models.* Cambridge, Mass.: Oelgeschlager, Gunn, and Hain.

Blaidsdell, M. (May 24, 2023). Hundreds of Chicago Cops can't testify in court. *The Tribe.*

Blakeslee, N. (2005). *Tulia: Race, Cocaine and Corruption in a Small Texas Town.* New York: Public Affairs.

Boey, V. (May 10, 2023). St. Cloud police officer responded to man's 911 call then stole his credit card information, authorities. *Osceola County Fox 35.*

Boyle, C. (January 26, 2023). About 10% of vetting files examined by HMIC shouldn't have passed. *Police Oracle.*

Bratton, W.J. (1995). Fighting crime as crime itself. *New York School Law Review.* 40 (1–2): 35–43.

Browne, D.G. (1956). *The Rise of Scotland Yard: A History of the Metropolitan Police.* London: George G. Harrap & Co.

Buchman, B. (November 13, 2023). School security guard who once ran for mayor charged with sexual battery of 17-year-old.

Burbank, K. (March 7, 2022). Members of Congress demand investigation into "rampant" abuse at Dublin prison (PleasantonWeekly.com).

Bureau of Justice Assistance. (1989). *Building Integrity and Reducing Drug Corruption in Police Departments.* Office of Justice Programs. U.S. Department Of Justice.

Burton, A.L., Jonson, C.L., Petrich, D.M., and Miller, W.T. (2023). Nefarious and Disconcerting Motivations for Choosing a Corrections Officer Position: A Deviant Case Analysis. *Criminal Justice and Behavior.* 30(10): 1506–1515.

Busby, M. (July 18, 2023). Ex-Met officer who took bribes from nightclub bosses jailed for seven years. *The Guardian.*

Byik, A. (August 18, 2023). More charges: Five Antioch, Pittsburg cops allegedly accepted bribes, including tequila, to make traffic tickets go away. *Bay Area News Group.*

Cabell, J.J., Moody, S.A., Yang, Y. (2020). Evaluating Effects on Guilty and Innocent Suspects: An Effect Taxonomy of Interrogation Techniques. *Psychology, Public Policy and Law.* 26(2): 154–168.

Cain, M. J. (2007). *The Tangled Web: The life and times of Richard Cain—Chicago Cop and Mafia Hitman.* New York: Skyhorse Publishing.

Caless, B. (2008). Corruption in the Police: The Reality of the "Dark Side." *The Police Journal.* 81.

Calhoun, A.J. & Coleman, H.D. (2002). Female inmates' perspectives on sexual abuse by corrections personnel: An exploratory study. *Women and Criminal Justice.* 13(2–3): 101-124).

Caruso, V. (September 10, 2018). 2 Chicago Officers Accepted $13k in Bribes in Alleged "Kickback" Scheme. *Chicago Tribune.*

CBS News Chicago. (January 17, 2013). Study Details History of Cop Crime in Chicago. *CBS News Chicago.*

CBS News. (September 1, 2015). White ex-chief of police makes plea deal in shooting of a Black man. *CBS News.*

Chamberlain, K. (July 14, 2020). After 9 years, my father is finally closer to justice for his death at the hands of police. *USA Today.*

Chan, J.B. (1997). *Changing Police Culture: Policing in Multicultural Society.* United Kingdom: Cambridge University Press.

Charms, D. (March 7, 2022). I-Team: Las Vegas police officer accused in 3 casino armed robberies reportedly used department gun. 8NewsNow.

Cheek, K. (December 9. 2023). New Study: Virgina spends over $283.3 K a year due to police misconduct. *WAVY.*

Cherone, H. & Ruterki, J. (August 22, 2023). Repeated Police Misconduct by 116 Officers Cost Chicago Taxpayers $91 M Over 3 Years. Analysis. *Chicago News WTTW*

Cherone, H. (May 16, 2023). Chicago ranks No. 1 in Exonerations for 5th year in a Row, Accounting for More Than Half of Total Report. *Crime & Law.*

Cheung, K. (2021). Cop who resigned after groping college student landed new job investigating sexual assaults. *Jezebel.*

Chevigny, P. (1969). *Police Power: Police Abuses in New York City.* New York: Vintage Books.

Chrisafis, A. (September 20, 2022). French police officers convicted over 2015 choke-hold death. *The Guardian*.

Ciaramella, C. J. (August 29, 2019). A DEA Agent Got a Drug Dealer to Buy a Truck so the Agent Could Seize it Through Asset Forfeiture. *Reason Roundup*.

Clarke, M. (May 8, 2023). Victoria Police chief Shane Patton says sorry for "trauma experienced by so Many Aboriginal families in our jurisdiction." *Herald Sun*.

Collins, S. C. (2004). Sexual Harassment and Police Discipline. Who's protecting the public? *Policing: An International Journal of Police Strategies and Management*. 27(4):512–538.

Colquhoun, P. (1806 and republished in 1969). *A Treatise on the Police of the Metropolis*. Montclair, N.J.: Patterson Smith.

Constantinou, A. C. (2018). How Do Police Officers Cope with Police Corruption and Corrupt Peers? A Typology in the Making. *Policing*. 14(3): 740–751.

Cooper, A. (October 20, 2021). BI Cop sues police officers and town over alleged sexual assault. *Yahoo News*.

Corey, E. (September 20, 2022). DOJ admits it has no idea how many people die in law enforcement custody. *The Appeal*.

Cox, B., Shirley, J., and Short, M. (1977). *The Fall of Scotland Yard*. Middlesex, England: Penguin Books.

Cray, E. (1972). *The Enemy in the Streets: Police Misconduct in America*. New York: Anchor Books.

Crepeau, (December 20, 2020). Wilson ruled innocent in a Burge-related case. *The Chicago Tribune*.

Cubitt, T. Gaub, J.E., and Holtfreter, K. (July 28, 2022). Gender differences in serious police misconduct: A machine-learning analysis of the New York Police Department (NYPD). *Journal of Criminal Justice*.

Dale, M. (August 1, 2019). Ex-Philadelphia sheriff gets 5 years for $675k in bribery case. *Yahoo News*.

Daley, M. (January 29, 2012). She dialed 911: The cop who came to help raped her. *The Daily Beast*.

Dash, M. (2007). *Satan's Circus: Murder, Vice, Police Corruption, and New York's Trial of the Century*. New York: Crown Publisher.

Davis, B. (January 18, 2023). Senior Met officer Richard Watkinson accused of having a secret room full of child Porn found dead at home. *Evening Standard*.

Davis, M. (January 25, 2023). Rooting out corrupt won't be rapid and it will be painful. *Yahoo News*.

Dehnel, C. (December 11, 2023). Ex-Glastonbury Cop Charged in East Hampton Restaurant Burglary. *Patch*.

Denham, R. (December 1, 2019). Normal Officer Accused of Stealing Money after 911 Call. *WGLT*.

Dillon, D. (March 7, 2017). Police: Former officer charged with stealing from crime scene. *Fox 5 Atlanta*.

Dinger, M. (February 5, 2014). Judge sentences former Del City captain in 18-year-old death. *The Oklahoman*.

Dodd, V. (16 October 2022). Huge failings that let racists, corrupt officers in the force, admits Met Chief. *The Guardian*.

DOJ press release. (December 2, 2020). In "Staggering" Conspiracy, Former Police Chief, Prosecutor, and Police Officers Sentenced for Framing an Innocent Man with a Crime. *U.S. Attorney's Office. Southern District of California. Department of Justice*.

DOJ. (1978). *Prevention, Detection, and Correction of Corruption in Local Governments*. Washington, D. C.: U.S. Department of Justice.

DOJ. (April 20, 2017). Former Louisville Metro Police Department Detective Sentenced to Five Months Incarceration and Five Months Home Detention—Pleaded Guilty to Theft from Interstate Shipment. *U.S. Attorney's Office. Western District of Kentucky*.

DOJ. (August 11, 2011). Majestic Auto Repair Shop Owners Plead Guilty to Paying Hundreds of Thousands of Dollars in Bribes. *U.S. Attorney's Office. District of Maryland*.

DOJ. (August 2, 2019). Former Narcotics Supervisor sentenced for Stealing Drug Evidence for his Personal Use. *U.S. Attorney's Office. Northern District of Oklahoma*.

DOJ. (August 20, 2015). Former Florida Highway Patrol Trooper Sentenced for Taking Bribes. *U.S. Attorney's Office. Southern District of Florida*.

DOJ. (August 24, 2022). Shreveport Police Department Office Indicted by Federal Grand Jury for Wire Fraud. *U.S. Attorney's Office. Western District of Louisiana*.

DOJ. (August 25, 2017). Bail Bondsmen and Secretary Sentenced for their Role in Bribery Scheme at Orleans Criminal District Court. U.S. Attorney's Office. Eastern District of Louisiana.

DOJ. (August 31, 2022). Federal Prison Chaplain Sentenced for Sexual Assault and Lying to Federal Agents. *Office of Public Affairs. Department of Justice*.

DOJ. (December 12, 2023). Former Police Officer Sentenced to 5 years in Federal Prison for Distribution of Child Sex Abuse Materials. *U.S. Attorney's Office. District of South Carolina*.

DOJ. (December 13, 2023). Former Massachusetts State Police Troopers Convicted of Conspiring to Steal Overtime Funds and Wire Fraud. *U.S. Attorney's Office. District of Massachusetts*.

DOJ. (December 13, 2023). Police Detective and Former School Resource Officer Indicted on Child Abuse Material Charges. *U.S. Attorney's Office. District of South Carolina*.

DOJ. (December 14, 2023). Former Special Agent in Charge of the New York FBI Counterintelligence Division Sentenced to 50 months for Conspiracy to Violate U.S. Sanctions on Russia. *Office of Public Affairs*.

DOJ. (December 14, 2023). Former Texas trooper imprisoned for lying to the FBI. *U.S. Attorney's Office. Southern District of Texas*.

DOJ. (December 14, 2023). New York City Police Officer Charged with Sex Offenses Relating to Minors. *U.S. Attorney's Office. Eastern District of New York*.

DOJ. (December 15, 2022). Former Baltimore Police SWAT Officer sentenced to 25 years in federal prison for sexually exploitation of a child to produce child pornography. *U.S. Attorney's Office. District of Columbia*.

DOJ. (December 16, 2022). Former Philadelphia Police Officer sentenced to nearly six years for child pornography offenses. *U.S. Attorney's Office. Eastern District of Philadelphia.*

DOJ. (December 21, 2022). Former Federal Special Agent Found Guilty of Civil Rights Crimes for Committing Sexual Assaults against Two Women. *U.S. Attorney's Office. Central District of California.*

DOJ. (December 21, 2023). Former Texas Police Lieutenant Sentenced to Nearly 13 years in Federal Prison for Attempting to entice 11-year-old Child to Engage in Sexual Activity. *U.S. Attorney's Office. Middle District of Florida.*

DOJ. (December 6, 2023). Former LASD Deputy Sentenced to Two Years in Federal Prison for Falsely Imprisoning a Victim and Then Trying to Cover Up His Crime. *U.S. Attorney's Office. Central District of California.*

DOJ. (December 7, 2021). Former East Helena police chief admits distributing child pornography. *U.S. Attorney's Office. District of Montana.*

DOJ. (December 8, 2022). Jury Convicts Former Federal Prison Warden for Sexual Abuse of Three Female Inmates. *Office of Public Affairs. Department of Justice.*

DOJ. (February 2, 2023). Additional Charges Brought against Four Boston Police Officers Involved in Overtime Fraud Scheme. *U.S. Attorney's Office. District Of Massachusetts.*

DOJ. (February 27, 2023). Former FBI Special Agent Sentenced to 6 Years in Prison for Accepting Bribes Paid by Attorney Linked to Organized Crime Figure. *U.S. Attorney's Office.*

DOJ. (February 6, 2014). Former Baltimore Officer Sentenced to 5 Years in Prison for Protecting a Heroin Dealer and Illegally Accessing Police Databases in Fraudulent Tax Refund Scheme. *U.S. Attorney's Office. District of Maryland.*

DOJ. (February 7, 2013). Former Bureau of Prisons Doctor Sentenced for Sexual Abuse of Three Inmates. *U.S. Attorney's Office. Southern District of Georgia.*

DOJ. (January 17, 2023). Federal Agent Arrested for Receiving Gratuity and Making a False Statement. *U.S Attorney's Office. District of Puerto Rico.*

DOJ. (January 23, 2023). Retired FBI Executive Charged with Concealing $225,000 in Cash Received from Former Intelligence Officer. *Department of Justice. Office of Public Affairs.*

DOJ. (January 25, 2023). Greensburg Police Chief Shawn Denning Charged with Federal Drug Crimes. *U.S. Attorney's Office. Western District of Pennsylvania.*

DOJ. (January 26, 2022). Former Metro East Police Officer Sentenced to Prison for Fraud. *U.S. Attorney's Office. Southern District of Illinois.*

DOJ. (January 26, 2023). Scranton Police Officer Pleads Guilty to Federal Program Fraud in Connection with Overtime Patrol Shifts at Scranton Area Housing Complexes. *U.S. Attorney's Office. Middle District of Pennsylvania.*

DOJ. (January 28, 2022). Two Former Federal Correctional Officers Plead Guilty to Bribery and Smuggling Contraband Scheme. *Office of Public Affairs. Department of Justice.*

DOJ. (January 4, 2013). San Antonio Police Officer Arrested in Bribery Investigation. *U.S. Attorney's Office. Western District of Texas.*

DOJ. (July 12, 2023). Federal Bureau of Prisons Lieutenant Pleads Guilty to Violating the Rights of an Inmate Resulting in His Death. *Office of Public Affairs. Department of Justice.*

DOJ. (July 31, 2019). Former Federal Bureau of Prisons Lieutenant Sentenced to 25 Years in Prison for Sexual Abuse and Violation of Civil Rights Conviction. *U.S. Attorney's Office. Eastern District of New York.*

DOJ. (July 21, 2020). Baltimore Police Officer Pleads Guilty to Federal Charge of Possession of Child Pornography. *U.S. Attorney's Office. District of Maryland.*

DOJ. (July 22, 2022). Former Philadelphia Police Officer Pleads Guilty to Child Pornography Offenses. *U.S. Attorney's Office. Eastern District of Pennsylvania.*

DOJ. (June 2023). PREA Data Collection Activities, Calendar Year 2022 (NCJ 306488). *Office of Justice Programs. Bureau of Justice Statistics.*

DOJ. (March 14, 2023). Former Kentucky Federal Prison Lieutenant Convicted of Covering Up the Assaults of Two Inmates by Correction Officers. *Office of Public Affairs. Department of Justice.*

DOJ. (March 16, 2018). Corrections Officer at Federal Prison in Victorville Arrested on Charges of Sexually Abusing Female Inmates. *US Attorney's Office. Central District of California.*

DOJ. (April 16, 2019). Twenty Defendants Indicted on Federal Racketeering and Related Charges at Maryland Correctional Institute Jessup. *U.S. Attorney's Office. District of Maryland.*

DOJ. (March 21, 2022). Perryton Police Officer Sentenced to 10 Years for Sharing Child Pornography on KiK. *U.S. Attorney's Office. Northern District of Texas.*

DOJ. (March 30, 2015). Former FBI Special Agent Sentenced to 10 Years in Prison for Bribery and Obstruction Scheme. *Department of Justice. Office of Public Affairs.*

DOJ. (May 11, 2022). Former DEA Supervisory Agent Sentenced to 135 Months in Prison for Accepting Bribes from Drug Kingpin. *U.S. Attorney's Office. Eastern District of Arkansas.*

DOJ. (May 11, 2022). U.S. Border Patrol Agent Charged with Attempting to Distribute Methamphetamine and Receiving Bribes. *U.S. Attorney's Office. Southern District of California.*

DOJ. (May 20, 2022). Former Norfolk Sheriff Sentenced for Public Corruption. *U.S. Attorney's Office. Eastern District of Virginia.*

DOJ. (May 24, 2022). BOP Corrections Officer pleads guilty to sexual assault of woman in federal custody in Los Angeles. *Office of Public Affairs. Department of Justice.*

DOJ. (May 5, 2008). Priest who sexually abused inmates at FMC Carswell in Fort Worth Sentenced to 4 years in prison. *Office of Public Affairs. Department of Justice.*

DOJ. (May 6, 2010). Former ATF Special Agent Pleads Guilty to Drug Conspiracy. *U.S. Attorney's Office. Eastern District of Arkansas.*

DOJ. (November 10, 2014). Former Jefferson Parish Sentenced to 92 Years in Prison for Civil Rights. Bank Fraud and Aggravated Identity Theft Violations. *Department of Justice. Office of Public Affairs.*

DOJ. (November 17, 2022). Former New Orleans Police Officer Pleads guilty to federal civil rights offense for sexually assaulting a 15-year-old crime victim. *Office of Public Affairs. Department of Justice.*

DOJ. (November 6, 2023). Knoxville Police Officer Arrested for Production of Child Pornography. *U.S. Attorney's Office. Eastern District of Tennessee.*

DOJ. (November 7, 2019). U.S. Attorney Announces the Arrest of 27 Individuals, Including NYPD Employees, for a Massive Bribery Scheme Relating to No-Fault Automobile Insurance Policies. *U.S. Attorney's Office. Southern District of New York.*

DOJ. (November 8, 2023). Assistant Attorney General Kristan Clark Delivers Remarks Announcing a Pattern or Practice Investigation of the City of Lexington, Mississippi, and the Lexington Police Department. *Department of Justice.*

DOJ. (November 9. 2023). Former High-Ranking DEA Special Agent and Current DEA Special Agent Convicted for Bribery Scheme. *U.S. Attorney's Office. Southern District of New York.*

DOJ. (October 11, 2019). Federal Agent Pleads Guilty to Embezzlement and Conversion of Government Property. *U.S. Attorney's Office. District of New Hampshire.*

DOJ. (October 13, 2023). Former San Diego Police Officer and Three Others Sentenced for Crimes Stemming from Years-Long Operation of Illicit Massage Businesses. *U.S. Attorney's Office. Southern District of California.*

DOJ. (October 18, 2023). Former Oregon Corrections Nurse Sentenced to 30 Years in Federal Prison for Sexually Assaulting Nine Female Inmates. *Office of Public Affairs. Department of Justice.*

DOJ. (September 15, 2017). Former Police Officer Convicted on Corruption Charges. *U.S. Attorney's Office. Middle District of Pennsylvania.*

Dolan, B. (2019). To Knock or Not to Knock? No-Knock Warrants and Confrontational Policing. *St. John's Law Review.* 93(1): 201–231.

Dombrink, J. (1988). The Touchables: Vice and Police Corruption in the 1980s. *Law and Contemporary Problems.* 51(1): 201–232.

Dorfman, D.N. (1999). Proving the Lie: Litigating Police Credibility. *American Journal of Criminal Law.* 26(3).

Droge, E.J. (1973). *The Patrolman: A Cop's Story.* Bergenfield, N.J.: New American Library.

Dunkle, S. (2021). The Air Was Blue with Perjury: Police Lies and the Case for Abolition. *New York University Law Review.* 96(6).

Dunn, L.T. (June 5, 2023). Timeline: Inside the case against Vincent Simmons. *48 Hours.*

Dyde, J. (January 27, 2022). What Are the Most Corrupt Countries in South America? Centralamerica.com.

Dziemianowicz, J. (March 24, 2023). Shocked at the Number of Shell Casings: Atlanta Sheriff-Elect Gunned Down in Hit Masterminded by Rival. *Yahoo.*

Emsley, C. (1991). *The English Police: A Political and Social History.* London and New York: Longman.

Engel, R.S., McManus, H.D., and Isaza, G.T. (January 2020). Moving beyond "Best Practices" Experiences in Police Reform and a Call for Evidence to Reduce Officer-Involved Shootings. *ANNALS. AAPSS.* 687.

FBI. (April 7, 2011). One Current and Three Former Chicago Police Officers, Once Assigned to Disbanded Elite SOS Unit Charged with Federal Civil Rights Violations. *U.S. Attorney's Office. Southern District of Illinois.*

FBI. (February 10, 2012). Former Connecticut Police Captain sentenced to prison for trading child pornography. *FBI Press Release—New Haven Division.*

FBI. (June 6, 2011). Rialto Police Officer and Orange County Defense Attorney Taken into Custody in Federal Bribery Case. *U.S. Attorney's Office. Central District of California.*

FBI. (September 28, 2011). Florida man indicted for Transporting. Receipt, and Possession of Child Pornography. *FBI Press Release—Minneapolis Division.*

Fellman, A.J. (2017). Correctional Officer Misconduct. Master's of Science in Criminal Justice. Minot State University. Minot, North Dakota.

Fenton, J. (September 25, 2023). Baltimore Police officer caught on camera stealing Envelope of cash from business. *Baltimore Banner.*

Florian, M. (February 28, 2019). Timeline: A Botched Houston Police Raid and Its Consequences. *Houston Public Media.*

Flowers, D.B. Jr. & Deaver, C. (2014). *Bangs: A Policeman's Guide to Corruption.* Palm Springs, Calif.: Bella Productions.

Fogelson, R. M. (1977). *Big-City Police.* Cambridge, Mass.: Harvard University Press.

Fohner, K. & Collins, C. (December 13, 2023. Former Gastonia police officer charged in trafficking conspiracy. *Gaston Gazette*

Forster, D. (March 31, 2022). Police Officer who killed Nelsonville Man enters plea loses badge. *WOUB.*

French, D.J. (2019). The Cutting Edge of Confession Evidence: Redefining Coercion and Reforming Police Interrogation in the American Criminal Justice System. *Texas Law Review.* 97:1038.

Fuchs, N. (December 18, 2023). Former Camden County deputy and school resource officer charged with numerous child sex crimes. *KRCG.*

Galicza, N. (June 24, 2023). The women that "Me too" left Behind. *Deseret News.*

Gambacorta, D. (May 1, 2012), Deputy Commissioner faces sex-harassment suit. *Daily News.*

GAO. (September 20, 2022). Deaths in Custody. *Government Accounting Office.*

Gardiner, C. (September 2017). *Policing around the Nation: Education, Philosophy, and Practice.* California State University: Fullerton Center for Public Education.

Garrett, B.L. (2009). Invalid Forensic Science Testimony and Wrongful Convictions. *Virginia Law Review:* 85:1–97.

Gee, J.L. (Winter 2020. Police Practices, Interrogation of Minors, and False Confessions. *Juvenile Justice Updates.*

Gilna, D. (November 8, 2017). Five Years after Implementation, PREA Standards Remain Inadequate. *Prison Legal News.*

Glaser, D. (1971). *Social Encounters.* Chicago: Markham.

Goldberg, M. & Wagster-Pettus, E. (August 3, 2023). White ex-officers in Mississippi plead guilty to racist assault on 2 Black men during raid. *AP News.*

Goldstein, H. (1975). *Police Corruption: A Perspective on its Nature and Control.* Washington, D.C.: Police Foundation.

Goldstein, H. (1977). *Policing a Free Society.* Cambridge, Mass.: Ballinger.

Goldston, M. (1990). Office of Professional Standards. Chicago Police Department.

Gonzales, D. (2010). The Act and Impact of Whistle Blowing on the Los Angeles Police Department. PhD Dissertation. Pepperdine University.

Goodman, A. (August 8, 2023). Family of Kenneth Chamberlain, Black Man Killed in 2011 by Police, Settles with City of White Plains. *Democracy Now.*

Goodman, J.D. (September 29, 2015). Officer Who Disclosed Police Misconduct Sues. *The New York Times.*

Gordon, J. (October 7, 2022). The Big Sleazy: Senior New Orleans cop is demoted from captain to lieutenant for payroll fraud: Traffic cam probe caught her performing private security work while clocked in at her precinct 26 times. *Daily Mail.*

Gordon, T. (November 11, 2020). Damning report finds bigotry and misogyny in Police Scotland. *The Herald.*

Gorner, J. & Hinkel, D. (March 26, 2021). Cop who allegedly lied about fatal shooting quits. *Chicago Tribune.*

Goudsward, A. (June 20, 2019). Ex-Harvey Cedars police sergeant gets probation for stealing donated ATV. *Asbury Park Press.*

Gould, J.B., Carrano, J., Leo, R., Young, J. (February 2013). *Predicting Erroneous Convictions: A Social Science Approach to Miscarriages of Justice.* U.S. Department of Justice.

Graham, H.D. & Gurr, T.R. (1969). *Violence in America: Historical and Comparative Perspectives.* Vol. 1. A Report to the National Commission on the Causes and Prevention of Violence.

Gross, S.R., Possley, M.J., Roll, K.J., and Stephens, K.H. (September 1, 2020). *Government Misconduct and Convicting the Innocent: the Role of Prosecutors, Police and Other Law Enforcement.* National Registry of Exonerations.

Gubi-Kelm, S., Grolig, T., Strobel, B., Ohlig, S., and Schmidt, A.F. (2020). When do False Accusations Lead to False Confessions: Preliminary Evidence for a Potentially Alternative Explanation. *Journal of Forensic Psychology and Practice.* 20(2): 114–132.

Gunderson, E. (April 29, 2023). 11 Men Exonerated of Murder Convictions File Civil Suit against Disgraced Ex-Detective Reynaldo Guevara. *Crime and Law.*

Gutowski, C. (October 30, 2020). Ex-prosecutors role in wrongful conviction spotlighted. *The Chicago Tribune.*

Guzzo, P. (September 6, 2016). Dirtiest of New York cops emerging from the shadows in Tampa Bay. *Tampa Bay Times.*

Hagedorn, J., Kmiecik, B., Simpson, D., Gradel, T.J., Zmuda, M.M., and Sterrett, D. (January 17, 2013). *Crime, Corruption and Cover-ups in the Chicago Police Department.* University of Illinois at Chicago Department of Political Science.

Hall. (March 23, 2016). German border police worked 2.7 million hours in overtime in the past year in the massive influx of migrants. *Daily Mail.*

Halter, N. (December 23, 2021). Ex-officer Kim Potter found guilty of manslaughter in killing of Duante Wright. *Axios.*

Hamacher, B. (November 17, 2023). FBI arrests Miami police officer accused of stealing cash and drugs during traffic stops. *NBC 6 South Florida*

Harper. T. (2022). *Broken Yard: The Fall of the Metropolitan Police.* London: Biteback Publishing.

Harrell, E. (April 2021). *Victims of Identity Theft, 2018.* Bureau of Justice Statistics: U.S. Department Of Justice.

Harris, J. (March 10, 2021). Dallas County DA's office seeks to free Benjamin Spencer after more than 30 years. www.wfaa.com.

Hastings, D. (December 15, 2022). Border Patrol Agent and Serial Killer sentenced to life in prison for murdering 4 women in 12 days. *Inside Edition.*

Hauck, G. (February 11, 2020). Prosecutors have thrown out nearly 100 convictions tied to "rogue" Chicago cop. *USA Today.*

Healey. J., Beauregard, F., Beech, A., and Vettor, S. (2014). Is the sexual murderer a unique type of offender? A typology of violent sexual offenders using crime scene behaviors. *Sexual Abuse:* 28(6): 523–533.

Hermann, P. & Scharper, J. (February 23, 2011). Towing scandals in the city are nothing new. *The Baltimore Sun.*

Hewitt, R. (December 9, 2019). E100k a day for police overtime: Exclusive Shocking bill revealed as one officer clocks up 1,759 hours. *Independent News and Media.*

Hinton, A.R. with Hardin, L.L. (2019). *The Sun Does Shine: How I found life, freedom and justice.* New York: St. Martin's Griffin.

Hohnstadt, C. (May 29, 2020). 18 complaints in 19 years, and a murder conviction. What we know about ex-Minneapolis Derek Chauvin. *AP*

Holdaway, S. (1983). *Inside the British Polic: A Force at Work.* Oxford, England: Basil Blacwell

Home Office. (January 19, 2023). Three former Met Police officers accused of child sex abuse image "conspiracy." *Independent.*

Hope, L. (March 21, 2023). 11 exonerees file federal lawsuits against former Chicago detective for coercing false confessions. *ABC7.*

Hopkins, E.J. (1931/1972). *Our Lawless Police: A Study of the Unlawful Enforcement of the Law.* New York: Viking Press.

Hostettler, J. (November 22, 2011). Pious Perjury. *The Garrow Society.*

House of Lords. (1 May, 2019). *Forensic science and the criminal justice system: A blueprint for change.* Science and Technology Select Committee. 3rd report on Session 2017–2019.

Hughes, M. (August 17, 2009). Police pay &ndash: The great overtime bonanza. *The Independent.*

Hughes, R. (February 7, 2023). 3 S.C. COs arrested, accused of taking inmate bribes and distributing contraband. *Corrections 1.*

Hughes, R. (February 12, 2023). Ga. Prison Warden fired, accused of taking payments in contraband smuggling. *Corrections 1.*

Human Right Watch. (2013). *Those Who Take Us Away: Abusive Policing and Failures in Protection of Indigenous Women and Girls in Northern British Columbia, Canada.*

Hunt, J. & Manning, P.K. (1991). The Social Context of Police Lying. *Symbolic Interaction.* 14(1): 51–70.

IBAC, 2022. Thematic review summary. IBAC Melbourn, Victoria.

IPCC. (2011). *Corruption in the police service in England and Wales.* Independent Police Complaints Commission.

Ivkovic, S.K., Haberfield, M., Kang, W., Peacock, R., Porter, L.R., Prenzler, T., and Sauerman, A. (2020). A Comparative Study of the Police Code of Silence. *Policing: An International Journal.* 43(2): 285–298.

Jacobson, D. (July 27, 2021). Still in seclusion, FBI agent who was real "Donnie Brasco" glad he took Down Mafia forty years ago. *UPI.com.*

Jaffee, D. (April, 2007). Industrialization and Conflict in America 1840–1875. *Heilbrunn Timeline of Art History.*

James, J. (September 25, 2023). Nightclub boss is jailed for four years for paying bribes to corrupt Met police officer "Sheriff of Soho" who turned a blind eye to crime by accepting free holidays, nights with call girls and whipping sessions with a dominatrix. *The Guardian.*

Jancsics, D. (2019). Law Enforcement corruption along the U.S. Border. *Security Journal.* 34: 28-46.

Johnson, M.S (2003). *Street Justice: A History of Police Violence in New York City.* Boston: Beacon Press.

Jones, B. (January 26, 2023). CPD officer fired for "stealing" time. *Columbus Dispatch.*

Joseph, J. & Smith, C.S. (2021). The ties that bribe: Corruption's embeddedness in Chicago organized crime. *Criminology.* 59:671–703.

Journey, J. & Donahue, L. (January 13, 2023). Ex-Rocky Mount police officer charged with trafficking cocaine. *Nexstar Media, Inc.*

Kane, R.J. & White, M.J. (2013). Exploring Career-Ending Misconduct in the NYPD: Who, What, and How Often, in Kane, R.J and White, M.J. (2013. *Jammed Up: Bad Cops, Police Misconduct, and the New York City Police Department.* New York: New York University Press.

Kania, R. (1988). Should we tell the police to say "yes" to gratuities. *Criminal Justice Ethics.* 7(2): 37–49.

Kark, B. (July 4, 2021). Bangor officials subject of federal lawsuit. *Herald Palladium.*

Kashbaum, W.K. & Goldstein (June 20, 2016). 3 NYPD Commanders are Arrested in Vast Corruption Case. *The New York Times.*

Kassin, S. (January 30, 2021). Police Must Stop Lying to Suspects. *The New York Times.*

Ke, B. (January 17, 2023). NYPD captain allowed to retire after admitting to collecting around $60k for fake overtime hours. *Yahoo News.*

Kennin, L. (June 9, 2023). Former MPD officer out on bond after allegedly kidnapping, murdering a man on duty in 2021. *PDS News.*

Key, V.O. (1935). Police Graft. *American Journal of Sociology.* 40(5): 624–636.

Knightly, R. (January 8, 2012). Diary of a "Corrupt" Cop: or, It was the custom. *The Crime Writers' Chronicle.*

Klockers, C. (1985). *The Idea of Police.* Newbury Park: Sage.

Klockers, C.B., Ivkovich, S.K., Harver, W.F. and Haberfield, M.R. (2000). *The Measurement of Police Integrity.* National Institute of Justice Research Brief. U.S. Department of Justice.

Knapp Commission. (1972). *The Knapp Commission Report on Police Corruption.* New York: George Braziler.

Koziarski, J. & Huey, L. (2021). #Defund or #Re-Fund? Re-examining Bayley's Blueprint for Police Reform. *International Journal of Comparative and Applied Criminal Justice*. 45(3): 260–284.

Kraska, P.B. (2007). Militarization and Policing—Its Relevance to 21st Century Police. *Policing*. 1(4): 501–513.

Krieger, S.A. (Summer, 2011). Why Our Justice System Convicts Innocent People, and the Challenges Faced by Innocence Projects Trying to Exonerate Them. *New Criminal Law Review: An International and Interdisciplinary Journal*. 14(3): 333–402.

Lambe, J. (June 2, 2020). Court Overturns Qualified Immunity in Police Killing of Marine Corps Veteran Who Accidently Activated "Life Aid" Device. *Law and Crime*.

Ladden-Hall, D. (August 18, 2022). Was a Kansas Cop Behind a Horrific String of Rapes and Kidnappings? *News Correspondent*.

Laporte, G. (April, 2018). Wrongful Convictions: Understanding the Role of Forensic Science. *NIJ Journal279*.

Lardner, J. & Reppetto, T. (2000). *NYPD: A City and Its Police*. New York: Henry Holt and Company.

Lawson, G. & Oldham, W. (2006). *The Brotherhoods: The True Story of Two Cops Who Murdered for the Mafia*. New York: Scribner.

Levitt, L. (2010). *NYPD Confidential: Power and Corruption in the Country's Greatest Police Force*. New York: St. Martins Press.

Lieberman, S. & Bandler, J. (April 6, 2023). Nicholas Tartaglione: Jury convicts ex-cop of "heinous" murders of 4 men in drug deal. *Lohud*.

Lindberg, R.C. (1991). *To Serve and Collect: Chicago Politics and Police Corruption from the Lager Beer Riot to the Summerdale Scandal, 1855–1960*. Carbondale, Ill.: Southern Illinois University Press.

Lissner, C. (June 8, 2023). Sheriff's officer charged with possession of child sex abuse material. *Patch*.

Livadeas, C. (10 November 2020). The true cost of undercover policing. *Police Oracle*.

Loevy, J. (2010). Truth or Consequences: Police "Testilying." *American Bar Association*. 36(3): 13–20.

Longley, R. (February 16, 2021). Firearms and Arrest Authority of U.S. Federal Agencies. *ThoughtCo*.

Lowe, P. (November 14, 2022). Former KCKPD detective Roger Golubski was paid to protect sex traffickers, feds charge. *KCUR News*.

MacFarlane, B.A. (December18, 2005). Convicting the Innocent—A Triple Failure of the Justice System. Revision of a paper first presented at the Heads of Prosecution Agencies in the Commonwealth Conference at Darwin, Australia on May 7, 2003.

Mackintosh, T. (August 11, 2018). UK police forces spend E1.7bn on overtime in five years. *BBC*.

Main, F. (March 21, 2012). Imprisoned cop blames partner for hit. *Corrections 1*.

Main, F. (September 15, 2016). Crooked ex-cop wants out early for informing on others. *Chicago Sun Times*.

Mannette, A. (October 20, 2022). Hutchinson officer signed up to defend justice. He is accused of a series of sexual assaults. *The Hutchinson News*.

Marcellin, C. & McCoy, E. (May 2021). Preventing and Addressing Sexual Violence in Correctional Institutions. *Urban Institute.*

Mareno, L. (June 26, 2022). El Paso cop gets federal time for helping family drug business. *Breitbart.*

Margaritoff, M. (December 1, 2021). How Michael Dowd Became the Most Crooked Cop in the NYPD. *Today in History.*

Marozzi. M. & Taylor, J. (December 14, 2022). Victoria police allegedly use LEAP database to pursue, stalk, Harass women prompting calls for inquiry. *ABC News.*

Marquette, C. (September 24, 2020). Exclusive: Capitol Police disciplinary reports show pattern of misconduct. *Roll Call.*

Mason, G. (2004). *The Official History of the Metropolitan Police: 175 Years of Policing London.* London: Carlton Books.

Mason, Y. (2008). *Silent Scream.* Dressing Your Book.

Mayo, B. (June 14, 2013). Former East Washington police chief pleads guilty in federal case. *Nowcast.*

McAlary, M. (1987). *Buddy Boys: When Good Cops Turn Bad.* New York: G P Putnam & Sons.

McAlister, M., & Franks, C. (December 2021). *Identity crime and misuse in Australia: Results of the 2023 online survey.* Australian Institute of Criminology.

McCarthy, B. (August 24, 2008). Ex-FBI Agent accused in murder, robbery plots. *The Times Picayune.*

McCarthy, C. (March17, 2021). New lawsuit alleges rampant corruption in NYPD's Internal Affairs Bureau. *New York Post.*

McCarthy, C., & Reilly, P. (February 5, 2022). Whistleblowing cops asks Mayor Adams to probe NYPD's Internal Affairs. *New York Post.*

McDevitt, J., Farell, A., and Wolff, R. (2008). *Creating a Culture of Integrity.* COPS Evaluation Brief No. 3. Northeastern Institute on Race and Justice

McNamara, M. (2018). *I'll Be Gone in the Dark.* New York: HarperCollins.

Medina, E. (August 17, 2023). 10 California Officers Face Corruption Charges in F.B.I Inquiry. *The New York Times.*

Meisner, J. (June 6, 2022). Ex-detective takes the Fifth over 200 times. *The Chicago Tribune.*

Meissner, C.A., Surmon-Bohr, F., Oleszkiewicz, S., and Alison, L.I. (2017). Developing an evidence-based perspective on interrogation: A review of the U. S. Government's High-Value Detainee Investigation Group research program. *Psychology, Public Policy, and Law.* 23(4): 438–457.

Meloni, R. (April 18, 2018). Detroit towing scandal: Former police deputy chief sentenced for taking bribes. *Click on Detroit.*

Miller, J. (August 19, 2022). Former Kansas Police Officer Accused of Being "Serial Sexual Predator." *Oxygen True Crime.*

Miller, W.R. (1973). *Cops and Bobbies: Police Authority in New York and London, 1830–1870.* Columbus, Ohio: Ohio University Press,

Mitchell, A. (September 6, 2014). Retired Flint police officer faces 16 counts of sexually assaulting children on duty. *Inquiter.*

Mitchell, C. (December 7, 2023). Payouts tied to a corrupt police sergeant could cost Chicago taxpayers $80Million. *WBEZ Chicago*.

Moore, W.H. (1974). *The Kefauver Committee and the Politics of Crime*. Columbia University of Missouri Press.

Moreno, L. (January 25, 2023). El Paso Cop Gets Federal Prison Time for Helping Family Drug Business. *Breitbart*.

Morton, D.E., Rao, A., and Sloan, L.R. (2009). Plagiarism, Integrity, and Workplace Deviance: A Criterion Study: *Ethics & Behavior*. 19(1): 36–50.

Morton, J. (1993). *Bent Coppers: A survey of police corruption*, London: Little, Brown and Company.

Muncaster, P. (November 8, 2019). Over 230 UK Police Disciplined for Computer Misuse. *Infosecurity Magazine*.

Murdock, S. (November 8, 2023). DOJ Opens Civil Rights Investigation into Lexington Police Department in Mississippi. *Huffington Post*.

Mustain, J. & Tucker, E. (June 11, 2021). "We mean it": FBI takes on sexual misconduct in its ranks. *AP News*.

NACJSA. (1973). *National Advisory Commission on Criminal Justice Standards and Goals*. GPO.

Nation. (May 5, 2023). 3 fired police officers under house arrest in gunfire death of 8-year-old girl. *PBS News Hour*.

National Advisory Commission on Criminal Justice Standards and Goals. (1973). *Police*. Washington, D.C.: Department of Justice.

National Council on Identity Theft Protection. (no date). What are the Different Types of Identity Theft. *National Council on Identity Theft*.

National Police Funding Database. (July 11, 2023). Settlements. *National Police Funding Database*.

National Research Council. (2015). *Forensic Science in Criminal Courts: Ensuring Scientific Validity of Feature-Comparison Methods*. Executive Office of the President.

Nedim, U. (May 5, 2016). Police Officers Misuse Private Information for Personal Gain. *Syndney Criminal Lawyers*.

Neely, P.R. & Cillo, J. (2019). Police integrity in the courtroom when testifying. *International Journal of Research*. 7(8): 287–291).

Nowlin, S. (December 15, 2023). Two former San Antonio police officers indicted for murder in Melissa Perez case. *San Antono News*.

O'Conner, J. (October 31, 2022). Lying Illinois prison workers go unpunished in 2018 inmate death, despite conviction of three guards. *Chicago Sun Times*.

O'Conner. J. (December 6, 2019). Illinois prison guards face federal charges in inmate death. *AP News*.

Office of Inspector General. (September 16, 2019). Dallas Police Officer charged with NHTSA grant fraud. *U.S. Department of Transportation*.

Office of the Privacy Commissioner of Canada. (October 2020). Identity theft and you. *Office of the Privacy Commissioner of Canada*.

OJJPD. (2010). *Child Molesters: A behavioral analysis: For professionals investigating the sexual exploitation of children*. Office of Juvenile Delinquency Prevention. National Center for Missing and Exploited Children.

Oosting, J. (January 9, 2009). Ex-Wayne County Circuit Judge admits there were lies at 2005 drug trial. Mlife.com.

Ortiz, E. (January 28, 2022). Alabama town's traffic ticketing scandal leads to chief's resignation. *NBC News*.

Ousley, W. (2008). *Open City: True Story of the KC Crime Family 1900–1950*. Overland Park, Kansas: Leathers Publishing.

Parnass, L. (August 2, 2021). Lanesborough officer fired over improper use of criminal records database. *The Lanesborough Eagle*.

Patrick, R. (2011). "A Nod and a Wink": Do "Gaming" Practices Provide an Insight into the Organizational Nature of Police Corruption. *The Police Journal* 84.

Peacock, W. (April 20, 2012). Sexual harassment allegations amongst top cops. *Philadelphia Employment Law News*.

Pegones, S. & Estanowich, L. (May 1, 2019). Long Island police chief among officials indicted on corruption charges. *New York Post*.

Pinkerton, J. (May 30, 2005). Corruption crosses the border with agent bribes. *Houston Chronicle*.

Porter, L.E., & Prenzler, T. (2016). The code of silence and ethical perceptions. Exploring police officer willingness to report misconduct. *Policing and International Journal of Police Strategies and Management*. 39 (20:370–386).

Potter, G. (no date). *The History of Policing in the United States*. EKU Online. Eastern Kentucky University.

Prenzler, T., Beckley, A., and Bronitt, S. (2013). Police gifts and benefits scandals: Addressing deficits in policy, leadership and enforcement. *International Journal Police Science and Management*. 15(4): 294–304.

Press Association. (March 28, 2003). Soham police officer jailed for child pornography offenses. *The Guardian*.

Presse, A.F. (October 17, 2022). London Police Chief Admits Misconduct Checks Failing after Damning Report. *Barrons*.

Puddister, K. & McNabb, D. (16 March 2021). When the Police Break the Law: The Investigation, Prosecution and Sentencing of Ontario Police Officers. *Canadian Journal of Law and Society*.

Punch, M. (2000). Police Corruption and It's Prevention. *European Journal of Policy and Research*. 8: 301–324.

Punch, M. (2003). Rotten Orchards, "Pestilence," Police Misconduct and System Failure. *Policing and Society*. 13(2): 171–196.

Rajakaruna, N., Henry, P.J., Scott, A.J. (May 7, 2019). Misuse of Police Information Systems: Predicting Likelihood of Misuse among Unsworn Police Employees. *Policing*. 15(2): 686–790.

Rayman, G. (March 11, 2021). He quits after slam over old conviction. *New York Daily News*.

Reed, K. (September 7, 2022). A Gang of Rogue Police in Baltimore Cost the City More than $15 million. *The Root*.

Reiss, A.J. (1992). Police Organization in the Twentieth Century. *Crime and Justice*. 15: 51-97.

Reith, C. (1952). *The Blind Eye of History*. Montclair, N.J.: Patterson Smith.

Reppetto, T.A. (2012). *American Police: A History—The Blue Parade 1945–2012*. Volume 2. New York: Enigma Books.

Reppeto, T.A. (1978). *The Blue Parade*. New York: The Free Press.

Roebuck, J.B. & Barker, T. (1974). A typology of police corruption. *Social Problems*, 32: 423–427.

Ross, M. (9 September 2022). "Rapist" Met Police constable, 29, attacked female colleague and a second woman within the space of 10 days, court hears. *Daily Mail*.

Rousey, D.C. (1996). *Policing the Southern City: New Orleans 1805–1889*. Baton Rouge: Louisianna State University Press.

Rubinstein, J. (1996). *City Police*. New York: Farrar, Straus, and Giroux.

Rubinstein, J. (1973). *City Police*. New York: Farrar, Straus, and Giroux.

Russo, G. (2001). *The Outfit: The Role of Chicago's Underworld in the Shaping of Modern America*. New York: Bloomsbury.

Samuels, A. (March 7, 2017). Study finds Harris County leads nation in exonerations. *Texas Tribune*.

Sanchez, R., & Santana, M. (February 21, 2023). Genaro Garcia Luna, former Mexican public security secretary, convicted in US of taking bribes from drug cartels. *CNN News*.

Scherr, C.F. & Normile, C.J. (2022). False Confessions Predict a Delay between Release Time from Incarceration and Official Exoneration. *Law and Human Behavior*. 46 (1): 67–80.

Schilke, R. (June 27, 2023). Chicago police under the microscope as internal affairs has opened 11,000 investigations. *Washington Examiner*.

Schmelzer, E. (April 21, 2023). Ex-Aurora police officer found guilty of failing to stop partner's excessive force under new state law. *Denver Post*.

Schwartz, J. (2023). *Shielded: How the Police Became Untouchable*. New York: Viking.

Shecter, L. & Phillips, W. (1973). *On the Pad: The Underworld and its Corrupt Police, Confessions of a Cop on the Take*. New York: G.P. Putnam's Sons.

Sherrer, H. (10/12/2020). The Tragedy of the Choctaw Three. *Justice Denied—The Magazine for the Wrongly Convicted*.

Sherwood, S. (December 6, 2022). Police officer who allegedly stole at work appears in court. *NZ Herald*.

Singh, T. (September 27, 2022). Anger against racist police violence swells in the UK after killing of Chris Kaba. *Peoples Dispatch*.

Smee, B. (November 6, 2019). Queensland police "brought into disrepute" by computer system police says commissioner. *The Guardian*.

Smith, B. (April 2021). The Verne Miller Story: From Lawman to Oulaw. www.southdakotamagozine.com.

Smith, C. (June 1, 2023). Police Scotland staff experience negative consequences for calling out sexism. *Police Oracle*.

Smith, C. (May 25, 2023). Outgoing Police Scotland chief admits the force is "institutionally racist." *Police Oracle*.

Smith, L. (November 14, 2012). Additional claims of sexual misconduct leveled against Totten in second civil right suit. *The West Virginia Record*.

Snell, R. (January 13, 2023). Detroit corruption crackdown nears new conviction. *The Detroit News*.

Sorace, S. (12/4/2019). Baltimore state attorney says 305 police officers have "integrity issues," can't be called to testify. *Fox News.*

Stacom, D. (April 21, 2011). New Britain police hit by another sexual harassment suit. *The Hartford Courant.*

Staff. (August 24, 2023). Who's the retired Ventura sergeant tied to the O.C. Bar? Here's what we know. *VC Star.*

Staff. (February 25, 2015). Huntsville Police Officer Pleads Guilty to Fix Cocaine Trafficking Charges. *Quad Cities News.*

Stamper, N. (2005). *Breaking Ranks: A Top Cop's Expose of the Dark Side of American Policing.* New York: Nation Books.

Stamper, N. (2016). *To Protect and Serve: How to fix America's police.* New York: Nation's Books.

Stana, R.M. & Roleff, T.L. (2003). Drug-Related Police Corruption Differs from Other Forms of Police Corruption. In *Police Corruption.* New York: Green Haven Press.

Stanton, S., Smith, D., and Waloo, E. (November 13, 2019). Hundreds of California police misuse law enforcement computer databases, investigation shows. *The Sacramento Bee.*

Steele, M. (June 9, 2023). House Bill 305: Accountability. *Cape Gazette.*

Steinberg, E.J. (March 7, 2018). St. Paul Police Department Reform. *MNOPEDIA.*

Stickings, T. (September 12, 2023). France urges calm after teenager's death on police Collision. *The National.*

Stinson, P., Liederbach, J., Buerger, M., Brewer, S.L. (2018). To protect and collect: A Nationwide study of profit-motivated police crime. *Criminal Justice Studies.* 31(3): 310–331.

Stinson, P.M., Liederbach, J., and Frieburger, T. L. (2012). Off-Duty & Under Arrest: A Study of Crimes Perpetrated by Off-Duty Police. *Criminal Justice Faculty Publications.*

Stockburger, G. (January 21, 2023). Pennsylvania State Trooper charged for alleged road rage incident involving gun. *ABC27.*

Stockler, A. & Bandler, J. (August 7, 2023). White Plains settles with Kenneth Chamberlain family for $5m. *Iohd.*

Storm, D. (September 28, 216). Cops run unauthorized searches on confidential databases for revenge, stalking. *ComputerWorld.*

Suliman, A. (January 17, 2023). London police officer fired after convicted of 24 counts of rape. *Washington Post.*

Sutton, C. (January 17, 2023). Australia's dirtiest cop makes last attempt to have his life sentence for murdering a drug dealer overturned—but will die in jail if appeal fails. *Daily Mail.*

Swarns, C. (June 1, 2023). Why the Trial Penalty Must Go. *The Innocence Project.*

Sweeting, F. Arabaci-Hills, P., and Cole, T. (2021). Outcomes of Police Sexual Misconduct in the UK. *Policing.* 15(2): 1339–1351.

Task Force. (2015). *Final Report of the President's Task Force and 21st Century.* Washington, D.C.: Office of Community Oriented Policing Services.

Taylor, F. (2019). *The Torture Machine: Racism and Police Violence in Chicago.* Chicago: Haymarket Books.

Tempey, N. (September 30, 2015). Whistleblower Cop Adrian Schoolcraft Settles Lawsuit against City or $600k. *Gothamist News.*

The Challenge of Crime in a Free Society. (1967). *The Challenge of Crime in a Free Society.* GPO.

Trainum, J.L. (2016). *How the Police Generate False Confessions: An Inside Look at the Interrogation Room.* Lanham, Md.: Rowman and Littlefield.

Trainum, J.L. (2021). In Snook, et al. "Urgent issues and prospects in reforming interrogation practices in the United States and Canada. *Legal and Criminological Psychology.* 26:1–4.

Tudor, S. (April 27, 2023). *Police Standards and culture: Restoring public trust.* UK Parliament: House of Lords Library.

Turner, D. (August 8, 2023). Crack Epidemic: United States History (1980s). *Encyclopedia Britannica.*

Turner, E. (May 30, 2023). 4 arrested in Butts County on child exploitation charges, GBI says. *ANF.*

U.S. Attorney's Office. (July 18, 2023). Jury Finds Former Correctional Sergeant Guilty of Perjury during Investigation into Cover-up of Assault of CSP Sacramento Inmate. *U.S. Attorney's Office. Eastern District of California.*

U.S. Attorney's Office. (July 3, 2023). Customs and Border Protection Officer indicted for receiving bribes, allowing drug-laden vehicles to enter the U.S. *U.S. Attorney's Office. Southern District of California.*

U.S. Attorney's Office. (July 7, 2016). Former Police Officer Charged with Accepting Bribe for Unlawfully Accessing a Law Enforcement Database. U.S. Attorney's Office. Northern District of Georgia.

U.S. Attorney's Office. (June 29, 2023). University of Oklahoma Professor and Wife Sentenced to Prison for Federal Fraud Grant. *U.S. Attorney's Office. Western District of Oklahoma.*

U.S. Department of Justice. (April 2021). *Victims of Identity Theft.* U.S. Department of Justice.

Uchida, C. (2015). The Development of the American Police: An Historical Overview. In Dunham, R. & Alpert, G. Eds. *Critical Issues in Policing.* Long Grove, Ill.: Waveland Press pp 11–30.

Van de Riet, E. (July 14, 2022). Correctional officer charged after having sexual relationship with inmate, sheriff says. *Gray Media Group.*

Van Dyke, J. (May 11, 2012). Update: LBPD officer rearrested for more offenses. *Gazettes.com.*

Vasilogambros, M. (June 21, 2016). The NYPD's Corruption Scandal. *Atlantic.*

Vigdor, N. (March 9, 2021). Illinois Prison Guard Pleads Guilty to Beating Death. *The New York Times.*

Vigdor, N. (November 8, 2021). Ex-officers who used tasers on a man over 50 times convicted of murder. *The New York Times.*

W. R. (2021). How the Rational Basis Test Protects Policing for Profit. *University of Michigan Journal of Law Reform.*

Waddington, P.A.J. (1999). *Policing Citizens: Authority and Rights.* New York: Routledge.

Walker, S. & Tribeck, D. (June 2013), *Police Sexual Abuse of Teenage Girls: A 2013 Update on "Driving While Female."* The University of Nebraska Department of Criminal Justice.

Walker, S. (2001). *Police Accountability: The Role of Citizen Oversight.* New York: Wadsworth.

Wambaugh, J. (1989). *The Blooding.* New York: William Morrow & Company.

Ward, R.H. & McCormack, R. (1979). *An Anticorruption Manual for Administrators in Law Enforcement.* New York: John Jay Press.

Warden, R. (May 12, 2003). The Role of False Confessions in Illinois Wrongful Murder Convictions Since 1970. *Center on Wrongful Convictions.*

WBUR Newsroom. (July 10, 2020). State Police: 22 Troopers Implicated in Overtime Scandal Will Be Disciplined. *WBUR Newsroom.*

Weiss, M. (March 29, 2016). 23 NYPD Officers Suspected in Karaoke Bar Protection Racket Scandal. *On the Inside.*

Wickersham Report on Police. (1931). Wickersham Report on Police. *The American Journal of Police Science.* 2(4): 337–348.

Wikipedia. (Accessed November 8, 2023). Vernon C. Miller.

Wikipedia. (Accessed March 16, 2023). Adrian Schoolcraft.

Wikipedia. (Accessed August 6, 2023). Sidney Dorsey.

Wikipedia. (Accessed August 8, 2023). *Killing of Kenneth Chamberlain, Sr.* [Some would argue that Wikipedia is not a scholarly source. I do not agree. By itself that may be true, but it is a valuable source of other data. Just like I have always told my students— check the veracity of any cited source.]

Williams, H. (December 2002). Core Factors of police corruption across the world. Forum on Crime and Society. *The Police Foundation.*

Wilson, M.D. (2010). An Exclusionary Rule for Police Lies. *American Criminal Law Review.*

Winston, A., Bondgraham, D. (2023). *The Riders Come Out at Night.* New York: Atria Books.

Winton, R. & Blackstein, A. (March 26, 2003). LAPD's Kalish relieved of duty. *LA Times.*

Winton, R. & Blackstein, A. (November 7, 2003). Deputy chief won't be tried. *LA Times.*

Winton, R. (August 9, 2023). LAPD officer arrested after stolen debit card used at home improvement store. *Los Angeles Times.*

Wolfe-Robinson, M. (11 October 2021). At least 750 sexual misconduct claims against UK police in five years. *The Guardian.*

Woods, B. & Soderberg, B. (2020). *I Got a Monster: The Rise and Fall of America's Most Corrupt Police Squad.* New York: St. Martin's Press.

Woodworth, W. & Kanik, H. (July 13, 2020). "Brady lists," of untruthful Oregon police officers consistent county to county. *Statesman Journal*

Wuthmann, W. & Jarmanning, A. (September 27, 2020). Suffolk DA releases list of 136 police officers with possible credibility issues. *WBUR Issues.*

Zurik, L. & Lillich, C. (November 17, 2021). Zurik: Police officers claiming to work two jobs at the same time. *WVUL.*

Index

About the Author

Dr. Tom Barker is a former police officer, a police academy instructor, a college and university instructor, and a college dean. He is a past president of the Academy of Criminal Justice Studies. He has authored or coauthored seventeen books, including six that have gone into multiple editions—one, nine editions. Dr. Barker is considered a national and international expert in several areas: law-enforcement practices, including reform, and adult criminal gangs—street, prison, and outlaw motorcycle gangs. Since his retirement from college teaching in 2000, he has devoted his time to full-time writing and research.

www.ingramcontent.com/pod-product-compliance
Lightning Source LLC
Chambersburg PA
CBHW050337270326
41926CB00016B/3490